The
World's
Rim

The World's Rim

GREAT MYSTERIES OF THE NORTH AMERICAN INDIANS

By HARTLEY BURR ALEXANDER
With a Foreword by CLYDE KLUCKHOHN

UNIVERSITY OF NEBRASKA PRESS
LINCOLN/LONDON

Copyright © 1953 by University of Nebraska Press
All rights reserved
Library of Congress Catalog Card Number 53-7703
ISBN 0-8032-5003-7
Manufactured in the United States of America

First Bison Book printing: February, 1967

Most recent printing shown by first digit below:

9   10

Foreword

PHILOSOPHER, poet, and anthropologist, Hartley Burr Alexander seemed in many ways to be a figure from classical Athens or Renaissance Italy or Elizabethan England strangely appearing on the twentieth-century American scene. Yet his vitality, many-sidedness, and robustness were as distinctively American, and indeed Nebraskan, as blue denim overalls. He drew richly from the great civilizations of the past, but he never retreated into them. He lived in the present and worked to build a new civilization which would neither forget the permanent achievements of human history nor blindly worship them. A great scholar, but no Alexandrine scholiast, he believed in man's capacities for growth and development, adapting to changed situations in terms of discoverable eternal laws. His own world view was woven of strands beautifully tapestried from Mediterranean antiquity, Asia, and the New World (both American Indian and contemporary). For the eye Alexander's spirit is magnificently represented in the Nebraska State Capitol which—together with the new University City in Mexico—most hopefully presages a truly great modern New World civilization. But one may say of this book as well as of the capitol what Plutarch remarked of the Acropolis: "There is such a certain flourishing freshness in it."

In a period of specialism in scholarship and domination of a behavioristic viewpoint in the human sciences, Hartley Alexander was not always appreciated by the orthodox. The time is now more favorable for a return to his unique contributions. Philosophy and anthropology are realizing that each has something important to say to the other as evidenced by the work of F.S.C. Northrop, Robert Redfield, Eliseo Vivas, David Bidney, Abraham Edel, Richard McKeon, John Ladd, and others. Ruth Benedict, the anthropologist-poet, has come into her own only since Alexander's death. Most anthropologists now recognize that there is more to cultures than is directly observable: that there are serious questions which can not be answered in accord with the canons of radical behaviorism.

Most of all, perhaps, anthropology today is less exclusively preoccupied with the differences between human groups. We know that cultural differences, real and important though they are, are still so many variations on themas supplied by raw human nature and by universal human situations. The common understandings between men of different cultures are very broad, very general, very easily obscured by language and the external trappings of custom. The universals or near universals are apparently few in number. Nevertheless they seem to be as deep-going as they are rare. Anthropology's facts attest that the phrase "a common humanity" is in no sense meaningless. This is also significant, and is one of the two major unifying thoughts in the present book.

The other seems to me to be that of the dynamic particularity of men's lives. I remember Alexander's saying something like this (I quote from rough notes) around the campfire in New Mexico:

"A true view of the world must be cast in the particular—i.e. the dramatic mode. Our understanding of experience must be historical and dramatic rather than abstract and mathematical. This is why Plato was a wiser man than Aristotle. Plato never built his house in a static sense. He used the myth to present a dramatic interpretation. To Aristotle the world was something which could be represented by an intellectual photograph, by an architect's drawing. Hence there was always a contradiction in Aristotle's metaphysics. Today too, philosophers like Russell write as if experience were all finished—as if all we had to do was to catch it as it is and describe it. No such abstract and mathematical models will suffice because of constant flux. Only drama catches things 'as they really are'."

Drama and mystery are almost two words for the same thing. This book is about the dramatic mysteries of the American Indians, about their special understanding of the dynamisms of our lives which constantly change in detail and in manifestation but never in essence.

Let me end with a remark of Plotinus which Hartley Alexander often quoted:

"It is for philosophy to point the way. It is for them that have eyes to see the vision."

CLYDE KLUCKHOHN

July, 1953

Contents

Author's Preface

WE JUDGE our own humanity by its white pages, not by
its black, especially when we are concerned with what
most gives us courage to live or what most deeply explains
our understanding of life. We should assess the thought
of another race by standards no less generous, nor can our
hope for humanity anywhere rest upon a lesser truth. In
the texts which follow, the white pages of American Indian
thought and understanding are definitely chosen with the
intention of showing his heritage and achievement at its
best, and of giving him the benefit of that type of judgment which we should most wish for ourselves and which
should be the last meaning of his culture for the whole
of humanity. Chapter V is a revision of the author's *Mystery of Life,* a brochure published by the Open Court
Company (1913). Chapter VII is largely a translation into
English of the fifth chapter of his *L'Art et la Philosophie
des Indiens de l'Amérique du Nord* (Paris, 1926). Elsewhere his sources are noted, although frequently he has
cited his volumes on North American (Vol. X) and Latin
American (Vol. XI) mythology in *The Mythology of All
Races,* where text references and other materials are ac-
cessible.

Editor's Preface

The World's Rim was first prepared for publication as early as 1935. However, it was still unpublished at the time of the death of its author in 1939. In view of the rich content, both in regard to vivid presentation of certain American Indian rites and ritual concepts, and in regard to the wider interpretation given in terms of a philosophy of religious culture, I have continuously sought to bring this volume into print. It is therefore with deep gratification that I wish to thank the University of Nebraska Press for making publication possible. Certain minor changes of terminology have been made in the interest of clarity and precision, and a few additions and corrections appear in the notes. Otherwise the volume remains as it was when first readied for publication by the author. It has not been possible to include any extensive critique of more recent anthropological data or hypotheses except for a note concerning the spread of maize culture. However, the merit of this volume lies elsewhere than in a scientific report on latest findings and theories. Rather its value lies in its deeper interpretation of the ritual concepts examined. In this capacity, I believe the material is as fresh and pertinent as ever.

I wish to express thanks to the following institutions, publishing houses, and individuals for permission to use quoted material:

EDITOR'S PREFACE

THE Smithsonian Institution for extensive selections from the *Reports* and *Bulletins* of the Bureau of American Ethnology; the Carnegie Institution of Washington for selections from its *Publications,* Nos. 17 and 59; the Pennsylvania Historical Commission for selections from its *Publications,* Vol. 2; the American Museum of Natural History for selections from its *Anthropological Papers,* Vols. 2, 16, and 25; the Museum of the American Indian, Heye Foundation, for selections from its *Indian Notes and Monographs,* Vol. 4; Peabody Museum of American Archaeology and Ethnology, Harvard University, for selections from its *Papers,* Vol. 1; the Chicago Natural History Museum for selections from its *Anthropological Series,* Vol. 4; the Archaeological Institute of America for the selection from *Art and Archaeology,* Vol. 9, No. 2; Houghton Mifflin Company for the selection from *Land of the Spotted Eagle* by Chief Standing Bear; Mr. Jeremiah Curtin Cardell for selections from *Creation Myths of Primitive America* by Jeremiah Curtin; Dodd, Mead and Company for the selection from *League of the Ho-Dé-No-Sau-Nee or Iroquois* by Lewis H. Morgan; Adam and Chas. Black Co. for selections from *Lectures on the Religion of the Semites* by W. Robertson Smith; Macmillan and Company, Ltd., for selections from *Malay Magic* by W. W. Skeat; Cambridge University Press for the selection from *The Thunderweapon in Religion and Folklore* by Chr. Blinkenberg; Oxford, The Clarendon Press for selections from *Cults of the Greek States,* Vols. 1 and 3, by Lewis R. Farnell; The University Press, Cambridge, Massachusetts, for selections from *The North American Indian,* Vol. 3, by Edward S. Curtis; Columbia University Press for selections from *Prairie Smoke* by Melvin R. Gilmore; Lathrop C. Harper, Inc., for selections from *Life, Letters and Travels of Father Pierre-Jean De Smet* by Hiram M. Chittenden and Alfred T. Richardson; Macmillan and Company for selections from *Mythology of All Races,* Vol. 11 (Latin-American) by H. B. Alexander; and Dr. Herbert J. Spinden for the selection from his *Songs of the Tewa.*

HUBERT G. ALEXANDER

Albuquerque, New Mexico
August, 1953

Introduction

THE PURPOSE of this book is to sketch the salient features of the American Indian understanding of human life. Every group of mankind which has developed a sense of its own solidarity and its own collective power and fate has brought to expression its appraisal of its own humanity, and this we call its culture or, in its more reflective manifestation, its philosophy. For a people whose culture is traditional rather than literate in its guidance, this expression takes form chiefly in ritual and art, which serve to objectify the broad pattern of its ideal of life, and so to vivify its philosophical understanding. Such has been the case with the North American Indian. His culture has been of the traditional type, with only the beginnings of literary record, and its reflective embodiment is to be found almost wholly in the elaborate ceremonials which incorporate the red man's conception of the natural world and of the human action which takes place within it.

Apart from the fact that many score of native rituals have been lost unrecorded, this centering of Indian thought in the ceremonial life of the tribes is by no means to be deplored. It affords us, certainly, the most instructive extant indication of what was the type and quality of our own ancestral thinking in that cloudy Age of the Gods which preceded the Fathers of our History—of what, for example, must have been the quality of the Hellenic mind in the period just anterior to the appearance of Thales and the birth of conscious Philosophy, at the time when the holy mysteries of Orpheus and Eleusis were flourishing and the epic sense of historic time was being fitted to ancient lore of monster-beings and of demi-gods. Indeed, the most direct approach to pre-Hellenic thought may be directly through the study of the forming speculation which the Indian rituals reveal: not only is the adumbration of Hesiod and the *Theogony* to be found there, but Thales himself and his successors and, most of all, Pythagoras are clearly prophecied in the ideas and teachings attached to more than one Indian ritual. The chapters which follow will attempt to demonstrate this. There is something that is universal in men's modes of thinking, such that, as they move onward in their courses, they repeat in kind if not in instance an identical experience—which, if it be of the mind, can be understood only as the instruction which a creative nature must everywhere give to a human endowment. The Indian gives us an understanding of life colored and adorned by his own unique familiarities with a hemisphere of Earth which for many centuries was his only; this understanding is delivered in his own imaginative guise and following the impulses of his own artistic genius. But the fact that so created—by a unique people in a unique continent—it still in substance echoes what other groups of men in other natural settings have found to be *the human* truth, so that Aryan and Dakota, Greek and Pawnee, build identical ritual patterns to express their separate discoveries of a single insight, is but the reasonable argument for a validity in that insight which cannot be lightly dismissed. It is easy to raise the cry of superstition, where our prejudices are touched, or to condemn with superficial epithets; but there is a ghost that will not be laid, a challenge to our self-understanding that is as deep-sprung as our remotest genesis, in those aspirations of our nature which in many lands and in many times take form in the human spirit and shape our humanity.

There are students today, as there have been in each generation since that of Columbus himself, who look to the Old World for the roots and indeed the direct plantings of American Indian

INTRODUCTION

ideas. Not merely a mythical Atlantis, or a Dispersion of Lost Tribes, or a dozen other Old World legends have been called upon to account for the native American cultures, but more recently theories of migrant adventurers out of the Orient, harking back even to Nilotic beginnings, have found scholarly favor. Such theories are not shared by the author, to whom they appear to be but the recent offspring of a frame of mind long-prejudiced by Adamic, Noachian and similar traditions which find it difficult to conceive that all things human may not spring from a single source. It is entirely true that there are analogies, at first glance astonishing, not only between the material forms of Old and New World cultures, but what is yet more impressive, between the reflective and imaginative expressions of the peoples of the two hemispheres. Consequently, it is facile to find striking samenesses of Chinese or Buddhist or Hindu thinking with American. The analogies with early Greek thinking, and indeed with Christian symbolisms, are no less striking, and these formed the stock of the earlier eighteenth-century commentators on Indian beliefs, who have left followers not yet rid of the notion of prehistoric Christian missionaries in America. But the evidence against all such theories is overpowering; nothing essential to the Indian cultures can be traced to other than native sources, while on the other hand, in the New World itself the origin and spread of numerous and fundamental cultural elements can be clearly traced. In brief, without the assumption of a long-seated and distinctive native development of American cultural ideas, we possess no intelligible picture of man in the Western Hemisphere.

There is no intention, then, of drawing analogies for the sake of tracing sources—even within the American continents themselves where migration of culture-traits is well evidenced. Far more interesting and revealing is the psychological, or indeed the metaphysical, problem as to what is human nature and what are the necessary forms of thought which emerge from the experiences of living to shape a philosophy of the world: what *must* men think in order to be human at all, and what in the constitution of nature and the world can inspire or validate this human thinking? This is perhaps the question which is finally the most important one that we can consider; and for its answer it should be considered especially fortunate that the ages so segregated a whole body of the human race from its fellow members that it was given season to develop for itself the salient outline of its own humanity. And if this thinking does not disagree with that which experience and reflection have elsewhere evoked among men, surely there is a more potent obligation to ask for its reason in the order of nature and in the roots of being. In this bearing, the inquiry is an ultimate and a metaphysical one.

This work is a series of studies of rituals and ceremonies developed by the Indians of North America, particularly of those within the limits of what is now the United States. The list is limited and consciously selected: a complete corpus of what is preserved would involve encyclopedic treatment. But the ceremonies treated are all of undoubted importance; with almost no exception they are inter-tribal and indeed inter-regional. No one of them is universal among the Indian groups, but on the other hand few of these groups lack the equivalent of the series, though in several the equivalent is perhaps rudimentary in form. That they are selected from varying cultural groups need not militate against their general truthfulness to the Indian mind. There are eight or nine primary cultural groups of the Indians of North America—ranging from the civilized to the primitive—but this may equally be said of Europe or of Asia. If we can speak with truth of a European or an Oriental mind, although the former may combine Classic with Gothic, Latin with Slav, and the latter Moslem and Hindu and Chinese, we may speak of an American Indian mind and understanding with even more assurance: the included differences in the New World are less.

In each chapter some fundamental Indian ritual is the base and, as it were, the metaphor of the study. With it may be compared analogous Indian or Old World rituals. Because the classical mysteries appear to afford the closest and best-known parallels to a number of the Indian ceremonies, these as a whole are here designated "mysteries" and indeed spoken of as Eleusinian or Orphic or Mithraic in substance. Others of the American rites are yet more universal in their analogues, though in every case they have some phase or interpretation individual to themselves and the continent, even while they throw light upon like customs of other peoples and times.

First in the series is the most distinctive of the native ceremonies of the American Indian, the Pipe or Calumet rite, from which may be deduced the Indian conception of the phenomenal and indeed of the unseen world, with even more picturesqueness than from any like-purposed ceremony of other peoples. It is also of widest dissemination in America. In the second chapter is discussed an American version of the tree-and-pillar cult, familiar to us from the records of the peoples of the most ancient East. Here it was developed into a poetry of symbolism that may possibly serve as a corrective for the extremely materialistic interpretations of similar old Oriental cults with which our scholarship has made us familiar. Third in the series, and closely related to the preceding, is the very widespread and significant rite of purification by the sweat-bath, which for the Indian is cosmic in its significance and poetic in its associated mythology: few episodes in Old World cosmogonies do not at some point touch the significances of the sacred stones as developed by the stone-age men of America. With the stone, as forming a fundamental dualism of nature, is associated in myth and rite Earth's vegetation, and before all the cereal plan upon which man is most dependent. The Corn Dance, or Corn Ritual, forms the theme of the fourth chapter, bringing with it not only a kind of ceremonial completion of the furniture of creation, as the Indian conceives it, but also profound and meaningful analogies to Old World corn-cults and myths, and in a way a whole philosophy of a sacramental nature.

If in the first four chapters a vision of the world is established in a ceremonial mode; the four that follow are devoted to rites that interpret human life, not only as the Indians but as all men open their eyes to it. Chapter V is occupied with what is perhaps the most beautiful of all Indian rites, not in its displays, which are slight, but in the wealth of poetic interpretation which it brings. The Hako ceremony is the key and theme, and its striking analogies to the mysteries of Eleusis certainly give rise to reflec-

INTRODUCTION

tions upon the origins in meaning of the most famed and honored of all the Grecian mystic cults. Here it is taken as type for the American rites which have as their symbol the Sacred Infant and as their meaning the victory of Life. Following this is the study of the Sun Dance, and with it the elaboration of American Indian conceptions of the discovery of understanding and the discovery of valor-of-soul as heights of human attainment: both lead to vision, in a kind of Sun-cult in which there are at least notable suggestions of Mithraic philosophy. A series of personal rites or sacraments forms the subject-matter of the following chapter, broadly analogous to those *rites de passage* which among all peoples and in all times give us a man's conscious image of his own lifetime and undeniably illustrate the fundamental individualism of American Indian thought and teaching. Finally, in a last study, the Algonquian Mystery of the Way, the Way that leads into a World and a Life and an Understanding beyond this, is made the theme, directly suggesting the Orphic mystery of the Greeks and in more than one particular the central mystery of the Christian religion.

Thus are sketched the Indian's view of the world and of man, and of man's place in nature, as composed and made conscious in life's experiences.

The
World's
Rim

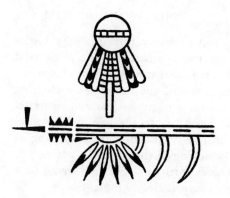

CHAPTER I

The Pipe of Peace

I

No SYMBOL native to the peoples of America has more profoundly stirred the imagination of the immigrant white race than that of the ceremonial pipe of the Indian—the hobowakan, the calumet, the pipe of peace, as it has variously been called. Hardly a trait of the Indian cultures, and certainly no ritual trait, was more widely disseminated among the tribes and nations of the red man before the era of the discovery than was the use of tobacco—its smoking and its symbolism. No gift of the New World found such ready and wide acceptance by mankind generally; it early entered every continent and archipelago, and its use rapidly spread beyond the outposts of European civilization, further than its nearest New World competitor, maize, or Indian corn. But maize, too, speedily found its way into remote lands. Africans and Asiatics of today are astonished to learn that it is to America and the American Indian that they owe both the food and the narcotic.

It was not, however, as a ritual act that tobacco smoking was adopted and carried by the Old World races. In the Old World smoking was what it has remained, an individual habit or a social convention; appetite, not idea, governed its expansion. For the

[3]

Indian, on the other hand, and probably from the very beginning, the use of tobacco was primarily ritual, and the plant itself
in some degree sanctified. It is true that the Indian also knew the
appetitive and social employments of the "weed"—for chewing
and for snuff as well as for the fume of pipe, cigar and cigarette;
but all this was, and is still, secondary to the first and essential
meaning of the smoked or breathed tobacco—a ritual offering or
a supplication. In the ritual smoking of the pipe it is not easy to
say whether the fume that goes forth is a gift of incense or a
breath of prayer: something of each is clearly present.

In any case, for the Indian peoples the whole complex that goes
with tobacco and its use is instilled with sanctions. The field in
which the plant is cultivated, the cured leaves, the decorated
pouch which contains tobacco and pipe, and above all the ceremonial pipe itself—all share in that hallowing which makes of
them the most potent and universal matter of Indian "medicine."
It may well be that tobacco first came into use as *materia medica*
in the European sense; for it was and is used for the healing of
bodily as well as of physical ills, and this might plausibly be associated with its original function. But whatever truth may be attached to this notion, it is to a far broader significance that the
full ritual of the pipe became developed. In the end the rite of
the calumet is the Indian's profound gesture to the World, whose
physical figure and inward being and powers he images and addresses in the ceremonial smoke. To bring his life, outward and
inward, into harmony with that of all nature is in essence the
meaning of the sacred fume which arises from the pipe whose
bowl is an altar and whose stem is the breath's passage. That the
instrument employed has been called "the Pipe of Peace" is due,
no doubt, to the fact that every Indian council in which men
sought to resolve their differences and every rite in which they en-
deavored to put themselves into tranquil accord with the powers
which participate with man in the life of nature, was inaugurated
with the ceremonial smoking. The whole meaning of human
existence is bound up with the ritual of the calumet.

II

In his account of the Iroquois, Lewis Morgan, historian of the Five Nations, gives this description of the opening of their councils: [1] "The master of ceremonies, rising to his feet, filled and lighted the pipe of peace from his own fire. Drawing three whiffs, one after the other, he blew the first toward the zenith, the second toward the ground, and the third toward the sun. By the first act he returned thanks to the Great Spirit for the preservation of his life during the past year, and for being permitted to be present at this council. By the second he returned thanks to his Mother, the Earth, for her various productions which had ministered to his sustenance. And by the third, he returned thanks to the Sun for his never-failing light, ever shining upon all." Père De Smet, one of the most wide-wandering of the Jesuit missionaries in North America, makes repeated allusions to the ritual use of the pipe.[2] "On all great occasions," he says, "in their religious and political ceremonies, and at their great feasts, the calumet presides; the savage sends its first fruits, or its first puffs, to the Great Waconda, or Master of Life, to the Sun which gives them light, and to the Earth and Water by which they are nourished; then they direct a puff to each point of the compass, begging of Heaven all the elements and favorable winds." Elsewhere De Smet remarks: [3] "It was really a touching spectacle to see the calumet, the Indian emblem of peace, raised heavenward by the hand of a savage, presenting it to the Master of Life, imploring his pity on all his children on earth and begging him to confirm the good resolutions which they had made."

An earlier and still more famous Jesuit explorer was Marquette, and few passages touching the significance of the calumet are more important than his account of its use among the Illinois, with whom, he says,[4] "there is nothing more mysterious nor more remarkable. So much honor is not rendered to the crowns and sceptres of kings as they render to the calumet. It seems to be the god of peace and war, the arbiter of life and death. It is enough to carry it with one and to show it in order to journey with assurance in the midst of enemies, who, in the height of combat, lower their arms when it is displayed. It is for this that the Illinois gave me one to serve as safeguard among all the nations by whom I must pass in my travel. There is a calumet for peace and another for war, which are only distinguished by the color of the plumage with which they are adorned. The red is the mark of war: they employ it only to end their differences, to confirm their alliances, and to speak with strangers. It is composed of two pieces, of a red stone polished like marble and pierced in such a fashion that one end serves to receive the tobacco while the other engages in the stem, which is a baton two feet long, as large as an ordinary cane, and pierced through the center. It is embellished with the head and neck of various birds of handsome plumage; and they add thereto great plumes, red, green, or of other colors, in fans and pendants. They make particular state of this, because they regard it as the calumet of the sun; and in fact they present it to the sun to smoke when they wish to obtain calm or rain or fair weather. They are scrupulous not to bathe themselves at the beginning of the summer or to partake of the new fruits until after they have danced the calumet." Marquette goes on to describe the dance of the calumets which, he states, they perform for making peace or war, for public rejoicings, or for the honoring of another nation or of important personages. The ceremony begins with songs, and when all are assembled the Manitou is saluted "by waving the calumet and throwing smoke from its mouth as if they were presenting incense. It was customary first respectfully to take the calumet, and supporting it with the two hands to cause it to dance in cadence, following the air of the songs. They caused it to make differing figures: now they made it to be seen of the whole assembly, turning it from one side to the other; now they presented it to the sun, as if they wished to cause it to smoke; now they directed it toward the earth; now they extended its wings as if for flight; again it was brought to the mouth of the assistants that they might smoke,— and all in cadence."

A second act, as described by Marquette, is still more interesting from the point of view of the symbolism of the pipe. In this, to the beating of a drum a combat was simulated in which one of the actors was armed with bow and arrow and tomahawk, while his opponent carried only a calumet, which nevertheless dramatically prevailed over the warlike armament. "The act could pass for a very pretty *entrée de ballet* in France," comments Marquette, "and the festival terminates, as usually among the Indians, with recountings of feats of arms by the warriors, and once more by the action of smoking, after which the chief presented the calumet to the nation which had been invited to this ceremony, as mark of the lasting peace which would hold between the two nations."

Probably the most instructive native account of the meaning of a ceremonial smoke-offering is that given by Sword, a Dakota shaman. According to this teacher, before a shaman can perform a ceremony in which deities participate, he must fill and light a pipe and say: [5] "Friends of Wakinyan, I pass the pipe to you first. Circling I pass to you who dwell with the Father. Circling pass to beginning day. Circling pass to the beautiful one. Circling I complete the four quarters and the time. I pass the pipe to the Father with the Sky. I smoke with the Great Spirit. Let us have a blue day."

Beginning with the West the mouthpiece is pointed to the four directions, or rather to the Winds of these quarters. Wakinyan, in the Siouan tetralogies,[6] is the Winged One, associated with the Rock, which is the deity of the West, and the Winged are the strong ones of the West. Next in turn the pipe is offered to the North Wind, the East Wind, and the South Wind. The North Wind is the companion of Wazi, the Wizard, "beginning day" designates the lodge of the East Wind, while the "beautiful one" is the feminine deity who is companion of the South Wind and who dwells in his lodge "under the Sun at midday." "It pleases the South Wind to be addressed through his companion rather than directly," said Sword. The Four Winds are the messengers of the gods, and for this reason should be first addressed. The shaman explained the meaning of the rite as follows:

When the offering has been made to the South Wind the Shaman should move the pipe in the same manner until the mouthpiece again points toward the west, and say, "Circling I complete the four quarters and the time." He should do this because the Four Winds are the four quarters of the circle and mankind knows not where they may be or whence they may come and the pipe should be offered directly toward them. The four quarters embrace all that are on the world and all that are in the sky. Therefore, by circling the pipe, the offering is made to all the gods. The circle is the symbol of time, for the daytime, the night time, and the moon time are circles above the world, and the year time is a circle around the border of the world. Therefore, the lighted pipe moved in a complete circle is an offering to all the times.

When the Shaman has completed the four quarters and the time he should point the mouthpiece of the pipe toward the sky and say, "I pass the pipe to the father with the sky." This is an offering to the Wind, for when the Four Winds left the lodge of their father, the Wind, he went from it, and dwells with the sky. He controls the seasons and the weather, and he should be propitiated when good weather is desired.

Then the Shaman should smoke the pipe and while doing so, should say, "I smoke with the Great Spirit. Let us have a blue day."

To smoke with the Great Spirit means that the one smoking is in communion with the Great Spirit. Then he may make a prayer. The prayer here is for a blue day. Ordinarily, a blue day means a cloudless or successful day. When a Shaman formally prays for a blue day, it means an enjoyable day and an effective performance of a ceremony.

Chief Standing Bear is a fellow tribesman of Sword. Reared in early life in the thought and customs of his people and later passing through the schools of the white man, he understands the ideals of the two peoples as few of either race can. It is from him that we have these words: [7] "The pipe was a tangible, visible link that joined man to Wakan Tanka and every puff of smoke that ascended in prayer unfailingly reached His presence. With it faith was upheld, ceremony sanctified, and the being consecrated. All the meanings of moral duty, ethics, religious and spiritual conceptions were symbolized in the pipe. It signified brotherhood, peace, and the perfection of Wakan Tanka, and to the Lakota [8] the pipe stood for that which the Bible, Church, State, and Flag, all combined, represented in the mind of the white man. Without the pipe no altar was complete and no ceremony effective. . . . Smoking was the Indian Angelus, and whenever its smoke ascended, men, women, and children acknowledged the sacred presence of their Big Holy."

III

DESCRIPTIONS SUCH AS those just quoted indicate the essential ritual form and the significance attached to the ceremonial smoking of the calumet. In practice the rite varies from tribe to tribe and ceremony to ceremony, and indeed from individual to individual. But there are universal features which indicate the primary symbolism and lead us into certain matters of human understanding and of the mind's radical metaphors which should enlighten us not only in the field of American Indian thought but also in the ideas and symbols of all mankind.

In the ceremonial gesture of the smoke offering, the several puffs may be directed to three, four, five, six, or seven points; but in every case these points belong to the one general system which in full is defined only by all seven. The smoke may be directed to the Above, the Below, and the Here; it may be directed to the four cardinals of the compass—East, South, West, and North, for it usually moves sunwise in sequence; it may be offered to the Quarters of the Earth and to the Above or to the Here, and this would yield a five-puff rite; or again to the Quarters, the Sky and the Earth, and this would yield six; and finally, in the full form, smoke will be blown to the six points which define the plane of earth's horizon and the zenith and nadir of its axis, and to that Middle Place where the axis cuts the plane to form the site of the ceremony and the ritual center of the World. Conceptually these seven points define man's primary projection of the universe, his World Frame, or cosmic abode, within which is to be placed all the furniture of creation. For it is only necessary to connect the four cardinals with a line marking the circle of the visible horizon, and, following the courses of the sun and stars, to draw the line of the wheel of day, circumvolent from sun-

rise to zenith, from setting to nadir and again downward and onward to returning dawn, in order to complete the great circles
drawn upon the face of the abyss which yield us the terrestrial
and the celestial spheres. It is clear that the Indian, after the manner of our compass, not only organized the plane of the earth
with respect to the radical four of the cardinal points, but that he
also subdivided the Above and the Below into zones and latitudes. First it is important to perceive that the red man's projection of his universe, incipiently at least, is a circumscribing
sphere with axis and equator, longitudes and latitudes, and that
the ritual of the pipe is schematically a recognition of the points
from which the great lines of the sphere are generated.

This primary projection of the physical world is of course not
uniquely a product of American Indian thought. The quaternity
of the cardinal directions and the trinity of heaven, earth and hell
belong to many lands and peoples. It is a mathematical construction, but it is one developed not from chance but from a reason
universal to mankind, and that reason is to be found in the
human skeleton itself. Man is upright, erect, in his active habit,
and he is four-square in his frame, and these two facts give him
his image of a physical world circumscribing his bodily life. In
the Indo-European and in many other languages of the Old
World and the New the primitive orientation of man is indicated
by those root-names for the directions which are, in meaning, for
the east, "the before," for the west "the behind," for the south "the
right hand," and for the north "the left hand." That the heavens
are figured as the crown and front, earth's middle as the navel
and the bowels, and earth's base as the footing of creation is
symbolized in the image of that Titan who adorns the symbolic
art of many peoples. The axial dimension of the universe is thus
deduced from the standing position of a man. So standing, there
at the middle, the human skeleton yields a world-frame with its
four quarters and its three bodily divisions. Certainly it is no
matter of merely idle imagination to note that the intellectual
feat which our conception of a "world" implies is profoundly associated with just those physical traits which most mark off man
from his fellow mammalians; for had we remained quadrupeds,

with horse and elephant, ox and dog, it is only to be assumed that (had any world been possible) our cardinal points must have been six and not four. Heaven could never have been so high nor hell so low for creatures whose mouth gives the main source of tactile definition. Geometry is the most human of sciences, clearly derivative from that bodily frame and carriage from which we formulate the dimensions of the world and the structures of that space which we are willing to call the real space.

In this connection it is notable that as for the Greek, so for the American Indian, numbers possess strongly a geometrical significance. They are symbols of order, and especially of the order of space, rather than indicators of class or quantity; and to certain of them there attaches also the glamor of fortune or fate, as reflected alike in tale and ritual. In the main, it is the number *four* that to the red man carried the notion of luck or charm which the European associates more readily with three; and this luckiness of four is perhaps because this most geometrical of all the numbers—symbol of the plane of Earth—accords with the vividly spatial and visual form which Nature takes on for the Indian's eyes. Four-part and cruciform emblems, crosses of every style and quartered designs are extremely common in Indian art, giving expression to the quaternities of his thought, and in his metaphysical moments the whole realm of distinguishable things is apt to be organized in fours or in multiples of fours. The kinds of living things, animals, birds, insects, plants are organized into fours; so are the meteorologicals, the winds and the stars and the heavenly bodies; so the hills and waters; and so also the storeys or regions of the world above and the world below, which for many of the native peoples are four. But perhaps the most significant and individual symbolism of all is that of color. Here again a fourfold order is established, each cardinal direction having its own color (not invariable for all tribes or societies), while the above is the realm of the union of the radical colors and the below the realm of their deprivation. Such primarily symbolic colors are associated with the living kinds of plants and animals, with beads and with minerals, and intricately with ceremony and costume; they even form a sound language, songs not less than

powers and "medicines" having their color values. One may say
that for the Indian more than for any other human race colors
are the elements of the whole phantasm of Nature and are, with
number, the teachers of its innermost wisdom.[9] It is not a little
odd that on another level of speculation our own physical science
likewise rests its claim to understanding upon formulary numbers
and the spectra of radiant energy.

IV

THE IMPORTANCE OF COLOR in the Indian's depiction of the world,
second only to number and to geometric form, brings us directly
to the rôle which vision—inner and outer—plays in the orientation
of his life. To begin with, we have stated that his world-frame is
a form circumscribed about his own body and deriving its generative points from projections indicated by his own skeletal structure—with the east as "the before" and the west as "the behind"—
a mode ancient for all mankind. But why is the east chosen as
the first of the cardinals once the Middle Place, the center of this
world, is established? The answer is very simple and is contained
in the rival names *orient* and *east;* for *orient* is from the verb
oriri, to arise, and *east* is a cognate of *eos,* the dawn. It is the
rising-point of the sun, the light of the dawning day, that estab-
lishes the fiducial primacy of the east among the cardinals and
introduces the dimensions of time into the static planning of the
world's spaces.

Man in his abode, his mid-earth station, arises from that night
which is his symbol of chaos and negation to greet the first rays
of the morning sun. This is the hour of his day's creation, and the
hour also of *cosmos,* of order, in his life. He looks to the east and
names it the before or the arising; and having established this,
the first radius of his universe, from his station and his own up-
standing posture, he gives to his awakening world its orientation,
its eastering, and perceives it as a field of action. Many a traveler
among the prairie tribes has been impressed by the frequent custom of greeting the rising sun erect and full-face, that the sun's
first ray may give strength and valor for the day. Both temporary

ceremonial lodges and permanent shrines and temples open to the eastern horizon, either to the seasonal point of the equinoctial rising or to the solstitial station of the sunrise. The Old World, of course, knows the same ancient adoration, for it springs from our essential habit as creatures of the day. *Fiat lux* is, in a more universal sense than the writer of Genesis could have guessed, the law of our world's creation.

There are many rites and myths in Indian lore elucidating this fundamental metaphor, which lies at the root of so much of man's philosophy and reflects perhaps most of the greatness of his understanding; but among these none more vividly combines the symbolisms of form and color than does the Navaho analogy to the Greek myth of Phaethon—the tale of the creation of the sun. The tale begins with an account of the ascent of the First People from the underworlds of Navaho cosmology.[10] "The first three worlds," the narrative continues, "were neither good nor healthful. They moved all the time and made the people dizzy. Upon ascending into this world the Navajo found only darkness, and they said, 'We must have light.' " Thereafter two cosmic women were summoned to their aid, symbols of East and West. Their names were Estsanatlehi (here rendered Ahsonnutli) and Yolkai Estsan (here Yolaikaiason). The Indians told these women of their desire for light. The narrative proceeds:

The Navajo had already partially separated light into its several colors. Next to the floor was white, indicating dawn, upon the white, blue was spread for morning, and on the blue, yellow for sunset, and next was black, representing night. They had prayed long and continuously over these, but their prayers had availed nothing. The two women on arriving told the people to have patience and their prayers would eventually be answered.

Night had a familiar, who was always at his ear. This person said, "Send for the youth at the great falls." Night sent as his messenger a shooting star. The youth soon appeared and said, "Ahsonnutli, the ahstjeohltoi (hermaphrodite), has white beads in her right breast and turquoise in her left. We will tell her to lay them on darkness and see what she can do with her prayers." This she did. (The old priest relating this myth now produced a pouch containing corn pollen and a crystal, which he dipped in the pollen and said, "Now we must all eat of this pollen and place some on our heads, for we are to talk about it.") The youth from the great falls said to Ahsonnutli, "You have carried the white-shell beads and turquoise a long time; you should know what to say." Then with a crystal dipped in pollen she marked eyes and mouth on the turquoise and on the white-shell beads, and forming a circle around these with the crystal, she produced a slight light from the white-shell beads and a greater light from the turquoise, but the light was insufficient.

Twelve men lived at each of the cardinal points. The forty-eight men were sent for. After their arrival Ahsonnutli sang a song, the men sitting opposite to her; yet even with their presence the song failed to secure the needed light. Two eagle plumes were placed upon each cheek of the turquoise and two on the cheeks of the white-shell beads and one at each of the cardinal points. The twelve men of the east placed twelve turquoises at the east of the faces. The twelve men of the south placed twelve white-shell beads at the south. The twelve men of the west placed twelve turquoises at the west. Those of the north placed twelve white-shell beads at that point. Then with the crystal dipped in corn pollen they made a circle embracing the whole. The wish still remained unrealized. Then Ahsonnutli held the crystal over the turquoise face, whereupon it lighted into a blaze. The people retreated far back on account of the great heat, which continued increasing. The men from the four points found the heat so intense that they arose, but they could hardly stand, as the heavens were so close to them. They looked up and saw two rainbows, one across the other from east to west and from north to south. The heads and feet of the rainbows almost touched the men's heads. The men tried to raise the great light, but each time they failed.

Finally a man and a woman appeared, whence they knew not. The man's name was Atseatsine [Atse Hastin] and the woman's name was Atseatsan [Atse Estsan]. They were asked, "How can this sun be got up?" They replied, "We know; we heard the people down here trying to raise it, and this is why we came." "Chanteen" (sun's rays), exclaimed the man, "I have the chanteen; I have a crystal from which I can light the chanteen, and I have the rainbow; with these three I can raise the sun." The people said, "Go ahead and raise it." When he had elevated the sun a short distance it tipped a little and burned vegetation and scorched the people, for it was still too near. Then the people said to Atseatsine and Atseatsan, "Raise the sun higher," and they continued to elevate it, and yet it continued to burn everything. They were then called to "lift it higher still, . . . ," but after a certain height was reached their power failed; it would go no farther.

The couple then made four poles, two of turquoise and two of white-shell beads, and each was put under the sun, and with these poles the twelve men at each of the cardinal points raised it. They could not get it high enough to prevent the people and grass from burning. The people then said, "Let us stretch the world"; so the twelve men at each point expanded the world. The sun continued to rise as the world expanded, and began to shine with less heat, but when it reached the meridian the heat became great and the people suffered much. They crawled everywhere to find shade. Then the voice of Darkness went four times around the world telling the men at the cardinal points to go on expanding the world. "I want all this trouble stopped," said Darkness; "the people are suffering and all is burning; you must continue stretching." And the men blew and stretched, and after a time they saw the sun rise beautifully, and when the sun again reached the meridian it was only tropical. It was then just right, and as far as the eye could reach the earth was encircled first with the white dawn of day, then with the blue of early morning, and all things were perfect. And Ahsonnutli commanded the twelve men to go to the east, south, west, and north, to hold up the heavens (Yiyanitsinni, the holders-up of the heavens), which office they are supposed to perform to this day.

V

THE NAVAHO MYTH of the creation of the sun of our world leaves us with the perfected creation of zenith day: God saw the work of his hand, and it was good. But the Wheel of Day, which is also the Wheel of Time, does not cease its revolutions with morning and noon. Morning, as we have said, is the moment of invigoration, when new life awakens and all creation is astir—it is creation itself, an "in the beginning." Just as man's awakening, after that lapse into the nothingness of chaos which is sleep, is a daily birth, so the dawning ray of the sun is the daily emergence of a world out of chaos—"a thing very mysterious," said Tahirussawichi,[11] "although it happens every day." So it is that the red man greets the dawn with raised palms, with a prayer, with a pipe, eager to receive into himself that power and life of which its first ray is the bearer. So it is also, in the great myths, that each renewed age of the world, each great historic "Sun" of time, as the ancients of Mexico spoke, began with its own creative dawn, when a greater and more glorious solar disk, awaited with vigil and prayer, first broke above its horizon.

But beyond the white light of dawn expands the blue day of our active life, nooned with achievement and upward zoned to the circle of Father Heaven himself; and still beyond this is the fated descent, as the sun sinks from maturity to age, into the fires and reflections of evening. Night, too, sunless for us, beyond the margins of the west marks the hours of the sun's more pallid journeyings through the caverns of the dead, our spiritual antipodes. Such conceptions belong to old Egypt and Babylon and Greece, to Scandinavia and the Mongol world, and not less to the peoples of America.

In Indian imagery this Wheel of Day is no less vivid with color than is the disk of earth. The wheel and dart game, like the ball game *tlachtli* [12] of the Mexican nations, is built upon solar symbolism, and it is in many cases a quadrated wheel which is used, each of the four sections being webbed with its own cosmic color. The four points of daily time are morning, noon, evening, and night, and it is perhaps inevitable that the number imagery which is born of our skeletal form and creates space should receive its flesh of color from that visual flow of light and shade, of tint, intensity and hue, which the great hours of the day changingly yield. Light gives us form and color, we say; light gives us also that union of rigid and defined space with fluid and transforming time which is the reality of a primitive no less than of an Einsteinian *physis:* physical nature is first conceived by bones and eyes, functioning in man's frame.

Not less does the wheel function in man's life. For the conception of the revolving day is again the simple and inevitable emblem of both the *daily life* and the natural *lifetime.* For the Egyptians Harmachis, boy and physician, was the sunrise; Horus was the victor youth of the ascending sun; Re was the lord of noonday, king and ruler; and Tum was the old man of the western horizon. More bloodily the Aztec conceived Tonatiuh, the sun disc, as the avatar first of the heart of his sacrificed herald, the Morning Star, red with new-throbbing life; thence, as he mounted to the zenith, he was a war-captain bearing in his train the host of those who had perished in the violence of battle, glorious as *Sol Invictus*. But he was dragged from his high throne, down toward the dark horizon of the west, by the anguished and vengeful claws of the Dark Mothers, the women who had died in child-birth, in life-giving. Here is the harsh concept of a daily birth and a daily death of the Lord of Day. But not all Indian thought is of this grim cast. With the nations of the prairies, and with all who are simply natural, the sun of morning is the life-giver; the sun of full day and of noon is the lord of high deed and full vision; and the sun of the vanishing day is the father of reflection and of the mind's meditation. "Farewell, our Father, the Shining One—farewell, whither thou goest! Thy thought this day thou has given us." This is the essence of a Huichol song-prayer of evening.[13]

So also of life itself, which is but a greater day in which years count the hours. From the dawn comes generation and birth. Love, Valor, and the Wisdom of Medicine—life's three great treasures, as Indian myth sees them—are all gifts of the day and of sunward-directed prayer. But the sunset is the blazed and streamered trail into the west, which souls must follow, where the Master of Day, gathering about him his clouds and his visions, vanishes into the dark. In American Indian myth generally the Morning and the Evening are Heroic Twins: one is lord of this life and of the illuminated earth; the brother, caught by underworld demons or thither banished by fate, is ruler and companion of the dead. The duality takes many forms: those of Sapling and Flint, earth's vegetation and earth's rock; those of Manabozho and Chibiabos, the hunter-sun and his hapless brother; those of the two diminutive giant-slayers, the Twin Gods of War of the Pueblo peoples; those of the morning and evening incarnations of Tezcatlipoca and of Quetzalcoatl among the Aztecs; but the ultimate image which underlies all is fundamentally that of the image of the daily sun in its simple correspondence with waking and sleeping, with life and death. No more profound and at the same time ironical myth of this meaning is to be found than the tale—already impressive to the first Jesuit missionaries in Quebec—of the four seekers who journeyed to the sunrise lodge of Manabozho, the White Hare of Morning, to implore divine gifts. The first prayed for hunter's skill, and this was granted; the second for success in love, and this was granted; the third, for skill in medicine and healing and in the preservation of life, and this was granted. But when the fourth asked of the Life-Giver freedom from death, life eternal, the favor came in the only form which the gods could grant: he was transformed into unchanging stone. In the end the Sun's course is the Course of Destiny.[14]

The Disc of Space and the Wheel of Time, the encircling quarters and the revolving years, are nature's two circumscriptions of man's station and range. All peoples have reduced them to ritual and emblem, of which our astrophysical science is only the most recent form. American Indian ritual everywhere follows this common prescriptive plan of our humanity, although at the same time it gathers into itself those experiences which were distinctive of America and which make of the Indian's ritual life a New World poetry and a New World wisdom.

VI

BUT IT IS NOT only as a definition of the dimensions of cosmic space and time, as a projection of the world and its years, that the symbolism of the calumet is significant. The regions which circumscribe the Here are, after all, only the projected environment fitted about the body and life of the Central Man, much as a mollusc's shell is given shape and order by its bodily life. *Cosmos,* order, is essentially physiological, or at most psychophysical, in its logic. The meters with which the world is diagrammed and so made comfortable to the mind (for order is such comfort) are derived from man's bones and muscles and organs, his senses, desires and intuitions—in brief from his conscious life. The world of understanding is anthropomorphic, which is but another way of saying that man is at its center and is himself the principle of its structural being. One of the most curious and interesting types of Mediaeval-learned illustration is that of the schematic man, each organ and part emblematically redupli-cated in a structure of nature, which in turn is no more than the counterpart of his organism—the world itself being conceived as a vaster man-being. Not even the heavens are remote from their especial and complementary relations to his organs and functions; the zodiacal signs betoken celestial influences upon his organs as well as vital forms projected into the starfield; and all astrol-ogy is only a more complex disquisition upon this impulsive sense that the world is somehow a figure conformed to man's own, like a vaster chart of his anatomy. Indeed, in subtler modes we have not yet escaped this sense of a man-centered cosmos; for the meas-ures of our physics and astrophysics are themselves, at their cores, imaginary numbers derived from our bodily life: man bone-lengths meter space, man paces yield us linear miles and motions, man work gives meaning to energy, man purpose to cause, and the whole cycle of our vital activities creates for us the intelli-gibilities of day and year and lifetime. Projected mathematically, by the numberings first counted out from our digits, all these give us our science-construed cosmos.

Indian thinking symbolizes this human centrality of man, no less than has European. This is true in both the social and the individual senses; for while it is evident that the Indian, like men of other continents than his, draws his spatial and temporal tokens from the body and life of a type-forming anatomical in-dividual, there is also, with him as with other men, a social sym-bolism, intrinsic in his cosmos. Man is at the center of the world not only individually, as a form of flesh and bone, but socially; and one may say that in most Indian ritual thinking the individ-ual *is,* vicariously, his human group—whether it be clan or tribe or ceremonial federation. This may be represented diagramati-cally, as it is in the way the encampment of a prairie people is set up on the occasion of festal celebration. There is the outer circle of the horizon, which defines "the place wherein the people dwell"; there is the great tribal camp circle, with its sky and earth divisions into which are assorted the living clans; and in the center there is the Medicine Lodge, usually circular, the site of the mystery and the Here-place of the world, with respect to which all else is oriented. The social form thus shapes itself after the pattern of the world whole, circumscribed by physical nature and circumscribing that central symbolic man-being of which it is in turn the reality.[15]

In his striking analysis of the symbolic man of the Osage tribe Francis La Flesche called attention to this triplicate relation as centrally symbolized by the ceremonial pipe. In the ritual devoted to this pipe upon the occasion of entering war, the pipe is offered by its tribal keeper to the men who represent the two great divisions of the tribe, the Sky-people and the Earth-people. In the chant the several parts of the pipe are spoken of as if they were the parts of the body of a man. This man, symbolized by the pipe, is for each warrior his own body, but he is also the tribe socially, which in its several parts is likewise thought of as a man, and as reflecting that world of sky and earth by which man is surrounded. The idea is probably quite akin to that which still impels nations to adopt some such anthropomorphic symbolism of their social life—in an Uncle Sam, a John Bull—just as in antiquity peoples deified their national existences in man-form gods or goddesses. When about to set forth upon a national venture, the Osage adds to such symbolism only his own form of ceremonial communion, that of the pipe and its smoking—American substitute for the sacrifice at the high altar of the Classical nations, or perhaps for the celebrant Mass of Christian nations. The words of the Osage chant, as abridged by La Flesche, are the vivid paraphrase of the symbol: [16]

Behold, this pipe. Verily a man!
Within it I have placed my being.
Place within it your own being, also,
Then free shall you be from all that brings death.

Behold, the neck of the pipe!
Within it I have placed my own neck.
Place within it your neck, also,
Then free shall you be from all that brings death, O, Honga!

THE PIPE OF PEACE

Behold, the mouth of the pipe!
Within it I have placed my own mouth.
Place within it your mouth, also,
Then free shall you be from all that brings death, O, Honga!

Behold, the right side of the pipe!
Within it I have placed the right side of my own body.
Place within it the right side of your own body, also,
Then free shall you be from all that brings death, O, Honga!

Behold, the spine of the pipe!
Within it I have placed my own spine.
Place within it your own spine, also,
Then free shall you be from all that brings death, O, Honga!

Behold, the left side of the pipe!
Within it I have placed the left side of my own body, O, Honga!
Place within it the left side of your own body,
Then shall you be free from all that brings death, O, Honga!

Behold, the hollow of the pipe!
Within it I have placed the hollow of my own body.
Place within it the hollow of your own body, also,
Then shall you be free from all that brings death, O, Honga!

Behold, the thong that holds together the bowl and the stem!
Within it I have placed my breathing-tube.
Place within it your own breathing-tube, also,
Then shall you be free from all that brings death, O, Honga!

When you turn from the rising sun to the setting sun to go against
    your enemies,
This pipe shall you use when you go forth to invoke aid from
    Wakonda,
Then shall your prayers be speedily granted, O, Honga!
Yea even before the sun shall o'er-top the walls of your dwelling,
Your prayers shall surely be granted, O, Honga!

This ritual prayer is clearly a half-magical spell, intended to
ensure life-preservation to the men going into peril. In this
sense it is individual. But it is also for the tribe, whose safety is
likewise at stake, and which is personified in the Symbolic Man.
The line "when you turn from the rising sun to the setting sun

to go against your enemies" makes this clear. For on the occasion of war the whole symbolism of Osage ritual life was reversed. In times of peace the Osage camp-circle faced the east, with the Earth-people to the south and the Sky-people to the north. In wartime this image was transposed: the Honga, symbolizing the vital energies of Earth, encamped to the north, the Tsizhu, the Sky-people, to the south; while the tribal man, symbolizing all and symbolized in the pipe, now faced the west. There are such changes in symbolism in other tribes, where the shift from peace to war is felt to shift the whole cosmic plan: the colors shift their quarters and into nature Discordia enters with Bellona.

VII

In the Osage ritual just described the pipe is in the charge of a leader who, while he is in a sense the actual chieftain of the war-party, yet does none of the fighting. It is his function to appoint the man who is to conduct the attack, but it is his more essential rôle to guard the sacred pipe and employ it in supplications for success: the pipe is, in brief, of the nature of a palladium, or at least of a sacred vessel such as the Hebrew Ark, and its keeper is a man who holds himself apart from actual bloodshed, even while his enterprise is that of war.

This is only one among many cases in which the calumet is not a Pipe of Peace but a Pipe of War. The Kiowa, for example, employed a red pipe as symbol for enlistment in a war-party: the organizer of the expedition sent this pipe to the several war societies, and while no man need accept it, to take and smoke it was the pledge of participation. Pipes of war and peace are mentioned from early times onward, so that it is clearly in part a misunderstanding to name the ceremonial pipe the "pipe of peace." In many uses it was so, and it is possible that this was its first and widest employment; but the mere fact that the pipe and its smoking, and in the main the cultivation of tobacco, were in the hands of men and warriors, with the women excluded, indicates that it was from early times much more than a symbol of peaceful pledges or intentions.

Its fuller symbolism is very clearly that of a sacred, or "medicine" emblem, to be employed wherever the issue was serious or fateful. This might be a purely social occasion, and every society appears to have had in its ceremonial bundle its own sacred pipe or pipes; the giving of a pipe to a group was, like a coronation, the token of the transmission to them of social rights; and in myth and in the ritual commemoration of myth the pipe is an accompaniment of the reception of a culture gift. In the Dakota legend of the gift of maize from the White Buffalo Cow, represented as a beautiful Woman-from-Heaven, a Brulé version tells how the divine giver appeared to two young men, and with kernels of maize of the four colors, she presented them with a pipe, saying: [17] "This pipe is related to the heavens, and you shall live with it. . . . Clouds of many colors may come up from the south, but look at the pipe and the blue sky and know that the clouds will soon pass away and all will become blue and clear again. . . . When it shall be blue in the west, know that it is closely related to you through the pipe and the blue heavens, and by that you shall grow rich. . . . I am the White Buffalo Cow; my milk is of four kinds; I spill it upon the earth that you may live by it." It is clear that the symbolism underlying the ritual gift is here more than social and more than a mere gesture to the structure of Nature: the pipe is itself, in some deeply indefinable sense, a mystic token of man's union with nature, and like the Christian cross, of his temporal and spiritual salvation.

No less than for the group this symbolism holds also for the individual. When the watcher goes forth to keep his vigil for the Sun Dance, he bears with him as first essential the pipe which is his offering, and the pipe itself may constitute a man's prayer. In her account of the Omaha attitude toward Wakonda, the Great Spirit or Mystery of the Siouan peoples, Alice Fletcher speaks in this fashion of personal prayers: [18] "A man would take a pipe and go alone to the hills; there he would silently offer smoke and utter the call, *Wakonda ho!*, while the moving cause, or purport of his prayer, would remain unexpressed in words. If his stress of feeling was great, he would leave the pipe on the ground where his appeal had been made. This form of prayer (made only by men) was called . . . 'addressing with the pipe.' "

No symbol could more specifically summarize the last and most intrinsic symbolism of the pipe. Central in the universe is man; central in man is his mind's thought and his heart's aspiration. The pipe of peace was the emblem of each.

CHAPTER II

The Tree of Life

I

FOR MILES THE PRAIRIES stretch treeless. To the northern horizon and the eastern horizon there is nothing but the undulating swales and swells moulded into unanticipated patterns by the continental ice-drifts, millennially remote. Here and there is a shallow hill-top basin filled with waters fed from nowhere, mere memories of the winter's snows, now formed into still mirrors of the inexhaustible blue of a wind-cleansed sky. Sedges grow about these upland lakelets, and water-fowl in myriads now rise with a sun-flash from every wing, now descended in showers to their perpetual bickerings, their pipings upraised only to be immediately absorbed in the silence of a space which is equally oblivious of birds and men. Before us shimmer all the iridescences of greens, violets, purples, softened into the velvety textures of the prairie grasses, now and again transformed into a wave of ethereal blue where a flax field has breathed into the high summer's blossoming. But the distance is the remotest of margins, the line of the great circle which marks the rim of Earth's drumhead where it hangs suspended before the Musician of the Skies.

Westward there is a long gash in the flow of the prairies, with repeated gleams of the Upper Missouri, where that river's great

bending turns on its southward course. Below the bluffs spreads
the green of tree-tops and brush, lithe willow and the flickering
leafage of cottonwoods, glossy berry bushes, the blue-gray sage,
and the dogwood that gives to the Indian's *kinnikinnic* a flavor
more native than his own tobacco.[1] Westward, too, just on the
bench over the river, shines the circle of tipis and tents and covered wagons which marks the ceremonial camp of the Arikara,
prepared for their summer festival, for the erection of the sacred
Cedar Tree and the Mystery of Mother Corn.[2] In the midst of
the vast prairies the nations of men are very small, camp circles
and council circles, ephemeral as the flocks of fowl that rise and
vanish into the air. . . . But evening is approaching and shadows,
and there is an intimacy in twilight that is friendly to small creatures. Smoke from camp-fires, and now the twinkling blaze, and
we know that the women are bustling about their kettles and the
men tending the horses. As we make our own camp, a quarter-
mile away, the rim of the sun sinks down and we hear the voice
of a man, long, clear, ululating, and we can discern his blanketed
form, erect upon the roof of the brown Medicine Lodge, beside
the bison skull which makes a white spot just over the long en-
trance-way. It is Crow Ghost, the priest, calling the opening of
the ceremony, and calling not alone to his tribesmen round
about, but to the whole assemblage of invisible Powers that abide
on earth and in sky and daily and nightly walk beyond the rim
of the world. His voice rings like music, pulsates on the evening
air, ascends, and is erased into the still breath above.

Night has fallen, and within the great lodge begins the rite of
purification. The lodge is circular; its entrance is from the east;
its roof is supported by four pillars, trunks of sturdy trees, the
names of which are Sunrise and Thunder and Wind and Night.
The central space within the pillars is for the fire, and four logs
are ended to the center, forming a cross pointing to Earth's four
quarters. Westward of the fire is the altar-place, and the station
of the chief priest and his musicians, while right and left, as far
as the eastern pillars, are the stations of the Medicine societies,
each with its drum before while above is suspended its sacred

bundle and its emblem of beast-skin or bird-feathers—Elk Society, Buffalo Society, Cormorant, Duck, Owl. Opposite the Sunrise pillar is the spectral society of the Ghosts, while across the lodge, at the station of Night are the Bears, potent in wisdom of the earth and strong in Medicine. The eastern portion of the lodge, beyond the pillars, is for attendants and guests.

The fire is lighted by the Fire-tender, and from its early sparks is ignited the tobacco in the ceremonial pipes, where, beginning with the priest, smoke is offered to the Quarters and the Above and the Below—to all that abide with man in this world-frame. "The ceremony is not of human origin," the priest explains; "it was given from Above long ago." The members of all the societies have painted their bodies with the sacred white clay brought from the magical Bad Lands. Now branches of sage are distributed to them; they arise; faggots are flung on the glowing log-ends and the blaze leaps up; the crier calls from the roof above the smoke-hole; the rattles sound; the motion begins. Closer and closer the white bodies move; they form a serried circle about the fireplace; knees and ankles, ankles and knees, almost a vertical motion, and the stamping of moccasined feet. The branches of sage move up and down; the musicians beat the drums and, even louder, the rawhide roll; voices chant. Dust, smoke, sound, the rhythm of whitened bodies, all is wraithlike and unreal. "What do they sing?" I ask. "They honor the fire. Fire is the oldest. Fire is the first living. That is what they sing."

A woman enters, an old woman, brown and wrinkled, and with nothing of ceremony about her costume. But she alone passes within the sacred space and joins the sage-dance behind the men. Her face is worn and strange, with that unforgettable admixture of voiceless tenderness and the long weathering of the wilds which one encounters on the faces of old Indian women. And as she dances, her voice is raised in a high, eerie keening that somehow impossibly combines the wail of a prairie wolf and the cry of a broken heart. "Why does she dance with the men?" "A woman who has fasted much and suffered much, a woman who has given much for the tribe, is given the privilege. She is like that. It was long ago." "Has she a name?" "They named her Lucky-in-the-House."

There is a song of praise, "Thanks for the Gift from the Power Above!" There is a prayer and a wailing. Then the dancers depart, to cast their sage-brush wands into the waters of the Missouri and to wash the sacred paint from their bodies . . . so that one recalls how also in ancient Athens the initiates ran to the sea and cast their wands into the waters and bathed in its waves, at their ceremony of purification, when the Mysteries were about to begin. . . .

But here, in this northern Indian lodge, the women stand with hands and voices upraised, and after the dancers the audience departs. Only Lucky-in-the-House remains in her station, east of the place of the Bears, forgetful of all, keening. . . .

II

AMERICAN INDIAN RITUALS of the type that marks the great tribal festivals most frequently have a four-part structure. There is first the preparation which usually occupies many days and is a matter primarily for the priests in charge, culminating in the purification, which as in the case of the Sage Dance just described, marks the opening of the ritual proper. Second, there are secret ceremonies, largely of consecration, but often interspersed with episodes and always with significant teachings. Third, there is the great dramatic miming of the Mystery—a spectacle which is for all to see, but is truly understood only by the initiate: this is what is commonly called the dance. Lastly, there is the tribal festival, a general rejoicing with much gift-giving, feasting, naming, and a large measure of both humor and pathos. This last feature marks a major purpose of the whole, which is to set the tribe at rights both with its own tribal world and with that world of nature by whose complaisance all life exists. The poor are taken care of at this festival; children are introduced and names given them; foster parents are designated for the needy; those who have served the tribe and the heroic whose deeds call for recognition are given honor; and not least all the participants are blessed, formally or

THE TREE OF LIFE

by their mere sharing in the revelation. The whole ceremony is
at once a prayer for prosperity and a blessing of the tribal life.
At the heart of it is a drama.

At the foundation of the world is the pillar of stone, the
"Grandfather," the "Aged One," the abiding rock. Fifty paces before the entrance of the Medicine Lodge the pillar stands, fixed
and unchanging through summer and winter, but now, for the
festival, anointed and painted with red, the sign of life. With
him must be associated the "Grandmother" of life, the living
Cedar Tree, green the year long, but because she is symbol of the
annually fading and renewing vegetation of the earth and of the
unceasing drama of human passing and renewal, each year she
must be upreared anew, fifty paces toward the sunrise from
Grandfather Rock. The ritual of the second day is the ritual of
Grandmother Cedar.

Early in the morning, from the roof over the entranceway of
the great Lodge, is heard the call of the priest, proclaiming the
ceremonies of the day and greeting the youthful sun just lifted
above the horizon. Within the Lodge the members of the societies
are being painted and adorned, each with his own regalia, and the
sacred objects are receiving offerings of smoke. Novitiates are introduced—sons to succeed fathers who have gone on to the Spirit
Lodge—and their bodies are anointed and their faces painted,
transforming them into *other* beings; for after the painted pattern is on a man's face he is not to be addressed except by one
who has been blessed and has become an intermediary. Finally
there is the song of departure, and except for the vigil-keepers,
the lodge is emptied, and the procession goes seeking the tree.
Grandmother Cedar has been felled in the mysterious Bad Lands,
and laboriously brought to the vicinity of the camp. New ceremonies there: paintings, sending out of scouts to the world Quarters, smoke-offerings, prayers, until finally the tree is taken up
and brought in by its bearers, to be greeted joyfully by the people
within the camp circle and smothered with gifts—yards of colored
cloth, blankets, feather ornaments, and the peeled willow wands
which are symbols of horses. Each giver is blessed with symbolic
movement of the priest's hands, never actually laid upon the

body whose form it traces, foot to thigh, thigh to shoulder, head, and down again. Meanwhile the members of the societies, in their animal maskings and mimings, are out in the open entertaining the crowd with gaieties. The Bears, heavy in their ponderous bearskin robes, are pursuing deer and elk and the other animals, each provided with whistles and dancing temptingly near to their lumbering pursuers. Should the Bear touch his quarry he may manhandle him as he pleases; that is the game; but escape proves easy for the nearly nude, agile men, who in their leafy ornaments seem most like classical fauns. Finally the Grandmother Cedar is borne within, for a new and ritual consecration beside the altar, and for a curious drama in which the leaders of the societies attack and strike the tree, as if it were an enemy—rattles, drums, singing, dancing all the time. At last Snow Bird, of the Elk Society, fastens a fan of hawk feathers at the crown of the tree, the butt of which has already been painted red. Once more the procession resumes, as the tree is borne out and set up not far from Grandfather Rock, there to remain standing until the ice breaks in the Missouri with the next spring thaw. Then mothers will fasten upon its branches the worn shoes of their little children, and Grandmother Cedar will be consigned to the flooding waters of the Missouri. Miles downstream, say the Arikara, from the bluffs where their ancestors dwelt, the spirits of their Ancients will be watching, and when they see the numbers of the children's moccasins tied to the branches of the floating tree, they will be happy in their spiritland, for they will know that the tribe is still powerful in the land.

The third day is given to the Mystery of Mother Corn. It is Mother Corn who has conducted man from the nether world of his olden origins, up into the light of day and the life of this land. She has been his guide and guardian, food-giver and life-giver, and the source of wisdom and intelligence, and animals no less than men are under her protection, and, with cereal food, game also is her gift. The whole Medicine Lodge is emblematic of her presiding presence, and the day's ceremonies are its lesson. Except in the hunting episode of the morning, when the symbolic hunt takes place and the devoted animal is slain, token of the good of man, and flesh for the feast, women play a large rôle in this day's celebration, for it is to their charge that food care is committed.

The hunt takes place, and the beef animal, replacing the ancient bison, is slain and ceremonially butchered. This is in the field. Afterwards all return once more to the camp circle, where now, within the Lodge, the symbol before the altar is the sheaf of green stalks which is the emblem of the Corn Mother. This is the day of festival and gift-giving, with namings and consecrations. But it is the day also of the drama which records first of all how the Ancients of the People came forth from the darkness, seeking their light; how they wandered naked and destitute, ignorant, cold, hungry, until there came the Woman from the South who brought the gift of the maize, that men might live. "Father Heaven placed Mother Corn in authority over all things on this Earth. She moves between men and the Spirit Above from whom all things come." [3]

The first dance is the dance of the hoeing. The women with shoulder-bone hoes, such as their mothers used, receive the sacred seed-corn from the priests; about the four pillars of the lodge they mime its planting, its cultivation, its reaping. Every woman seems to wish to take part, and one succeeds another in the scene. There is humor, too. A man jumps in and sportively imitates the weeding of a held—a playful insult which the woman resents. An Indian gotten up as a Negro, cocky straw hat, cowhide coat, turkey-feather tail, joins with comedy dancing. [4] Meanwhile gifts are continuous, and the excitement grows. Every gift must be called by the criers, and the recipients answer with loud thanks. An old blind man stands with streaming eyes holding blankets and food and the willow-wand emblem of a horse, his voice breaking with emotion as he praises the givers. Elder women are keening, the long piercing note cleaving every other sound with its eerie wail and its palpitant lament for the long ago and the life-fellows who are now but ghosts out of the past. Tears flow from many eyes, and the Fire-tender wipes them from the wet faces and with a reverent gesture presents them at the altar. For tears, too, are offerings to Mother Corn.

Later there is the drama of the hunt. Women in cowskins represent the buffaloes. They lumber along the lodge, curiously convincing in their movements, and one brings her young daughter in calfskin, representing the buffalo young. Then the hunter appears, an old man who in his youth had hunted the buffalo with the bow and arrow which he now carries. He dances mimetically about the little herd, and one after another, drawing his arrows from the coyote-skin quiver, thrusts an arrow under each victim's arm, symbol of the hunt. Each buffalo-cow in turn sinks to earth, and the hunter gathers up his arrows, wiping them carefully. But before the maskers may throw aside the heavy hides, the priest must mark each, there between the horns, with a wisp of featherdown, symbol of the breath of life.

The last dance is before the altar. The men stand with wands raised, emblems of the Mystery. But the dance is for the women, each of whom, at the last, receives from the Corn Priest an ear of seed-corn, for to their charge are committed the fields. The Song of Ending closes the rite.

Early on the fourth day the camp is broken. But before the people depart, an elder woman, one who had given much for her people, stands beside Grandmother Cedar and speaks. The people must live in harmony; they must do no evil, hold no ill thought; anger and bitterness must be banished; they must be of one heart. She lifts her hands and prays to the Power Above that he be compassionate to all, and that Indian and white man alike, all who have taken part in the ceremony, may find peace. . . . Tents are struck; wagons rumble away in every direction; from the lingering embers of the morning fires the thin wisps of smoke dissolve into the blue. As we drive eastward toward the thin line of trees that records a frontier planting, the scenes of the ritual days rise and fade phantasmagorically. But most vivid and most lingering is the image of the solitary dancer, behind the men, body swaying, feet and half-lifted hands rhythmic rather than active, and in her upraised face, weathered and tear-stained, the stamp of a vision, deathless and remote. . . .

III

THE CADDOAN TRIBES, of whom the Arikara are the northernmost representatives, probably represent the elder group among the Indians whom the white man encountered in the country of prairies which lies between the Missouri and the Rocky Mountains, and on southward into Texas. The Wichita of Kansas and the Pawnee of Nebraska, from whom the Arikara have branched in relatively recent times, were encountered on the Plains by the Spanish adventurers repeatedly from the sixteenth century until early in the eighteenth when, in 1720, the Pawnee inflicted upon the Spaniards such a defeat that movement in this direction was stopped. Meantime, however, the northern Caddoans themselves were being hard pushed by incursions of Siouan tribes from the axis of the Missouri River: the Arikara were forced up that river from their old homes in Nebraska by the Omaha, who replaced them, while the Pawnee were constantly at war with the Osage from the lower Missouri and with the Sioux of Dakota. It was possibly because of this pressure from peoples numerically much stronger than themselves that both Pawnee and Arikara became friends and allies of the French and American traders who gradually followed in the wake of De Bourgmond's expedition from St. Louis up to the mouth of the Platte in 1714. These Caddoan nations were never at war with the eastern Americans, and in the last fatal struggle with the Plains tribes there were still Arikara and Pawnee scouts in the service with Custer at the Little Big Horn. It was about this time, too, that the Sioux, surprising a Pawnee tribal hunt, inflicted upon them such terrible losses that they the more willingly retired from their ancient home in Nebraska to the relative safety of Oklahoma, then Indian Territory. The Arikara, moving farther and farther to the Upper Missouri, meantime became associated with the Hidatsa and the Mandan, both peoples of Siouan stock, though of another division than the Dakota, whose enmity they have shared with the Caddoan peoples.

There are many indications that the Caddoan culture, which has proved profoundly influential even upon its Siouan enemies, takes its origin in the Southwest. When Coronado in 1541 made his incursion into the central prairies in quest of the mirage cities of Quivera, his guides were Caddoan tribesmen whom he found residing in the Pueblo fortress of Pecos; and it was from the Pueblo, and later the Spanish New Mexicans that the Pawnee obtained the horses which they possessed by 1650 in considerable numbers, a half century before these animals became common among the Siouan peoples. The horse, however, did not so profoundly alter the manner of life of the Pawnee as it did that of Siouan and other Plains peoples, probably because they were already organized for an agricultural life—which plausibly derived from contacts with the agricultural peoples of the Southwest—in times long antedating the period of Coronado.[5]

In the ritual which has just been described the basic symbolism is obviously upgrown from the prairies themselves. The circular lodge and the camp-circle which surrounds it are in turn circumscribed by the circle of the horizon, which defines man's abode—"the rim of the world about which walk the winds." Above is the sky-dome, of which the dome-shaped lodge is itself a kind of replica. The four pillars of the lodge represent the structure of this intermediate space, symbolic of the sun and its course, of the thunderstorm, of the winds and the air, and finally of night and the ending of the day's and year's course—for this fourth pillar is also the pillar of the harvest. At the very center, the Middle Place, is the tribal and ceremonial hearth, a veritable Hestia, its fire fed by four logs oriented to the four cardinal points. The entranceway, facing the sunrise, is the path of all beginnings, and the true ceremonial circuit is sunwise—east to south to west to north, following the path which the sun's beams chart in his daily passage. The priestly station is at the west, just below the sacred bundle, and between this and the fireplace is the altar-space, sacred to Mother Corn, leader of man's way and the bread of his life. Outside, dawnwards, are Grandfather Rock, imperturbable, and Grandmother Cedar whose green carries through the winter's snows and whose annual renewal is the image of man's generative years. All this is elemental and simply structural, forming as it were the natural frame about which is shaped the flesh and form of the tribal life, hardly a trait of which is not somewhere symbolized in the festival. Indeed, ultimately the whole complex ceremony can only be interpreted as an essential prayer for the health and continuity of this life; and this is no doubt true also of all the great major rituals of the American Indians. Hardly less is to be said of the greater rituals of other races and creeds, for religion itself is, at the heart of it, man's expression of his aspiration for the afterlife.

IV

"THE CEDAR," says the priest, "is addressed as 'Grandmother'; the Cedar is turned and twisted by the winds, but she endures their buffetings even as the People must endure through adversity." [6] In this simple statement is probably to be found the root idea which governs the symbolism of the evergreens of coniferous type in whatever part of the world or from whatever source—the Christmas tree of Germanic origin being only a Christianization of the ancient Teutonic emblem of enduring life. Among the Pueblo Indians of New Mexico the use of pine, spruce and fir is frequent in ceremonial costumes, where the symbolism seems everywhere to be that of life and the powers of life. Coniferous evergreen is employed for collars, arm-bands, belts and kilts in ceremonial dances, where often branches of spruce are carried in the hands of the dancers, while the *jacal,* or ceremonial booth, is adorned with evergreen along with bright blankets and other ornaments. In the Pine Tree Dance of the Rio Grande Pueblos pine or spruce or fir trees are brought in from the forest and set within the dancing plaza. These may be two or four or eight; where two are used apparently one is devoted to each moiety of the community; where four or eight appear they are arranged singly or in pairs with respect to the cardinal directions. This dance is celebrated in the autumn, and it has something of the character of a harvest-home. It combines with a thanksgiving for the crops that have matured a plea for the frosts that will harden the corn and season the grapes for drying. But animal food is not forgotten, and with the dance is a tribal rabbit-hunt, followed by feasting, fun, and gift-giving. At the end the trees erected in the plaza are either returned and reset in their native forest or consigned to a stream, as is the sacred Cedar of the Arikara.

In still another Pueblo ceremony an evergreen is set in the dancing plaza in connection with a ritual plea for game. The Deer Dance, as it is called, is a winter ceremony devoted to the miming of the hunting of the greater game animals—bison, elk, mountain sheep, antelope—and here again the tree is introduced. The close association of the deer-kind with the pine tree may in part be mere forest-imagery, for, say the Indians, the deer loves the pine forest; but it is not improbable that far more deeply lies that symbolism which associates the deer not only with the east and the dawn but also with the beginnings of life at the creation of the world. In more than one American Indian cosmogony it is the elk or the buck that bays into existence created life, and sometimes in Indian art the tree is shown as springing from the pronged horns of the animal—as in the European lore of the vision of St. Hubert, the huntsman.[7] That the tree is transformed into a cross in the Christian version is only another example of transferred symbolism; for to the Indian as to the European the roman cross is symbol of the Tree of Life, shown sometimes in its simple geometric idea, sometimes with branched or foliated extremities, as in the famous crosses of Palenque.

When the sacred tree is introduced into the plaza in the ritual dance, sacred meal and pollen, symbols of food and fecundity, are sprinkled over them, and sometimes the feathers of birds are fastened to the upper tip, recalling at once not only the hawk plumage which is bound to the crest of the Arikara ceremonial cedar, but also the birds which mark the summits of the symbolic trees of Aztec and Maya art. The symbolism of spruce and fir is definitely that of the female life-giving powers. These are the trees which "make the world green," and like Grandmother Cedar they symbolize the vital energy of earth itself. Furthermore, it is the great fir tree of the underworld, which in Pueblo cosmogony furnishes the ladder by means of which the Ancients ascended from the underworld into their present abode, the earth of our Sun. An idea so similar that it seems to be a variant of the same conception appears in the myth of the heaven-piercing fir-tree by means of which the bride of the Sun ascends into the heaven above this world. As in the European tale of Jack-and-the-Bean-stalk, the tree grows as the maiden climbs, pursuing a porcupine, which is none other than the Sun himself. The tale tells of her marriage in the skyworld; of her disobedience to her husband's commands; of her fall to earth; and of the birth on earth of the twin heroes, who become the champions of the humankind. In most particulars it follows the cosmogonical type of the Indians of the eastern forests, for whom the shapers of this world are thought as descending from a sky-world rather than as ascending from an underworld. But the episode of the fir-tree, with its symbolism of life and strength and of cosmic plan, is clearly analogous to the mythic lore of the Southwest.[8]

The most striking artistic elaboration of the conception appears in Aztec and Maya learning. The famous initial illumination of the Codex Ferjérváry-Mayer represents the cardinal regions of the earth each by a cross-shaped tree, surmounted by a bird. The tree of the red region of the east rises from an image of the Sun and is surmounted by a glowing quetzal, the sacred bird of the Mexican peoples, the long green plumes of which were emblematic of the curving blades of the Indian corn. The tree of the west, which quarter is here represented by blue, is a thorn-tree rising from the body of the dragon of the eclipse and surmounted by a humming-bird, which the Aztecs believed to die with the dry and to revive with the rainy season. The tree of the green south, which rises from the jaws of earth and is surmounted by a parrot, is represented as half-living, half-dead, and is accompanied by the Maize-god and the Lord of Death, one on each side—as indeed each of the other trees is accompanied by regional tutelaries. Finally, the thorny tree of the north, represented by yellow, perhaps because arid and desert lands lie in this direction from the Aztec seat, rises from a bowl and is surmounted by the eagle: the Rain god and the Heart-of-the-Mountains whose voice is the voice of the jaguar are the tutelaries of the north. For the eastern tree the Sun and the Flint Knife, for the western, Flowing Water and Earth are the attendants. Central to all, in the Middle Place, is the Dart-Thrower, Lord of Fire. The image is clearly that of a world's orientation, symbolizing the visible universe with just such an imagery of earth and sky, of emblem, plant and bird as is to be found abundantly in the lore of the peoples of the Maya-Aztec and Pueblo-Navaho terrains.

But the Aztec knew also of a Life-giving Tree of the Underworld. Codex Vaticanus A depicts such a tree, the many fruits of which are the swaddled souls of infants who here await rebirth into the world above, from which they have been too cruelly snatched. Milk distils from this tree for their nourishment, until that hour when once again they shall see the light of the sun of this world. Certainly the idea is a picturesque counterpart to the Arikara notion that the worn moccasins of their little ones, tied to the sacred Cedar, will refresh the spirits of the Ancients with tidings that the tribe still flourishes.

V

BUT THE SACRED TREE, while it carries this cosmological symbolism and in its primary significance seems to be an emblem of the female life-giving energies of nature, becomes also a social and humanized emblem. The very process which in Classical and other Old World mythic developments is so frequent, that of a Nature Power passing over into a political or social tutelary or deity, is evidenced in America by the acquisition of such meanings by Grandmother Cedar among the Arikara.

An even more striking example is in the legends of the Omaha tribe concerning the miracle cedar which saved the tribe from disruption and instituted the cult of the Sacred Pole, itself a veritable palladium.[9] According to this Omaha tradition, at a time when the jealousies of rival chieftains were threatening the tribe with disruption the son of one of the ruling men, wandering in the forest, came at night upon a miraculous cedar. The tree was burning without being consumed, the trails of animals from the four cardinal points led to it, thunderbirds alighted in its branches. When this was reported to the tribe, the warriors put on their ornaments and gear; they ran for the tree as if it were an enemy; they struck and felled it, and then brought it into the camp, where it was adorned as if it were a man, a scalp being placed at the top for its hair, and its keeping placed in charge of one family. "You now see before you a mystery," said the chiefs. "Whenever we meet with troubles we shall bring all our troubles to him [the Pole]. We shall make offerings and requests. All our prayers must be accompanied by gifts. This [the Pole] belongs to all the people, but it shall be in the keeping of one family . . . , and the leadership shall be with them. If anyone desires to lead . . . and to take responsibility in governing the people, he shall make presents to the Keepers [of the Pole] and they shall give him authority." The civic character of the emblem is apparent in this legend of its institution, and its symbolism is further indicated by the ornaments placed upon it, which were those of a warrior, protector, and provider for his people. The whole imagery, indeed, is closely analogous to that of the Symbolic Man of the Osage, whose emblem was a pipe, and it apparently reflects the same central conception of a tribal personification, half deific.

The Sacred Pole of the Omaha, as finally conserved and as transferred to the Peabody Museum, was of cottonwood, not of cedar as the legend indicates. Again, it is conceived as male and not female. This brings the palladium into another cycle of tree-symbolism, characteristic of Siouan rather than of Caddoan Indians and only remotely cognate with the cult of the cedar. Among the Omaha, older than the institution of the Sacred Pole was an analogous ceremonial cult in which the pole was devoted to war rather than to peace. This was the He'dewachi ceremony. Here again a tree was selected, attacked and felled as if in war, adorned with colors emblematic of night and day, earth and sky, and also of the Thunder to which the tree was dedicated, as to that warrior's death which befalls him who is by the Thunder fated. Finally, the pole is spoken of and addressed as a man. About it, during the period of its erection, was performed the great tribal dance, in which the warriors were painted with the heraldry of their deeds, in which they "counted coup," and into which all—youths, men and women—finally entered with the gift-giving and rejoicing which characterized the great tribal festivals. What perhaps most sharply distinguishes this older Omaha ceremonial from that of the Sacred Pole is precisely the fact that the symbolic tree was renewed each year and not preserved *in perpetuum* as a tribal palladium.

There can be little question but that the He'dewachi is only a simpler variant of the Sun Dance, characteristic of the ceremonial life of the major portion of the Plains peoples and especially of the Siouan tribes of this region.[10] This ceremony is interbound with military and social ideals to a degree which calls for its fuller interpretation. Here it is important merely to call attention to the tree symbolism central within it. The tree chosen is usually a cottonwood, possibly from some remote symbolism of the fleeces of cotton that float from its seed-pods and suggest the fleecy clouds of summer, when the dance was held. The tree was scouted for, attacked and felled in warlike mode, painted with the colors of the Sun's domain, and at the forked top adorned with rawhide symbols of man and the buffalo, with the sun-banner, and with a bundle of green cherry twigs, which is symbolic of the woman as the pole is of man. A curious and persistent custom is the presence of a Holy or Devoted woman in connection with the cutting and bringing in of the ceremonial tree. Sometimes this woman is a member of the clan in charge of the sacred objects, as among the Omaha; again she represents a captive, as with the Kiowa; or, as among the Oglala, she is representative of the Holy Woman of yore, who came in ancient times bringing the ritual and the laws of morality to the tribe. There is a dim possibility that the devoted woman was originally a ceremonial sacrifice. The Creek Indians, far to the southeast, record in tradition the discovery of a victory-bringing tree, felled with warlike assault, to which an orphan was sacrificed: thereafter, like the Sacred Pole of the Omaha, it became a tribal palladium. And early explorers in Florida record also a sun-worship, centering about a pole to the summit of which was attached the effigy of the deer, the eastern equivalent for the bison of the Plains.

Far and wide throughout North America are to be traced examples of cults of poles or pillars, consecrated from captured trees, and emblematic alike of the principle of life, of the order of the world, and of the valor and prosperity of the tribe. Almost universally, too, in close association is the Holy Woman, who in some sense represents earth and the food which earth brings. In the ancient East and in the old Aegean, cults of the same sort prevailed. There was the Holy Woman and her Tree and the Son or Lover who was sacrificed before the shrine: Rhea, Cybele, Demeter, Isis, Ishtar, the Lion-Queen of the Hittites, and the Ashtoreth of the groves of Palestine, seem one and all to share something of that revelation from growing nature which among our Indians seems most intelligibly preserved in the rites of Grandmother Cedar as the Arikara observe them. Beyond this are whole worlds of symbolism—with the Tree of Life central in Eden.

CHAPTER III

The Abiding Rock

I

EASTWARD OF THE DOOR of the Medicine Lodge of the Arikara are placed two emblems—a pillar of stone and an evergreen tree. The pillar of stone is addressed as "Grandsire"; the cedar tree is honored as "Grandmother." The stone, a low ovoid, deeply earth-seated, stands unchanging through the seasons, an emblem of the unchanging. On occasion of the great festival it is painted red and covered with a cloth of red—red is the color of life at the heart of it, and of the Morning Star which heralds the new life of day. The cedar tree is renewed each summer season, for while the tree also is a symbol of life, its symbolism is of the foodbringing vegetational life, annually renewing and annually fading, though through the winter emblematically sustained by the evergreen boughs. Conjoined, the two symbols typify permanence and procreation, being and becoming, the stony ribs of the earth-body and its living flesh.

"Yes, the Rock is the oldest. He is grandfather of all things. Which is next oldest? The earth. She is grandmother of all things. Which is next oldest? *Skan* (the Blue or Sky). He gives life and motion to all things. Which is the next oldest after *Skan*? The Sun. But He is above all things." This is the statement of a wise man of the Sioux.[1] Each of the four has its own symbolic color: red for the Sun, blue for the Sky, green for the Earth and a yellow for the Rock. The rock, who is the core of Time, is lord of the abiding mountains, but his domain extends over all the earth. In him lies authority; he is the avenger; he constructs and destroys; what is in hand, man's implements and utensils, are from him; he also is the associate of the Winged Ones and of the Thunders which fly abroad from the rocky summits and peaks. Natural monoliths or imposing cliffs or buttes of stone are the emblems of *Inyan,* the Rock, in the Siouan country, like Standing Rock in South Dakota or Inyan Kara, a volcanic spire in Wyoming. It is on the primeval Rock, too, lifted above the abyss, that the Great Elk stood forth in the dawn of time, and baying across chaos, summoned the first morning of the world. But in the Siouan philosophy, while the Rock is the grandfather of all, nevertheless with Earth and Sky and Sun he is combined into the one being and substance of *Wakantanka,* the Great Spirit, just as the four colors of the quarters unite into one creation.

From the Omaha tribe, Siouan in speech and kinship but profoundly affected culturally by their Caddoan neighbors (Pawnee and Arikara), are preserved the most instructive of the ritual prayers which interpret for us the meaning of Grandsire Rock. "At the beginning," said the Omaha,[2] "all things were in the mind of Wakonda. All creatures, including man, were spirits. They moved about in space between the earth and the stars (the heavens). They were seeking a place where they could come into a bodily existence. They ascended to the sun, but the sun was not fitted for their abode. They moved on to the moon and found that it also was not good for their home. Then they descended to the earth. They saw it was covered with water. They floated through the air to the north, the east, the south, and the west, and found no dry land. They were sorely grieved. Suddenly from the midst of the water uprose a great rock. It burst into flames and the waters floated into the air in clouds. Dry land appeared; the grasses and the trees grew. The hosts of the spirits descended and became flesh and blood. They fed on the seeds of the grasses and the fruits of the trees, and the land vibrated with their expressions of joy and gratitude to Wakonda, the maker of all things."

This reads amazingly like a fragment from an early Ionian cosmogony; so might Heraclitus have expressed himself, with his doctrine of the fiery flux, or Empedocles with his epic tale of the primal elements "seeking union meet," and forming at last a world core where life and humanity should come to birth. The cosmic symbolism possesses a certain philosophic magnificence, preserved for us in the ritual hymns. . . .

> Toward the coming of the sun
> There the people of every kind gathered,
> And the great animals of every kind. . . .
> Verily all gathered there together,
> By what means or manner we know not.
>
> Verily one alone of all these was the greatest,
> Inspiring to all minds, the great white rock,
> Standing and reaching as high as the heavens, enwrapped in mist,
> Verily as high as the heavens.
> Thus my little ones shall speak of me!

These lines are from the ritual of the Pebble Society of the Omaha,[3] whose emblem was a white or translucent pebble, symbol of the primeval waters whence the Rock of the World emerged, and potent as a vision-inducing charm. Mystically "shot" with the pebbles, which were part of the "medicine" of the society, the members fell into trance, which in Indian lore is the road of understanding and of insight into things unseen. The practice suggests the custom, widespread in Indian America, of employing transparent or translucent stones—rock crystal, quartz, obsidian, and the famous greenstone of the south—as talismans and as inducers of vision. Such must have been the crystal of judgment in Iximche, built into a shrine in the plaza of the capital city of the Cakchiquel; and in the Navaho myth it is the life-endowed crystal which first lifts up the all-illuminating sun.[4]

Indeed, it is for us, with our physical and chemical achievements and so richly the masters of nature's material wealth, a difficult adventure to think ourselves back into the Stone Age man's reverence for the one half-magical natural gift which had most lifted him up. Stones were the tools and weapons and treasures and charms of the human race through long thousands of years; it was the stone primarily which gave to the first-born of the ape new means for food and defense, shelter and power, and in the end made a man of him. We recognize this in our very designations of the Dawn Stone and the Old Stone and the New Stone eras of human culture; and we recognize it also in our still-cherished superstitions of the merits of gems and jewels and all lustres reaved from the matrix. Doubtless it is in our attitude toward gems that best of all we can realize what the dump stone meant for the man who knew only this material for the dependence of his life. To him a piece of flint was not first of all a mere material; it was an individual being to be handled respectfully as a tool, to be caught up magically as the prison of a jinni of fire, to be fondled as a charm or besought in the hour of peril. In his "medicine" paraphernalia the Indian carried stones which when rubbed together yielded dimly a phosphor, light of the spirit within, or which when ground into their colors were painted into the emblems of the quarters, and which when placed upon or within the body of man gave him power from the healths of all creation. Stones are fashioned by nature or by art into the shapes of helpful animal beings; and in their translucent depths fate and fortune should be read. The Urim and Thummin of the high priests of Israel were stones of this kind, and if today one were to tour the circuit of the Mediterranean with an eye for it, he would see that the Stone Age has there not only created the ancient culture, but that it has survived more intimately there than elsewhere in the civilized world. To the north is the Age of Steel, but it is still to Italy that we go for the marble worker and the quartz worker, for the skillful sculptor and the cunning handicraftsman of the precious cameo. The age of stone has been supplemented, not superseded.

Probably more completely than in any Old World culture we are carried back imaginatively to the spirit of the Stone Age in Europe by the rituals and lore of the American Indians, whose institutions and ideas are surely much what must have been those of our own ancestors in the late Neolithic. Not only are implements and modes of living much the same, but from what we can gather from Old World survivals, so also must have been beliefs and fantasies. It is as if America were a belated Neolithic Europe, preserved that we might greet our own more ancient life still in the flesh.

II

No RITE of the Indian leads us more directly into this spirit of the past than does that of the sweat-lodge and bath, one of the most widespread of Indian customs. In its typical form it is a rite of purification and healing, undertaken both to restore and to maintain bodily health, but undertaken even more generally as a preliminary for participation in religious exercise. The sweat-lodge was ordinarily composed of a light framework of saplings over which were spread coverings of skins or blankets. Within was room for the extended bodies of two or three men, while near the entrance was dug a hole into which were thrust heated stones. Water thrown upon the white-hot stones brought the clouds of steam and the nude bodies of the bathers broke into perspiration, from which, after a period, they were relieved by running to an adjacent stream and plunging into the cold flood. Such was the simple form of the treatment, but in the Indian's eyes the sweat-bath was of far more than a simple physical efficacy. It brought him intimately and directly into contact with the Powers which uphold his world, giving the universal health and sanity of nature. All the elements, fire, stony earth, water and vaporous air, entered into the ritual healing, which was preceded by chants and prayers and was felt to bring a new birth into the life of that greater community of being in which man's existence is only a participation. The use of heated stones was not universal in sweat-bath practices, but it was widespread and probably pertains to the original form from which other customs arose. And where stones were used, a direct and medicinal power was ascribed to them as symbols of the being, immovable and steadfast, which is the "dwelling-place" of all. This is why the rock is addressed as

"Grandsire," as the "Aged One." Thus, in one of the several sweat-bath chants of the Omaha, whom we have already cited, the priest cries: [5]

Ho, Aged One, eçka, [I implore thee!]
At a time when were gathered together seven persons,
You sat in the seventh place, it is said,
And of the Seven you alone possessed knowledge of all things,
        Aged One, eçka.

When in their longing for protection and guidance,
The people sought in their minds for a way,
They beheld you sitting with assured permanency and endurance
In the center where converged the paths,
There exposed to the violence of the four winds, you sat,
Possessed with power to receive supplications,
        Aged One, eçka.

Where is his mouth, by which there may be utterance of speech?
Where is his heart, to which there may come knowledge and under-
        standing?
Where are his feet, whereby he may move from place to place?
We question in wonder,
Yet verily it is said you alone have power to receive supplications,
        Aged One, eçka.

I have desired to go yet farther in the path of life with my little ones,
Without pain, without sickness,
Beyond the second, third, and fourth period of life's pathway, . . .
O hear! This is my prayer,
Although uttered in words poorly put together,
        Aged One, eçka.

A commentary upon this chant would lead far toward the heart of Indian metaphysics. In the first place the familiar cosmic frame, or world projection, is there: the seven places which define the cardinal points and the above and the below and the here of man's natural orientation, and the converging paths which lead to him—central in his world. But the seven places are not merely places, they are also powers or persons, imbued with that life and meaning which is the cement and bond of creation, giving it sense and bearing. The powers are endowed with the power of receiving supplications and of answering them, and most of all the Rock, which holds, creatively, the steadfast center of the world, untouched by wind and change, immovable, enduring through all things. The physical world, in brief, is not only a body, it is a thought-structure, and a living being, somehow in the end curative of man's ills and a solace to his soul—as we poetically conceive nature today. The rock at the core of the universe is not only an abiding rock, it is the Rock of Refuge; permanence and consolation are somehow united in the one image.

It is instructive, too, to follow the inner promptings of the questions, "Where is his mouth, by which there may be utterance? . . . His heart, giving understanding? . . . His feet, whereby he may move from place to place? . . . We question in wonder." The wonder is certainly aroused by a *conviction* of an animism, an inner life in all things for which there is no outward and responsive sign in the dumb object. It is a conviction that reaches very deep into the heart of a human instinct which natively compels mankind to ascribe spirit to nature. Socially we attribute life-impulses to bodies analogous to our own and to conduct which may be interpreted in the language of our own needs and appetites; but metaphysically we are not content with such a limitation of life, but expand its realm out and beyond the range of forms such as animate bodies show. This is that animism, apart from which little in human lore can be understood, yet which of itself is one of the least obvious of our modes of understanding. It is both an older and subtler thing than anthropomorphism to which, indeed, it eventually leads, as shown when on the sacred stone first are crudely scrawled facial features, then shapings of limbs, and finally the sculptured marble of the idol—all steps in skill of representation of the form of a body which itself is the alphabet of thought, yet steps which are no more than interpretations of the deeper-lying, instinctive ascription of life to nature. The Indian's questions as to speaking mouth and understanding heart and moving limbs are prompted fundamentally by a desire for interpretative tokens, for *theophany*, in last resort; but they in no wise express doubt as to the metaphysical vividness of the cosmic life, pervading all things.

It is instructive once again to turn to the backgrounds of European metaphysics, there to find the similar question asked. Empedocles chants the boundless Sphere, exultant in its solitude, without arms or feet or bodily member. And in the *Timaeus* [6] Plato gives to the idea its classic locus: "Now to the animal which was to comprehend all animals, that figure was suitable which comprehends within itself all other figures. Wherefore he made the world in the form of a globe, round as from a lathe, having its extremes in every direction equidistant from the centre, the most perfect and the most like itself of all figures; for he considered the like as infinitely fairer than the unlike. This he finished off, making the surface smooth all round for many reasons; in the first place, because the living being had no need of eyes when there was nothing outside of him to be seen; nor of ears when there was nothing to be heard; and there was no surrounding atmosphere to be breathed; nor would there have been any use of organs by the help of which he might receive his food or get rid of what he had already digested, since there was nothing that went from him or came into him: for there was nothing beside him. Of design he was created thus, his own waste providing his own food, and all that he did or suffered taking place in and by himself. For the Creator conceived that a being which was self-sufficient would be far more excellent than one which lacked anything; and, as he had no need to take anything or defend himself against any one, the Creator did not think it necessary to bestow upon him hands: nor had he any need of feet, nor of the whole apparatus of walking; but the movement suited to his spherical form was assigned to him, being of all the seven that which is most appropriate to mind and intelligence; and he was made to move in the same manner and on the same spot, within his own limits revolving in a circle. All the other six motions were taken away from him, and he was made not to partake of their deviations. And as the circular movement required no feet, the universe was created without legs and without feet."

William James, in a picturesque passage interpreting the

thought of Fechner,[7] gives a similar image of the body of Earth as a higher kind of animal, uncrippled by limbs; and it is not a little instructive that modern physics, facing in refined form the same ancient problem, is moved subtly to ascribe to its bodily universe those abstractions of light and motion which in the end are but the imaginative gift of eye and limb: till the whole cosmos is conceived as a sense-endowed thought, the *Zoön empsychon* of the Platonist. That the American Indian, via his own routes, should have arrived at an analogous view of the world is perhaps only an added evidence that nature among all men has one truth to impart.

III

FOR THE MAN OF active hands mere matter is but the corpse of a living world, and from the very beginnings of the mind's instincts the life is discriminated from the brute body. Anthropomorphism, truly understood, is not a manner of conceiving after bodily shapes, but after bodily functions and activities, after the model of the living body. This with emphasis, for the dead body is not a man, and even an inactive body is only potentially a man: Mors and Somnus are twins. Unceasingly we study the bodies of our fellow human beings as the expressive agencies of their life-impulses; it is there, in the mind's intention, that lie their realities; outwardly they are but symbols of power and meaning. Only to recall the great number of poetic metaphors likening unfamiliar nature to the familiar form and action of man is to see how inevitable is this way of thinking; and in our vocabularies there are numberless compounds on "head" and "mouth" and "arm" and "hand" and "foot" which have long since lost their metaphorical feeling yet remain to attest the fact that man's frame and motion give his first great measures of the cosmos. Even more intimate are the functional similitudes. Next to his own bodily life the imagination most readily seizes upon the life-impulses of animals, and most readily upon the impulses of those animals that are endowed with organs and functions analogous to the human. Hence his earlier gods are often personified in the cousinly likenesses of animal kindreds, not because men have not been able to discriminate the human form from the animal, but because man feels in animal conduct his conduct. The animals have eyes, limbs, organs, dimensions, and hence senses, affections and passions like his own. With him they share breathing and heart-beat and pulse, vision and hearing, assimilation and procreation, desire and feeling and thought, and it is these that shape the alphabet of intelligibility.

And as it is for the animal world, so also for all nature; the life-breath is in all things and it is our human energy that is the *work* of creation. At first blush stocks and stones would seem to be of all natural objects the farthest removed from any proper candidacy for divinity; they are the very emblems of the senselessly material, without organs and without motive. Yet if we reflect that in the instinctive way of thinking *the life of an object is its use,* and also that the earliest and most familiar of human tools are sticks and stones, the oddness disappears, and there issues a subtle and fitting sequence uniting primitive staff and god's sceptor, paleolithic celt and the idealized marble.

Certainly the cult of Tree and Pillar lay in the misty backgrounds of the classical culture of the Old World, even as it appears in the native rituals of the Western Continents. The numerous revered *baetyli* of the classic peoples were little more than fetish stones, in many cases reputed to be fallen from heaven; while rumored as images or symbols of the gods, they were treated rather as magical beings than as mere emblems. At Delphi such a stone was each day annointed with oil, the tale passing that this was the stone in swaddling clothes swallowed by Cronus when Rhea deceived him into accepting it as the infant Zeus. Rhea Cybele herself came to Rome in 205 B.C. in the form of an irregular black stone brought in a sacred ship from Pergamon (whither, in turn, it had come from Pessinus). The stone is called a meteorite, but it is not necessary to suppose that all reputed images "from heaven" actually were meteoritic. In one of the shrines at Knossos were found three fetish idols which were natural concretions, one suggesting a woman's form, one that of an infant, and the third ape-like. Similar concretions are found in

the kiva chambers of ancient pueblos in the American Southwest, and indeed not a few are from the living pueblos. The city
of the Ephesians is reputed to have had for its palladium (the true
Palladium, the old *xoanon* of Athens, was a stock) an image of the
great goddess, the Diana of the Ephesians, fallen from Jupiter.
The familiar pillar-like form of this image is a particular instance of the multitudinous pillar-cults which prevailed not only
in the Aegean world (mainly associated with the Earth-Mother
worships), but extended throughout hither Asia among the Ana-
tolians and the Semites.

And Jacob rose up early in the morning, and took the stone that he
had put for his pillows, and set it up for a pillar, and poured oil upon
the top of it. And he called the name of that place Bethel: [8] . . .

Greek βαίτυλος is probably but a form of this Semitic *bethel*, and
the cult which both represent far antedates the Classic Age. Yet
still in classical Greece Apollo Agyieus and Zeus Meilichios were
represented by simple conical or pyramidal stones.

At Knossos it was not the fetish-like concretion, but the stone
pillar inscribed with the image of the double axe, or the double
axe itself, which was the cult object of paramount interest. It is
altogether plausible that this axe is nothing more than a special
form of the almost universally venerated "thunderstone." For
worldwide is the notion that the lightning-riven earth or tree has
been cleft by a material missile—a "stone from heaven" hurled by
the powers above. Sometimes these stones are natural formations
—fossils of a special type or stones of a particular color, as black;
very often, in regions where the use of stones for implements and
weapons has been replaced by metal or other materials, stone arrows or spearheads and especially stone celts, the primitive axes,
are regarded as the veritable thunder's bolt. Such stones are talismans, "medicine," strong to protect their bearers from the wrath
of heaven or again strong to give them more than human powers.
Thus the axe becomes more than merely a man's tool; it becomes
an object of veneration, eventually the attribute of a god, or the
god himself: for Thor, we are told, was the Hammer from heaven

before he became the cloud-riding Hammerer. Surely there is a dramatic appropriateness in this ascription by man of a heavenly power and origin to the celt, the baetyl which marks the place of god's descent; it is the most ancient and far-cast of all human implements, the universal symbol of the liberation of human-nature from brute-nature, and so of the conception of divinity.

We may turn to the New World for the clearest exemplifications of the living significance of "stones from heaven." The association of lifeless stone with living heavenly fire appears in various forms. Among the Zuñi, thunder is the sound made by the gaming-stones of the rain-makers while lightning is the arrows of Kupishtaya, mighty warriors above: a man with a good heart, they say, need have no fear of these, for none are ever struck save those who possess bad hearts. Near the summit of the Coteau des Prairies, in eastern South Dakota, a number of large round boulders are pointed out as the eggs of the Thunderbird—reminiscent of the famous roc and his huge eggs. The Thunder Society of the Omaha originated with those men, each of whom had received in a vision, as token of the special form of Wakonda which was to be his own, some sign of the thunder. A black stone represented the thunder, just as a translucent pebble was the symbol of the water's potency (the "black stone" of Mecca is pre-Moslem, and the meteorite from Pessinus—if meteorite it was—was black). Such a stone was "a sort of credential that served to connect its possessor with the potentiality of the species or class represented by the form seen in the vision, through which man's strength or faculties could be re-enforced by virtue of the continuity of life throughout the universe. . . ." [9]

"Thunderstones" primarily are themselves charged potencies, magical, fetishistic. Later the arrowheads and axes and other stones which are viewed as "bolts" from on high are taken to be the missiles hurled down by a Thunderer or Fulminator. Then man-made emblems of these bolts—the Minoan double-axe, the pronged image of the lightning, the Roman *bidens*, the Hindu *trisula*, the Greek *triaina*, weapon of "earth-shaking" Poseidon, and the *keraunos* of Zeus which seems to combine the lightning's fork with the double-striking power of the two-blade axe—all these become symbols of the awesome Power, and later were pictured attributes of the God to whom the power is ascribed.

At first the god is the stone—*Juppiter Lapis* is perhaps such a one. Then he becomes the fire out of heaven. "The lightning is not merely the sign through which the Heaven-God manifests his mind and will, but he himself descends in the lightning and thence bears the name of *Juppiter Fulgur*." This is the primitive Roman view. It was the same with the primitive Greek:

The thunder-god was worshipped as Κεϱαύνιος in Olympia and Κεϱαυνοβόλος in Tegea, as 'Αστϱαπαῖος in Antandros, and probably every spot struck by lightning was consecrated by the same rite to him. An interesting worship, showing probably a very primitive view, is that of Zeus Κέϱαυνος at Mantinea, in which Zeus appears, not as the god who directs the phenomenon, but as the phenomenon itself: the thunder is regarded as personal, and in this, as in other cases, we find traces of a very undeveloped stage of belief in Arcadia, . . .[10]

The Romans erected a kind of tomb where the fire from heaven had fallen—a *bidental,* sanctified to Jupiter and tabu to the profane touch. In Rome "the most solemn oath was that sworn by *Juppiter Lapis* . . . The sacred stone was used when the *fetiales* took the oath and made sacrifice upon the formation of an alliance with a foreign power. Such an alliance, according to the Roman view, received its highest sanction from the lightning god himself." [11] *Audiat haec genitor, qui foedere fulmine sanctit.* "The God that answereth by fire, let him be God"—this is the world-wide conviction.

The Chavin stone represents the Peruvian Zeus, Viracocha, armed with a double bolt amazingly like the *keraunos,* emblem of the classical sky-god; and it is in the Peru of the Incas that there occurs that association of the moral and natural which is represented by the Zuñi conviction that lightning will not strike the man of good heart, and a custom almost identical with the Roman habit of erecting *bidentalia*. The Incas, says Garcilasso de la Vega,[12] "called the thunder, the lightning, and the thunderbolt, the servants of the Sun. . . . But it does not follow from this that the Incaic peoples took these phenomena for gods; on the contrary, if it happened that a house or other place were struck by a thunderbolt, they held it in such abomination that they forthwith walled up the door with stones and mud, in order that no person might enter therein; while if the bolt were fallen in the country they marked off the place with boundaries that none might set foot therein. In a word, they called such places unlucky and ill-spoken, and they added that the Sun had shown this malediction by means of the thunderbolt, his servant." Surely here we have a Zeus or an Apollo in the making!

IV

As it is for the stone so also for the stock—human form is suggested once the magic of power has been ascribed to it. When the pole which was the tribal palladium of the Omaha had been cut down and brought in, "the chiefs worked upon the tree; they trimmed it and called it a human being. . . . They said: 'It has no hair!' So they sent out to get a large scalp-lock and they put it on the top of the Pole for hair." [13] The Herms and Terms of the classical peoples, and Dionysus as the manheaded tree Dendrites, represent a similar anthropomorphizing expression; and the African fetish tree in which the *kulu* of a human being was imprisoned was hewn to the full figure of a man. In Arabia, "the sacred date-palm at Nejrān . . . was adored at an annual feast, when it was all hung with fine clothes and women's ornaments"; while for the modern Arabs, "it is deadly danger to pluck so much as a bough from such a tree; they are honoured with sacrifices, and parts of the flesh are hung on them, as well as shreds of calico, beads, etc. The sick man who sleeps under them receives counsel in a dream for the restoration of his health." [14] Such a tree, hewn and set up beside an altar becomes an *ashera:* "Thou shalt not plant thee an Asherah of any kind beside the altar of the Lord thy God, which thou shalt make thee. Neither shalt thou set up a pillar; which the Lord thy God hateth." [15] " 'All trees,' according to the Malay tradition, 'were planted by "the prophet Elias," and are in "Prophet Noah's" charge. In the days of King Solomon, trees could speak as well as birds and animals, and several of the trees now to be

seen in the forest are really metamorphosed human beings.' " [16]
Elsewhere whole races of men have been metamorphosed into
rocks—but these magical metamorphoses of men and animals into
trees and stones are only the backwash of our more conscious
humanhood; the real order is the reverse, first, the fetish-strong
boulder or stock, second, the demand that it be given organs and
dimensions that will account for its senses and appetites.

The intensifying anthropomorphism appears in the notion
that the tree is but the habitat of the tree-soul, Nymph or Dryad,
once perchance a mortal maiden but now transformed by the
music-loving god into singing leaves. In the first derivative from
utter fetishism the idea will be more material. The Malay find
"a strangely shaped piece of eagle-wood which possesses a natural
resemblance to some animal or bird. It is believed to contain the
soul of the tree, . . ." [17] Animal forms are akin to our own animal body: they have speaking mouths and seeing eyes and carrying limbs. Long after men have ceased to be content with the
puzzling formlessness of stocks and stones, they continue to make
images of animal powers; gradually these take on human parts,
and we get the strange and monstrous shapes which make the im-
press of the ancient art of the Orient—a cow's head on a woman's
body, a human-headed lion, a winged bull, or such grotesque
composites as amazed Maundeville in the Far East. "Summe," he
says, [18] "worschipen symulacres and summe ydoles. But betwene
symulacres and ydoles is a gret difference. For symulacres ben
ymages made after lyknesse of men or of wommen or of the sonne
or of the mone or of ony best or of ony kyndely thing. And ydoles
is an ymage made of lewed wille of man, that man may not fynden
among kyndely thinges. As an ymage that hath iiij hedes, on of a
man, another of an hors, or of an ox, or of sum other best that
no man hath seyn. . . ."

Usually, by the time men have progressed from "ydoles" to
simulacra, cult images have come to be recognized as symbols
rather than as seats of power. They are objects of artistic ideali-
zation, and hence rapidly they tend to assume for us the most expressive and hence most beautiful of all physical forms, those of
the human body. Behind this full-blown anthropomorphism the

old ambiguous fetishism persists, but falls more and more under the domination of the conviction that life is expression, and that the truest expression is human expression. In the Navaho myth of the creation of the sun, when Ahsonnutli would intensify the power of the charms by which she was endeavoring to generate light "with a crystal dipped in pollen she marked eyes and mouth on the turquoise and on the white shell beads" and for the first time the reign of Night was broken.[19] The light of the human countenance is man's nearest revelation of the divine in the physical universe.

V

THUS, both for stones and stocks we have indicated paths whereby the block is transformed into the idol, the fetish into the symbol. The Arikara Grandsire Rock and Grandmother Cedar, marking the sacred plaza before the Medicine Lodge, are typical of the early and aniconic phase of the development which in the end gives us a symbolism of the Rock of Ages and the Tree of Life, or in material form yields the great art of Phidias and Michelangelo. In the promptings of man's instinctive thought there are few symbols that spring forth more vividly, Old World and New alike yielding example. Yet the full meaning of this ancient symbolism is still to be revealed, and for it we must turn not to cult but to myth.

The Iroquoian cosmogony, recorded in several versions by J. N. B. Hewitt and others, begins with an archetypal world, in the heavens above the heavens, whence falls a woman-being, who has been bride of the Chieftain of the Skies. She falls toward a waste of waters, the chaos that was before the Earth was, where she is received upon the carapace of a turtle, which is the core from which the Earth grows and is shapen. Here she gives birth to a daughter, who in turn, impregnated by the winds, becomes mother of the twins, Sapling and Flint. Even before they have issued from the womb Sapling and Flint are at war, and their birth is the death of their mother, so that they are left with their half-malevolent grandmother, Ataentsic, the sky-fallen. Speedily they grow into heroic powers, and it is they who become the demiurgic earth-shapers, but chiefly Sapling, who incarnates the whole vegetal energy of creation, the vitality of all that grows and multiplies, whereas Flint is but a chill imitator of life or produces but evil and barren things. It is, indeed, easy to see in the twins the two great primitive seasons, Summer and Winter, each conceived as an energy rather than a time and the two unceasingly in conflict. In the tale, Flint is conquered by Sapling in their final struggle, and is slain by him. Say the Mohawk: [20] "Now, at this time, to-ward the west, where the earth extends thitherward, there lies athwart the view a range of large mountains that cross the whole earth. There, so it is said, his body lies extended." But of Sapling it is said that after he had completed the earth he also de-parted. As the Onondaga recount it: [21] "Moreover, it is said that Sapling, in the manner in which he has life, has this also to befall him recurrently, that he becomes old in body, and that when, in fact, his body becomes ancient normally, he then retransforms his body in such wise that he becomes a new man-being again and again recovers his youth, so that one would think that he had just then grown to the size which a man-being customarily has when he reaches the youth of man-beings, as manifested by the change of voice at the age of puberty. Moreover, it is so that con-tinuously the orenda immanent in his body—the orenda with which he suffuses his person, the orenda which he projects or ex-hibits, through which he is possessed of force or potency—is ever full, undiminished, and all-sufficient; and in the next place, noth-ing that is otkon or deadly, nor, in the next place, even the Great Destroyer, otkon in itself and faceless, has any effect on him, he being perfectly immune to its orenda; and in the next place, there is nothing that can bar his way or veil his faculties. More-over, it is verily thus with all the things that are contained in the earth here present, that they severally retransform or exchange their bodies. It is thus with all things that sprout and grow, and in the next place, with all things that produce themselves and grow, and in the next place, all the man-beings. All these are af-fected in the same manner, that they severally transform their bodies, and, in the next place, that they retransform their bodies, severally, without cessation."

It is evident enough in this myth of origins that nature is interpreted as a conflict of forming and transforming forces, and again that these forces are the elemental ones, mineral earth and soil-bursting vegetation. They are personified as shaping and creating seasons, and their emblems are stone and tree, Flint and Sapling. Here indeed is a stone-age man's philosophy of nature, and gifted with not a little metaphysical understanding.

The Iroquoian myth is an Indian interpretation of the origin of the world, with Flint and Sapling in the heroic rôles. A continent's width to the westward dwelt the Wintun of the Sacramento Valley, and it is in their tale of Olelbis, recorded by Jeremiah Curtin, that a second fine myth, less cosmogony than palingenesis, gives an interpretation where Flint and Acorn are the crucial emblems. Olelbis is the Sky-Father, a Wintun Zeus, whose home is Olelpanti, where he dwells in the Sweat-Lodge of the Skies, which is the most beautiful abode that ever was or will be. A great white oak was the central pillar, and other oaks formed the pillars, while their uniting branches formed the roof, which was bound together with withes of a beautiful ever-blooming flower. Flowers of the same rich color formed the walls of the lodge to the east, while those of the north were of red flowers, those of the south of white flowers, those of the west another beautiful blossom, blue and white. All kinds of beautiful flowering plants formed a bank around the base of the lodge, which was adorned with every color and sweetened with every fragrance. The roots of the trees and plants were so deep that the growth knew no seasons: the flowers were perpetually in bloom and acorns were ever-falling from the trees. "That sweat-lodge," say the Wintun,[22] "was placed there to last forever, the largest and most beautiful building in the world, above or below. Nothing like it will ever be built again."

But on the day on which the celestial lodge was completed, in the world below, the magical flint was stolen from the Swift, who through it was the greatest hunter in the world. And in revenge, aided by Fire-Drill, Shooting Star and Yonot, the buckeye-bush, whose child is Pohila, fire, the Swift kindled flames, east and west, which swept the whole world and consumed life everywhere. From Olelpanti Olelbis looked down upon the burning world. "He could see nothing but waves of flame; rocks were burning, the ground was burning, everything was burning. Great rolls and piles of smoke were rising; fire flew up toward the sky in flames, in great sparks and brands. Those sparks became kolchituh (sky eyes), and all the stars that we see now in the sky came from the time when the first world was burned. The sparks stuck fast in the sky, and have remained there ever since the time of the first wakpohas (world fire). Quartz rocks and fire in the rocks are from that time. There was no fire in the rocks before the wakpohas."

But when Olelbis saw the destruction that was assailing the world, he summoned Mem Loimis, the Old Woman of the Waters, who raised up waves mountain high to contend with the flames, and he summoned Kahit, the Old Man of the Northwind, to aid her. "Closely after Mem Loimis came Kahit. He had a whistle in his mouth; as he moved forward he blew it with all his might, and made a terrible noise. The whistle was his own; he had had it always. He came flying and blowing. He looked like an enormous bat, with wings spread. As he flew south toward the other side of the sky, his two cheek feathers grew straight out, became immensely long, waved up and down, grew till they could touch the sky on both sides."

Thus the flood swelled and the fire was extinguished. "When Mem Loimis and Kahit had gone home, all water disappeared; it was calm, dry, and clear again everywhere. Olelbis looked down on the earth, but could see nothing: no mountains, no trees, no ground, nothing but naked rocks washed clean. He stood and looked in every direction—looked east, north, west, south, to see if he could find anything. He found nothing." Then Olelbis sent the Mole and the Gopher—for these two had survived the fire by digging into the soil—to bring up earth from the underworld; and he had this rained upon the soil like a fine dust; and then he had seed and acorns from the everliving plants and trees of the celestial lodge sown upon the soil; and he restored life there and renewed the races of the animals. "All people that were good on this earth only, of use only here, Olelbis sent down, to be beasts, birds, and other creatures. The powerful and great people that were good in Olelpanti and useful there he kept with himself, and sent only a feather or a part of each to become something useful down here. The good people themselves, the great ones, stayed above, where they are with Olelbis now." [23]

In each of these myths, from the Atlantic and from the Pacific coastal regions of Indian America, the essential characters of Rock and Tree, as the ancient shapers of nature's reality, stand clear in their symbolisms. The rock, be it flint or quartz, is the stuff of the ribs of the world, the bone under the flesh of soil in the body of Earth, and it is deeply grained with the magical powers of the earth-stuff; imprisoned within it are the fire-spirit and the power of destruction; within it also is the power of shaping; and most of all, within it is some magical and mystic power, making medicinal the heated stones of the sweat-lodge, and in the colors and glints of crystalline forms creating charms and talismans and the letters of geomancy. The tree, on the other hand, is the symbol of the richness and glow of renewing life: all the flowers of the world, all the sweetnesses, are its kindred and its gift, the vital saps whose liquid strength so swells the young plant with vigor that it parts the rocks themselves, and with the power of life seems to defy the very stone of Earth.

Yet this defiance itself has limits and to the triumph of life is set a bound which it cannot ever reach without its own Nemesis. Not less than other peoples the American Indians have discovered a law of Destiny, and a sense of powers clamping with futility a life that would demand too proudly of the world. In the end the Rock is the master, even up from the Underworld. In Indian myth no note is more frequent than that of the metamorphosis of creatures that are earth's futilities into dull and senseless stone, meaningless save as grim emblems. Every tribal lore is adorned with tales of the giants of yore, First Peoples, now become just shapeless rocks; and there are Stone Giants, Stone Heads, and Stone Masks, monstrous and bogey-like creatures.

With one such tale we may turn from this theme, because it strikes so deeply into human understandings, and into what is

THE WORLD'S RIM

tragic in the life of man. The story is an ancient one, already recounted in the earliest of the Jesuit Relations,[24] and even then
widespread, although it originates, apparently, with the Eastern
Algonquian tribes. A certain man, fasting in the face of mystery,
decides to journey into the Dawn-Lodge of the White One of
Morning, the great Messou, who is the same as Manabozho, the
Demiurge, and is probably none other than the Morning Sun,
life's daily creator. After the Indian fashion, this man associates
with him a group of fellows, each like himself gift-seeking. They
journey, with many perils and hardships, until they arrive at last
before the shining lodge, whose lord greets them and gives them
entertainment. There each beseeches the gift that is most on his
heart. The first asks for success in love, that he may be attractive
in the eyes of women, and this human thing is granted to him.
The second asks for success in chase and war, that he may become known as a man among men; and this also is granted, being
what a man should seek. The third demands skill in medicine,
that he may heal the sick and may be wise with the insight of
doctors and medicine men; and even this greater gift is granted.
But the fourth, he who has inaugurated the fasting and the toils,
asks only for life, but for life unending. When his prayer has likewise been conceded he is transformed into stone—for it is only
thus that such a petition as his might be granted. In the end life
itself is reclaimed by the Abiding Rock, which was the first of
beings, which will be the last.

CHAPTER IV

The Corn Maidens

I

AT THE CROWN of the head each of the male-dancers is nodding a pompon-like tuft of variegated feathers plucked from the soft plumage of subtropical parrots, green-blue and turquoise flashed with orange and red and silver-gray. All the colors of a rainbowed land gather themselves into the bubble of day at its shining zenith. Seen there above they are predominantly blue or deep turquoise; but with morning, noon and sundown the milk-opals and the fire-opals of the changing clouds and the prismatic arcs of the sky-bows (often double and even treble) adjoin to the purer celestial hues those crimsons, oranges and vivid greens which festally splendor the native earth of the Pueblo Plateau. At the zenith of day all the colors of the world combine into the one great mystery of light, which is the creator of all things and the energy and substance of all things. It is also the energy and substance and life of man, of all his tribes and of all that life of plant and animal which with him walks this phantasmal earth and shares in its many-tone being. Thus each male dancer wears as his crest this symbol of man's innermost and vital nature—which in the male is most signally akin to the Sky-Half of the World-Whole, where-unto he uplifts himself with the whole vigor of his dancing mo-

tion, limbs rising repeatedly with the effulgence of ascension—
like the great sweeps of wing of strong eagles, mounting.

Not that the male has no invincible tie binding him to the
Earth herself. He is of the Sky-Half of the world, but never with
an utter liberation. In Aztec iconography even He the Supreme,
Tezcatlipoca, the "Fume-swept Mirror" (that is, the azure of
heaven) is portrayed with one foot wrenched away at the ankle-
bone. The grim myth recounts how only by this desperate mutilation was the Lord Above able, in the days of all dawnings, to free
himself from the clamped Jaws, toothed with obsidian, which
clutched at his heel. Man, after all, is mortal in his dust, and
Earth which gave him birth reclaims him, prone at the end. It
is as if he had been given, of all unwinged creatures, fullest leash
to rise from crawler to quadruped, from quadruped to biped, and
there for his brief noon to stand heaven-gazing from the tiptoe
of mammalian being, just for his one zenith-worship; but in the
end no staff can save him from the long reclining, earth-embosomed. So it is that while every man-dancer of them wears the
proud pompon nodding at his crown, yet his feet are masked
with the rigid-patterned black-white of the skunk-skin, beast of an
earth-hole. Again it is from ancient Mexican iconography that we
guess the meaning, for the ankle-mask in Aztec and Maya art is a
death's-head.

Thus the male-dancer in the crown and foot of his costume,
like the Homeric Titan, touches Earth and Sky and sets his man-
measure of the united worlds: he is central and in-between; and
his dance—which is man's utter life—is the spectacle for which the
gods of the colors above and the gods of the colors below alike assemble. Somehow their union is for his sake and is sacramentally
enabled through him, who is at once the offering and the bloom
of a creation that apart from him would fade into chaos, heaven
and earth alike, formless and empty. So he stamps the red earth
with vigorous feet and uplifts knee, forearm and painted face
while the drum-beats count life's hour, and the sky quivers.

Between earth and sky fall the streamers and filaments of rain—
the masculine fluid of heaven—to fertilize the soil and awake the
responsive greens, neither a red of the soil nor a blue of the skies,

but other-color to both parents, and the strong food of all blooded flesh. The dancer (if he is not school-cropped, after some bald man's idea) has loosened his Pueblo chignon and lathered it plentifully with soapy yucca, so that now it hangs in a loose wave, itself like a threaded rain from the black cloud. He wears, too, over his kilt the streamered cord which is called the rain-sash, while the kilt itself is embroidered with the terraces and lozenges that are rain-cloud signs. Furthermore, as he moves—the drum beating—his whole body is a music as of rain upon the feathered maize-fields. Loops of dried hooves across his shoulder rattle with every movement, and belled garters with them, and in his right hand a great gourd which gives the very echo of the swish and splatter of the long rain upon the fields. Armlets and collars of evergreen spruce, and a green bough quick with every motion in his left hand represent that for which the rain falls and to which life gives answer: something beautiful before the face of the sky. For it is after this fashion that the dance is a prayer, and the dancers' bodies also, as they trick them out with every ornament of silver, turquoise, iridescent abalone, and of all sky-glorifying colors.

The female is beside the male in the dance. The old women with gray hair with the elder men, women in the bloom of their years beside the vigorously matured men, girls with the youths, and at the streamer end of the dancing processional tiny maidens, vaguely striving after the unlearned rhythm, paired with diminutive stomping boys, just out of their cradle months, but all gravely earnest. The whole life-body of the tribe, age and sex, enters into the celebrant rhythm—for it is this very being of the tribal whole that is deploying before its Creators, the great powers of its parent Worlds. Man, collectively, makes brave show to prove his mettle and to qualify for his inheritance.

The costume of the women is not less symbolic than that of the men, for their domain also is a World-Body, the Earth-Half of nature. The Pueblo female is radically shorter than her male, but on the occasion of the great tribal fiesta a kind of compensation is achieved in the most conspicuous feature of her costume. This is the *tablita,* a panel reared above the crown of her head, usually turquoise blue or green-blue in color, and pierced with star, crescent, tau-cross, zig-zag or other symbolic aperture (whose origin is half lost in tradition, but which may be, as some Indians have said, derived from clan emblems, so harking back to ancient matrilinear custodianships of the blood of the tribes). More certainly symbolic is the terraced comb of the *tablita,* like the terraces of ascending mountains whence the sky-blown terraces of the rain-clouds spring—which are limned with yellow or red, as of the rainbow, and from the peaks of which float flakes of white featherdown, itself symbol of the sky-fleeces that float athwart the blue, at once vapor of heaven-breath and token of that breath of life which man draws from the loft of the world. And even the tiniest of the little girls bear this proud *tablita.*

Thus the woman, like the man, wears at her crown a heaven-beseeching token, although there is a difference, for hers is not the mingling of the colors there above and the descent of the fructifying rain, but the uplifting of the body of Earth herself to greet the Sky-Father, as the ancient myths describe. In her hands she does not carry the gourd rattle, which is for the male, but in each hand is the sprig of the evergreen which betokens the life-response arising from the mothering earth with her seasonal blessing. The woman's hair (like that of the unshorn male, only richer than his) falls loose at her back in a lustrous black river, and on each of her cheeks is a glow of vermilion; silver and turquoise are her ornaments also, and her dress, leaving bare one brown shoulder and arm, is the black chiton cinctured with the red girdle, token-inwoven. But most distinctive of all are her bare, unmoccasined feet, and as we note in the dance how they delicately pat the dust-soft earth, lifting only hoveringly above it, clinging, adhering, as if loath to leave this kindred element of the woman's body, and as again we see this in her perpetually downcast gaze, in the curiously restrained and bodily intimate motions of her arms and ankles—all so at odds with the vigorous earth-abandonment of the motions of the male dancers, even while the two are in one rhythm—we are brought back abruptly to an image found among many Indian peoples of the woman's barefoot print in the cornfields as in itself a kind of magic of growth and an act of agriculture, her body's touch imprinting her own native genius of increase to the growing fields.

So the Osage woman, as she tamps the hilled kernels at the corn-planting, chants the mystery of her own bodily magic: [1]

> Footprints I have made; a sacred act.
> Footprints I have made; to lie in even lines.
> Footprints I have made; they are broken.
> Footprints I have made; in which stand leafy stalks.
> Footprints I have made; the leaves wave in the wind.
> Footprints I have made; the ears cross in profusion.
> Footprints I have made; I pluck the ears. . . .
> Footprints I have made; there is joy in my house.

Like the footprints the songs also are a magic, and in the Corn Dances of the Pueblos these songs are many; for the most part they are each year composed afresh, though their central tradition is always maintained and the rhythmic form shows no radical alteration. For the songs that are sung by the chanting choirs are the breath of the people and belong to the hour—as a supplication should which is the expression of an essential need and indeed of the breath of a living society. Previous to the celebrant day there have been assemblies and conferences whereat each man who has felt within himself the voice of a song-petitioner has offered his contribution—his melodic plea for such blessing as the season should bring. This may be for the bounty of the fields, for an abundant yield, which is the prime good ever-present in the minds of all. But the songs are by no means restricted to just this; for all good things which are associated with tribal prosperity and honorable human desire—all in which god or saint might show interest—are likewise the subject of song-supplication: prayers for children and health and substantial goods, and for clean minds and friendly hearts. All is poured into the meaning of the festival, and as the circle of the elders and the choristers listen to the new-made melodies and phrases, their minds and hearts are stirred, and perchance another and another adds phrase or strophe. An elder may find his memory suddenly reviving a long-faded fragment from other days, which with kindling affection he sings again, and his tribesmen, as if it were a

new thing, may cry out that it is good and cause it to live again
in the program of the feast and the hearts of the people. . . .

> For even while I call myself poor,
> Somewhere far off
> Is one who is my father.
> Beseeching the breath of the divine one, . . .
> His life-giving breath,
> His breath of old age,
> His breath of waters,
> His breath of seeds, . . .
> His breath of fecundity,
> His breath of power,
> His breath of strong spirit,
> His breath of all good fortune whatsoever,
> Asking for his breath
> And into my warm body drawing his breath,
> I add to your breath
> That happily you may always live.
>
> To this end, my fathers, my children:
> May you be blessed with light.[2]

The dancing itself is many-patterned. Day's zenith is not much
more than passed when from the clean-swept plaza is heard the
sudden tremor of the great drum and thereafter the chant of
men's voices. Then into the plaza emerges the procession: foremost the fantastic body and visage of the Koshare,[3] who are at
once ghosts and seed-givers, and who, as their bodies are quick-
ened into a preternatural agility, cast antic shadows, vivid upon
the sun-bright sand. Next is the bearer of the banner, thrice the
height of a man, that earlier in the day protruded flauntingly
above the kiva entrance to proclaim the approach of the festal
hour. This banner is of a form native to America, like those pictured on ancient Mexican codices, not far-streaming, but vertical
and close to the shaft; here it is formed of an embroidered sash,
attached lengthwise, with pendants of eagle feathers and the skin
of a fox such as each man-dancer wears from the back of his
girdle. But above all, at the summit of the banner, is a painted
puppet-head surmounted by a splendid panache of parrot and

macaw plumes, each a ray of sun-glory. In the patterns of the dance, from time to time, the banner-bearer swings his great emblem over the heads of the rhythmic people, as if asperging them with the liquid light of sun-blessing. And it is a strong man who carries the banner, and labors with it for his hour.

Following him enter the people, man and woman, youth and maiden, infant and infant, timing their swinging movements to the drum and the choristers who enter beside them. For the choir is held curiously apart, and is genuinely a chorus, as in a Greek tragedy. It is composed of men only, attired not ceremonially but in the gala fashion of the Pueblo people: for the man, a bright kerchief or fillet binding the hair, a colored shirt with free skirts, belted with an ornamental girdle perhaps of Navaho silver-work, ankle-split trousers, and red-brown moccasins fastened at the ankle with a silver conch. In a dense cluster, near to the drummer who leads them and all the dancers with his booming instrument, these men chant the planting, birth and growing of the maize, its fructification and maturation in answer to the mighty summons of the Sun and to the growth-strength which falls upon the fields in the descending rains. They chant it, and they mime it, stooping and spreading their palms earthward, as if to foster the tiny plants, lifting them higher and higher as the strong stalks mount, opening their palms to heaven as if to cup the falling showers and extending their arms in broad gestures to the wide spans of the fruitful fields. Most moving of all is the deeply psychical intensity of their facial expression: each singer's face is rapt and remote, blind to the plaza and the people and to aught which the hour may bring save that one imperative mastery of song which merges with the relentless pulsing of the drum and mounts into an earth-thunder commanding the myriad dancing feet that echo and augment its rumbling. For somewhere hidden still beyond the horizons of his reason, the man-creature is carried into an exaltation by the rhythms of his own heart-beat and his own breathing and by his limb-motion and body-motion, as if his whole vibrant being were but the full throbbing of the Earth, itself the commanding drum. So athwart the plaza the dancers move in varied figures, pairing, facing, reversing, interweaving, circling sunwise and counter-sun, with sudden bursts from the gourd rattles arresting and changing their motions. They pass under the sweeps of the great banner as if they were one man—being answering the sudden pauses and shifts of the drum-time, or the shrill-yelped directions of the Koshare, oblivious to all save the sound and the color and the united motion into which flesh has become transfused.

After their cycle the dancers recede to their rest in the kiva, to make way for a second group which is entering even as the first go; for the dance is continuous from the high sun until the sunset. The Rio Grande villages are in the main divided into moieties, each half forming a ceremonial and indeed a residential unit within the village. And these moieties are commonly known as the Squash or Summer People and as the Turquoise or Ice-Blue or Winter People; for the World is halved not only by the sky and the earth, in space, but also by the year's two seasons, in time, and the life of nature is in truth a dance of these seasons, summer and winter reciprocally occupying the places where the people dwell and the dancing-plaza of creation. Could there be harvest upon harvest with no period of earth-quiet? None has taught or observed this, any more than birth without gestation, or life with no quiet of death. There is little to distinguish the two bodies of dancers: there are some minor variations of symbolism, chiefly a difference of colors in the drum-painting or the costume, and in certain villages the Men of the Squash paint their bodies red or yellow and the Men of the Turquoise paint themselves blue. At times the dance figures vary, from party to party, but the rhythm is much the same and only a sharp attention will note the differing figures. But at the end of the day, just before the feast and gifting which is to close all, both seasons may dance together—the full year in a world of halves united, sky with earth, male with female, summer with winter: for the dual is nature's shrewdest number.

Yet this is not all. The subtlest beings which have appeared in this beautiful pageant of the Corn Dance were the Koshare, who have already crossed the plaza with their shadow. The morning of the fiesta day in the devoutly Catholic villages has been given to the priest's mass and to marriages and baptisms with Christian name. Thereafter the saint of the town has been carried through each of the streets and past all the households, and has finally been set up in a gaily decorated booth, right in the center of the plaza, where, with governor and cacique and visiting chief men, the saint also might bless and enjoy the dance, and receive the gifts which the dancers bring upon entering. This is, to be sure, not their very first dance, since the first honoring of the saint has been rendered beside the church, not intimately, but at a near distance. In all this there is something curious: one wonders why the Christian saint should not linger within the Christian church; why come out into the plaza and the booth? And were there not possibly in remoter days other images in the gay booth, which is assuredly long pre-Christian? The suspicion is more than supported by the descriptions left from early chroniclers of the customs of the New World, clearly implying that smoke-offerings and food-offerings were made where now candles and loaves are brought to Christian saints.

And if, during the late hour of mass, you stood, not within the church, but in a by-street of the village, you would likely have seen a pagan thing, having nothing to do with any church and older than any church. For a group of men of this curious society of the Koshare, excitedly yet timorously regarded, by a scattering of women and children, first assemble from the kivas and then pass rapidly from street to street and house to house, striking lintels and doors and women and children with light boughs of leafy foliage, now prankish, now food-receiving, until finally they have passed the rounds of the village. Immediately the mind turns back to the Lupercals of antique Rome, on the day when dignity faded from the Imperial Hills, racing through the streets and striking women and children with thongs of goat-skin, emblems and magic of fertility. This blessing, this ritual of fecundation, is no doubt older in origin than the prim Christian street-passing of the patron saint, with priest and choir—but perchance similar in ultimate intention.

At any rate the Koshare represent a society oddly mixed in character and function, and wholly and anciently pagan. The men and boys who appear in it—and of the younger some are mere children—are not fair to look upon. Except for a loin-cloth their bodies are naked; they are painted head to toe, usually a clay white, striped or splotched with black, like rib-men or infected men. Their hair is matted with clay and bound up with dried corn-husks, and in older days the switches or boughs which they carried were of dry leaf: there is nothing of the gala in the black-and-white and the sere yellow of the typical Koshare adornment. Yet in the afternoon dance they appear somehow lighter and less bodied than any of the other dancers—among whom they weave, about and before whom they dance, whom indeed they seem to command with their sharp yelp-like cries, yet by whom they are apparently never seen: for to the dancing corpus of the village, the Koshare are like invisible beings out of another realm and moving in another dimension. Their acts are an odd combination of solicitude and impishness: if a little child is lost in the dance-action, it is a Koshare who gently directs him; if a costume needs adjustment, it is a Koshare who is quick to assist; but in a no less quick fashion, he polices any misstep or any infringement of ritual law; and again with a freedom which is clearly license he indulges in pranks and antic motions with no disguise of gravity, yet always with an Ariel-like humor and a levitation of the body past the skill of most dancers.

A Tiwa name for the Koshare is *Khobyonin,* and it means Cold-Dead-Being, or perhaps Afraid-of-the-Cold-Being. Is, perhaps, this clownish performer actually the ritual embodiment of the ghost of a tribal ancestor? This has been affirmed, and it is certain that in some uncanny sense he belongs to the realm of the ghostly and the unseen, and perhaps does indeed represent that care for the life of the people which runs through its generations, like a single wave of energy transbodied in time. It is of interest that among so many folk the heroes and the ancients of their nations have exercised a similar care. But this alone is not enough: for these Koshare ancients are more than guardian spirits; they are also sprites of fertility and authors of life; they are the seed-bearers as well as the ghosts of tribal life, and in a magical manner are intimate with the world's great medicine powers. Nymphs and fauns were in other times such beings, and the genius which was not lastingly distinguishable from the manes of the tribal past; so that the Roman heir who caught into his own body the expiring breath of the passing gentile Pater was in another day and mode but subscribing to that sense of the continuity of the life-stream of a people, its *spiritus* in the full sense, which still pervades the whole moral and metaphysical consciousness of the Pueblo Indian, and which is ritually embodied in the Koshare and credally echoed in his chant: [4]

> "Do not despise the breath of your fathers,
> But into your bodies draw his breath."

II

"IF ONE LOOK closely at these Indians he will find that everything they do and say has something to do with maize. A little more, and they would make a god of it. There is so much conjuring and fussing about their corn fields, that for them they will forget wives and children and any other pleasure, as if the only end and aim of life was to secure a crop of corn." [5]

Such is the observation of the unknown author of the *Crónica Franciscana,* writing in the seventeenth century of the Indians of Central America. Actually the Indians did make gods of their maize, or more often goddesses; for the bearers of the Seeds of Things, the Corn Maidens, each with a pollen-wafting butterfly at her lips like another Psyche, were divine not only among the Maya and the Aztec, but also far to the north in New Mexico, and in varied guise wherever the cultivation of the maize had created an aboriginal agriculture. With them were associated all those powers with which rest the fates of the fields: the flute-playing daemons of fecundity, the sprites of fruitfulness, the birds of flowing plumage, the lords of the dews, the masked thunders, rain-bringing, the swift archers of the skies, and over all the heroic sun whose lances open the caverns of the rainbow and reveal in their beauty the silken-haired maidens of the pollinating corn. A whole plan of living and a newer interpretation of nature came into the Indian world with the miracle of the maize—how many tens of centuries in the past only surmise may count—and it came in time to absorb the aboriginal life with such intensity that it stirred the early chronicler's wonder even while it lay beyond his understanding.

It is the received opinion (credible for many reasons) that the primal conquest of maize was in Mexico, and at a period so remote in prehistory that its beginnings in the New World are comparable to those of the domestication of barley and wheat grasses in the Old. Certainly it is in terms of millennia that we must reckon the development of an agriculture which at the period of the Discovery was extended from the estuaries of the Plata in South America to the mouth of the St. Lawrence in North America, and which had not only made of the maize a cereal totally dependent upon human cultivation for its survival (for it is nowhere found wild and is incapable of self-propagation), but which, during its long period of domestication had been developed into varieties adapted to every climate from the tropical to the almost sub-Arctic. Only the long and leisurely migrations of the years could have made this possible, especially under the untutored conditions of tribal transmission and cultivation; and it is no marvel, therefore, that among the Indian peoples the lore of maize culture had since generations out of mind become shrouded with fable and mystery—like the lore of the wheat among Old World folk.

Along the northern margins of the maize-growing area the coming of the corn was still recent enough to be remembered in myth, although only a few tribes could ascribe the gift directly to a neighboring people (as do the Omaha to the Arikara). Usually the myth is of another type: of a people hungry and ignorant, for whom subsistence is hard and precarious, of a tribal kinsman seeking through daring or vigil the discovery of a redemptive food, and of the triumph of finding it through the aid of the Corn Spirit itself. The Algonquian myth of Mondawmin is one of the most splendid of this type: the youth, sent for his fasting into the forest, there praying to the Great Manito for that which should enable his people to live; the coming of Mondawmin as a superb young man in feathered head-dress; the wrestling unto the fourth watch; and then the burial of the Corn Spirit and the growth of the maize from his grave.[6] It is a myth that at once suggests the Old-World analogues of Tammuz and Adonis and of all the annually slain and annually restored corn-gods of the Ancient East and of peasant Europe; but it suggests no less, similar vegetation myths and rites of the New-World continents: for at the heart of man's dependence for food upon plant life lies deeply a doctrine of transubstantiation, wherein the bread becomes flesh, and the flesh in turn is rebodied in the earth-born grain. Rites dark and bloody, where human flesh has been torn that the fields may bring forth their yield, as well as the most powerful sacraments of many faiths, and in the end the highest symbols of immortality, have sprung instinctively from this far-ancient miracle of domesticated grain.

Among the Plains tribes, Siouan and Caddoan, the myths of origin have quite generally ascribed the coming of the corn to the magical bison, which in bovine rather than human shape, has brought to man this blessing. For the Dakota the event appears to be set at a period about a thousand years remote from our own day; and this may reasonably be assumed as a plausible dating for a happening which so powerfully regenerated their lives. Cognate Siouan peoples—Mandan, Omaha, Osage, and others—may have brought the secret of maize-culture in their up-river migrations from the down-river territories where it assuredly flourished in past times, as the archaeology of the Ozark region testifies; or, following some of their own legends, the corn may have come to them along with the earth-lodge and certain rituals from the Caddoan Pawnee and Arikara, who, among living peoples, have best right to be regarded as the autochthones of the Plains (even if back of them may have lain yet other agricultural races). Certainly, of all the Plainsfolk, the Caddoans had most developed and ritualized their corn-culture with certain traits which seem to indicate that they may have derived it from the peoples of the great Southwest Plateau, with whom they were in contact at the coming of the Spaniard, and to whom the mystery had already been transmitted from Basket-Maker times, more than one millennium before.[7]

There are three routes following which the civilization of the maize—for in effect it is this—moved northward from ancient Mexico. Of these the easternmost, following the curve of the Gulf and thence of the Atlantic Coast, reached New England and Nova Scotia, and laid the foundations for not less than three widely disseminated village cultures, in which there were approaches to settled economies and established states: the forest-land agriculture of the Northeast, in which the Confederacy of the Iroquoian tribes, a century before the coming of the whites, had set up a notable polity; the more ancient Mound-builder culture of the Lake Region and South; and, surely still anterior, the culture of the Muskhogean tribes and their neighbors of the Southeast, which into our own times has carried ritual conceptions strikingly analogous to those of the Maya and the Aztec. The antiquity of this movement can only be guessed, but it represents the region which has given to the world as a whole the major varieties of cultivated maize, and with the maize the accompanying vines of bean and squash. For everywhere in the Indian world the hilled fields of the native peoples have brought forth in association these three staples of life, forming the true complex of the maize.

The second path of migration northward has been up the great continental rivers. This is clearly the most recent of the three routes, for while on the lower Mississippi maize-culture is many centuries old, it is within remembered times, as their myths indicate, that the cereal has reached several of the tribes of the Missouri Valley. Nevertheless, these are times of sufficient range to have permitted the acclimatization of the plant to the brief summers of lands lying north of the last great bend of the Missouri River, a process which could hardly have been possible except among peoples seasonally slow in their northward movements.

Whether the third path, presumably up the Rio Grande and Pecos valleys, may have antedated that into the Atlantic regions is once more only surmise. But at least it is evident that on the Southwestern Plateau, among Pueblo and pre-Pueblo peoples, the maize early became the very flesh and bone of the Indian civilization which there grew into being. Moreover, there are such affinities southward as to make clear that the antique culture of the highlands of New Mexico is only a northern spur of the un-remembered mother civilization—maize-planted—which yet earlier ages had transmitted along the highland ridge of the two continents, from Mexico south to the Andean north, thence to Incaic realms, and on into Chile and Argentina. This was in days long before the sub-Pedregal, or the civic splendors of Aztec and Maya and Chibcha and Inca, which were each but a local flowering from a deep-rooted parent stem.[8]

Myth and ritual as attached to an important culture trait are significant indices of its deep-seatedness and long establishment. In the Plateau regions of the two Americas the agricultural color of mythic traditions and ritual practices gives its fundamental tone to the whole complexion of the civilizations which evolved there. It is not only, as the chronicler noted, that the Indian's whole life is engrossed in the welfare of his fields; but even more that the patterns of his thought and his conception of the world turns pivotally upon the life-sustaining cereal. In ancient Mexico the origin of maize-culture had long since passed out of mind: mythically the maize is as ancient as the existing race of man, for it is from the maize that the gods first creatively fashioned man's flesh. There is no remembrance of a day when all men were nomad hunters, as the more northerly traditions testify. Accordingly, the corn-sprites are already deities, male and female—although the latter predominate, each goddess with the pollen butter-fly fluttering at her lips, symbol at once of increase and of life-breath. Such are Cinteotl, Lord of the Yellow Maize, Xilonen, Lady of the Red Maize, and Chicomecoatl, "Seven-Snakes" (for there is a profound association of the serpent and the corn) who represents the matured fields of the Seven-realmed Universe. Indeed, the World-Tree itself is shown pictographically with twinned maize-ears sprouting from its stalk, just as it is sur-mounted by the quetzal, whose bladed tail-plumes are the full symbol of the bladed corn. We realize, then, that this tree is no longer simply a schematic frame of the cosmos, but, like the foli-ated Cross of Palenque and of the Aztec codices, it has become

the living symbol of all nature. Even in the marginal north the
Roman cross may signify either man or maize, and it is not fanci-
ful to find this imagery rooted in the notion that man and maize
and world are ultimately one inter-substantiate being.

World time as well as the world's structure enters into this
complex of ritual thought. The festal year of the older Mexican
peoples is seasonal with corn-fêtes. Every stage of the annual
maize-growth, soil-breaking to harvest, is occasion for a feast or
prayer. Every power upon which maize-growth depends—above
all, the water-bringers, the Nahua Tlalocs and the Maya Chacs,
tutelaries of the cloud-summoning mountains and of the pools of
the Earth-Quarters—calls for its cult and its sacrifice. That such
sacrifices were so often of human flesh and of human blood
(kneaded into the maize-meal) is only another indication of the
strangely passionate conviction of agricultural men that the gods
who give the grain-yield must themselves be sustained by the life
of the flesh into which the grain has been transmuted. It is a conviction and practice familiar in Old World corn rites also—curiously testifying to some deeply instinctive sense on the part of
mankind that we who live as parasites on earth's vegetation must
yet make restitution. Thus in Aztec lore, the Earth-Goddess is
patroness of increase but claimant also of the dead: all-mother-
ing and all-devouring. The kernel of all sense of destiny lies here.

Assuredly in old Mexico the passing of millennia could alone
have produced this total engrossment of the conceptual and the
physical life, as if, in the kneading, bread and life were made one
—so that even for late initiates into the Mexican culture (like
the Nahua) every vital significance had been blood-adopted.
Maize had become the life-measure of the civilization, to such an
extent that men counted by it rather than by years; for the
tonalamatl, the curious 260-day cycle by which the Mexicans
reckoned their civil time and which they periodically "tied" in
with the solar years to form their 52-year cycle of destiny, was
plausibly derived from the seedtime-to-harvest span of the maize-
crop.[9] The unit of time, then, was not given primarily by the
Sun, in his annual career, but by the Sun's offspring, the corn.
That this period so nearly corresponds to that of the gestation of

human life would have been but another indication of that unity of maize-life and man-life which we have noted, giving an added emphasis to the fact that for the ancient American the unit of time is a biological and not an astronomical year. In Virginia and other parts of the Southeast the year was similarly measured by the corn-seasons rather than by sun-seasons; and it is worth noting that the great annual festival of our Southeast, the Pus-kita, the Feast of the New Corn, in many ways profoundly resembled the Tying of the Years of the Aztec—as if the latter might have developed from it with the maturing of the agricultural folk-spirit and its expansion into a complicated urban civilization.

In the American Southwest, the Pueblo region, is another maturation of the maize-culture, again akin to the Mexican. Its unique traits are doubtless due to the special conditions of a semi-arid plateau life, where the cult of the Tlalocs, the rain-sprites, is first in mind; for in many ways the entire culture seems built up out of a prayer for rain. In all the villages the rain-plea is the one theme of the women's pottery. Each olla is filigreed with the streaming, the laced, the sun-broken, the dense, the rainbowed rain; the cloud-terrace takes on manifold forms, zig-zags, steps, and crescents super-piled, fringed with streamers and jagged and tongued with lightnings; in the interstices are leaves and seeds and flowers and pollens; feather-plumes and birds are there, the latter often themselves composed of leaves and flowers; and there are the insects that frequent pools and fields, the dragonfly, the butterfly; and now and again the deer, which to American peoples is widely the symbol of the East, of the White Light, and of Life and Increase, so that even the Maize-Goddess is at times known by this name. On ceremonial jars, to be sure, there are frogs and serpents and yet more sacredly the Plumed Serpents of the Cosmic Waters; but these are for the great rituals. What is significant is that even the commonest utensils of life are figured with the all-engrossing emblems of the peoples' one concern—which is for the Bread of Life. Whether the feast be Rain-Dance or Snake-Dance or Flute or Butterfly, or the great Corn-Dance of the annual fiesta, all turn upon and embody the central mystery of the corn.[10]

III

MAN IS OF THE SKY, woman is of the earth: Zeus is πατήρ, Gē is μήτηρ, and from their union issues the Birth, which the Hellenes named the *Physis*, and we, after the Latins, call *Nature*. There is something chill and austere and battlefree in the wind-swept blue; the squadrons of the clouds are there, and the birds of war, with their flashes of levin and their heavy bolts; and there the Sun, *Invictus*, is chieftain, and leads his war-bands in the seasonal Titanomachies of the heavens; thence also descends the bearded rain of *Pluvius*, whereby recipient Earth is made fertile and life-productive. The green, on the other hand, is a warmer and more intimate and sedentary being; it is she who is the nourisher of life, she who gives breast to her children, she, too, who cherishingly receives back into herself the bodies of her brood—tenderly, like the poor Australian Blackwoman who, refusing the grave its due, for months bore with her the corpse of her babe, until her own body had again given vital form to its transmitted life. Earth, also, receives the bones of her offspring, so that they may be born again, and nature be ever renewed. . . . Quite directly this is the image which underlies cosmogonies—procreation and birth, parents and child—where with an understanding deeper than has perhaps been surmised, men have everywhere mythically divined that nothing less than a *vital* force could have produced a world wherein man himself vitally stands, the conscious off-spring of Sky and Earth. Metaphysics is far more than a sophisticated critique of science; it is an instinct of a life-sensing mind which without such a homing of its intelligence is no better than a frighted ghost, unlaid in chaos.

It is probably true that for nomads, whether hunter or pastor, the Sky-Father, with his tribesmen the Stars, is patriarchally supreme and the Earth no more than passingly his woman. The idea is only the reflection of his daily condition, wherein, under their leader, the men circle the camp and scout beyond its borders, and as out-riders discover new ways to reave what they can from the wilderness of the hunter or the settlements of farmer clans. But within these settlements the woman's function is the more profound, for to her is committed the giving of food and the magic of increase; and the shrines which the villagers serve are dedicated to the goddesses and the Earth-Mother, and their temples are groves and grottoes and pools, not the sky-facing altars of Father Zeus. The earth-embosomed life of agricultural man is a sedentary life, and when the man-animal changes his ways from wandering after prey and from war and mastery into what we usefully term a "productive life," there is a certain feminization or woman-centering of his thought, and the goddesses come into their own.

It is thus that there grows up even a kind of gendering of the tribe itself, so that one moiety is of the blue, the northerly and the protective but wintry male, whereas the second is of the summery south and of the earth-life. Even the camp circles of the Plains tribesmen—which are in inspiration only defensive formations, like a Roman castrum—are thus divided, with a northerly sky-moiety and to the south the earth-clans; but with the more seasoned agricultural folk of the Pueblos the whole ordination of living, their social cosmos, is symbolized, or rather *lived*, in this dual mode, as if the tribe were Man and Woman, like the elemental human pair, the two-fold world, which is also Man-Woman. Such was the first naming of spaces and things, as Cushing[11] recorded in Zuñi belief a generation ago how in the age of the beginnings "the Twain Beloved and priest fathers gathered in council for the naming and selection of man-groups and creature-kinds, spaces, and things. Thus determined they that the creatures and things of summer and the southern space pertained to the Southern people, or Children of the Producing Earthmother; and those of winter and northern space, to the Winter people, or Children of the Forcing or Quickening Sky-father." The planned village and the ceremonial year of the Pueblo peoples and the antiphonal dances themselves correspond to, and are to be understood, to this day, in this gendered form. For sex is a mode of thinking which colors tradition and shapes ritual, a prime category of the human understanding—as Pythagoreans long ago defined it.

In this mythos of the Origins, as disclosed by Cushing, the clans of the Fathers are represented as having issued from the four-fold womb of Earth, still uncleansed of animality either in body or mind, for in body they are scaly and tailed and goggle-eyed and webbed in foot and sun-shunning, while in disposition they are war-makers and plunderers. But led by the Twin Heroes of Light—the "Twain Beloved," who are in fact the smiting Sun-beams—they journey in search of that Middle Place, over the beating heart of Earth, which is the home of their desire. En route they come to *Shipololon K'yaia,* the Place of Misty Waters, and there they encounter the People of the Dew, who are also the People of the Seed, for these are the custodians of the Corn Maidens and hence of the fruitfulness of the fields. When the clans of the Fathers, after their male custom, advance hostile, there occurs a curious fliting and wrangling, like a folk-courtship. For as the calmer nature of woman might withhold the impetuous man, so the People of the Dew bid the hostile clans that they forbear attack until each has proved his magic and rulership. "We have powers above yours, yet without your aid we can never exert them; even as the mothers of men may not be fertile save of the fathers" . . . and they challenge the comers to show of powers.[12] Whereat, the clans of the Fathers, aided by their medicine, call forth rains from the Sky-Father and fields of tasseled stems. But of fruit there is none, not until the People of the Dew, who are the matriarchs of nature, summon forth the Corn Maidens, and they, jointly with a certain youth of the father-clans, Yápotuluha, foster-child of the Sun-Priest and a water-being, perform a dance in the maize-fields, rendering them heavy-eared and fruitful. This is the first Corn Dance, and the meaning of all corn dances, whose magic is seen annually in the Pueblos, where Summer and Winter enact yearly the fliting of nature in her twained yet uniting bodies. This is the description of it in the Zuñi myth:

Now THERE WERE in the village of the stranger Seed people seven maidens, sisters of one another, virgins of one house, and foster-children of Paíyatuma (the God of Dew) himself. And they were surpassingly beautiful, insomuch so that they were likened to the seven bright stars and are sung of in the songs of the Seed people and told of in their stories. They, too, were chosen and breathed upon by all the fathers and matrons of the Seed, and with the youth Yápotuluha, instructed in the precious rites and incantations of their custom. And during all the time of preparation rain fell as before, only gently and warm, and on the eighth day the matrons and fathers led the maidens and youth, all beautifully arrayed, down into the plain before the bower where watched the people and grew the grasses. And there they danced and were breathed of the sacred medicine seeds. All through the night backward and forward danced they to the song line of the elders, and in accordance therewith by the side of the growing plants, motioning them upward with their magic wands and plumes, as we, with implements of husbandry, encourage the growth upward of the corn plants today. As time went on, the matron of the dance led the youth and the first maiden apart, and they grasped, one on either side, the first plants, dancing around them, gently drawing them upward as they went, even as the Two Beloved had caused to grow the canes of the underworld. So also did the youth and each maiden in turn grasp the other plants in their turn, until all had grown to the tallness of themselves and were jointed where they had grasped them; yea, and leaved as with waving plumes of the macaw himself. And now, in the night, the keepers of the great shells brought fire with their hands from roots, and kindled it in front of the bower toward the east, that its heat might take the place of the Sun and its light shine brightly on the dancers, making their acts verily alive; and as the dawn approached, the youth and first maiden were led apart as before by the Mother-making matron, and together embraced the first of the full-grown plants, and so, in turn, the youth and each of the other maidens embraced the other plants.

And as they embraced the first plant, the fire flamed brightly, with the first catching and flush of the wood, and yellow was its light; and as they embraced the second plant, the flames were burning smokily with the fuller grasping of the wood, and blue was the light; and as they were embracing the third plant, the fire reached its fullness of mastery over the wood, and red was its light; and as they were embracing the fourth plant, the fire was fumeless and triumphant over the wood, and white was its light; and as they were embracing the fifth plant, the fire gave up its breath in clouds of sparks, and streaked, of many colors, was its light; and as they were embracing the sixth plant, the fire swooned and slept, giving more heat, as 'twere, then light, thus somber was its light; yet as they were embracing the seventh plant, it wakened afresh, did the fire, in the wind of the morning, and glowed as does the late fire of the wanderer, with a light of *all* the colors.

Now when the day dawned, lo! where the mid-persons of the youth and the maidens had touched most unitedly and warmly the plants, new parts appeared to the beholders, showing, through their coverings, many colors, soft hair shrouding them, as if to make precious their beauty.

Whilst the people still gazed at these, wondering, out from the East-land came Paíyatuma and Ténatsali of the All-colored flowers (God of the Seasons), followed by Kwélele with his flame-potent fire-wand. Paíyatuma touched the plants with the refreshing breath of his flute; Ténatsali with the flesh-renewing breath of his flowers; Kwélele with the ripening breath of his torch, whereby the new parts were hardened, some to fruitfulness; others, being too closely touched, burned to the very heat of generative warmth, unfruitful in itself, but fruitful making! Then, as Paíyatuma waved his flute, lo! following Ténatsali, the maidens and the attendant Kwélele went forth and disappeared in the mist of the morning. As they vanished Paíyatuma turned to where, full in the light of the rising sun, stood the seven plants. Lithe and tall stood he there beside them like a far journeyer, and said to the awed watchers:

> Lo! ye children of men and the Mother,
> Ye Brothers of Seed, elder, younger,
> Behold the *seed plants of all seeds!*
> The grass-seeds ye planted, in secret,
> Were seen of the stars and the regions,
> Are shown in the forms of these tassels!
> The plumes that ye planted beside them
> Were felt in the far-away spaces,
> Are shown in the forms of their leaf-blades!
> But the seed that ye see growing from them,
> Is the gift of my seven bright maidens,
> The stars of the house of my children!
> Look well, that ye cherish their persons,
> Nor change ye, the gift of their being,—
> As fertile of flesh for all men
> To the bearing of children for men,—

THE CORN MAIDENS

> Lest ye lose them, to seek them in vain!
> Be ye brothers, ye people and people;
> Be ye happy ye Priests of the Corn!
> Lo! the seed of all seed-plants is born!

As the people eagerly looked, the mists of the morning were seen to be clearing away, and gone with them, even as his voice, was Paíya-tuma! "Thanks this day," together said the fathers and their people, as they looked upon the plants before them, then at the stranger people. "Verily, ye are our elder brothers, and as children and sisters, yea, as our very mothers, will we cherish thy maidens and the substance of their flesh!" [13]

This striking myth has more than one implication. Plausibly, the union of the People of the Fathers with the Seed People, guardians of the Corn Maidens, may well hark back to the ritual and social union of a nomadic with an agricultural tribe or folk, representing such a ceremonial beginning of a revolutionary mode of life as is not infrequently remembered in myths of acculturation. Again, the story is obviously a scenario of the Pueblo Corn Dance itself, with its plea for rain and fruitfulness, its magical evocation of growth, its symbolism of the seven-regioned cosmos of the Pueblo peoples, each with its color (yellow-corn of the North, blue of the West, red of the South, white of the East, speckled of the Above, black of the Below, and vari-colored, ripened corn of the kindled fire-place of the Here—such, even today, is the key-symbolism of the whole Pueblo culture). But in a third and yet wider symbolism the myth propounds a dogma of the fundamental metaphysics of mankind: that which makes of Earth the Mother and of Corn her daughter or daughters, such that the home-half of man's primary universe, the food-giving and life-bringing half, is the female element of a sex-twained world-whole. And the myth marks, if not the full surrender, at least the cultural subordination of the heroic Sky-Realm to the fostering Earth-Domain, the *alma mater* of humanity.

This entire conception of the matriarchate, or perhaps better, the *motherhood* of the earth—which still hues our poetic and intimate thought of nature—becomes the very body of the culture of farmer-minded men. The cult of the Corn Maidens of the

Pueblo peoples is a local example of what in analogous forms appears among other agricultural Indians: among the Iroquois, for example, and in forms which seem to imply intimate relationship with the Southwest, among the Pawnee, Arikara, and other tribes of the Plains. Most striking, of course, are its affinities with Nahuatlan corn-cults, where the goddesses of the maize, with their pollen butterflies and their intimate associations with the Breath- or Flute-God, with the Flower-God, with the Fire-God, argue precisely the complexion of thought which the Zuñi myth images.

Indeed, in Mexico, as again in the Andean south and in the Pueblo Plateau, the maize-cult develops a whole understanding of the world, a cosmogony, of which, in spite of its changing versions, the single origin can hardly be questioned. It may suitably be called the "earth-womb cosmogony," the *autochthon* conception of life-genesis, or in another relation the "maize-cosmogony." The general features of this cosmogonical cycle are of a four-period past, each period staged in a subterranean world-realm, one below the other: of a "Sun," or life-age, passed in each world-stage but ending either in a cataclysmic destruction (the Mexican mode) or in a migration to a higher world (as the Pueblo versions relate); of a final emergence into this upper or earth-world, and of the upraising here of the full-powered Sun which we know, and which is the sun of the present age and also of vegetation and of a furnished creation. The Hero Twins, gods of morning and evening, are the guides and discoverers of the way, the monster-slayers and the transformers of old, imperfect things into new. In general they are the deliverers and leaders of mankind. When, for example, the Corn Maidens have been lured away to the flower-bordered Pool of Mist and Dews in the far south and there concealed under the wings of water-birds, the Hero Twins finally rediscover them and lead them back to the people who await them with fast and anguish in a land from which summer has departed. The episode is clearly that of the seasons; and remembering that Persephone is but the leader of the *korai* of the spring, the nymphs of the Grecian returning springtime, we see that here is an American version of the rape —of winter broken by the all-powerful rays, and of the corn-goddesses and the flower-sprites seasonally celebrating their festival of increase under the smiling blessing of their mother the Earth.

There is yet one further trait of this mythic cycle which gives it distinctive character. In the *Popul Vuh*, at once the most dramatic and the most subtle of versions, the Makers and Formers of mankind first shape men of clay, but these are without speech or intelligence, and they are destroyed in a great flood which ends the first Sun of the world. The creators strive once more, creating carved men of woody fibre; but they are again disappointed in what they have produced, for neither memory nor intelligence graces the creatures; and a resinous rain is sent to wipe them out. But in a third attempt men are moulded from the maize, and from this was formed their strength and their flesh. "Only yellow maize and white entered into their flesh, and these were the sole substance of the legs and arms of man; thus were formed our first fathers. . . . Men they were; they spake and they reasoned; they saw and they understood; they moved and they had feeling; men perfect and fair, whose features were human features." Similarly, in the cosmogony of the people of Sia, Utset, the Mother, who "had always known the name of corn," planted bits of her own heart, whence the cereal grew; and she said, "This corn is my heart, and it shall be to my people as milk from my breasts." In a wholly analogous vein the White Buffalo Woman of the Sioux brought as her gift to the people her milk, which was corn of four colors, the white and the yellow and the red and the blue, which was likened to the clouds of four colors, rising from the quarters of the terrestrial world; and this was to be the nourishment and the life of man. Thus is the corn, as in the Zuñi chant, "fertile of flesh for all men." [14]

IV

IN THE NEARER EAST of the Old World the star-guided nomads brought with them out of the desert and into the coastlands the cults of the heavenly wanderers and of the fiercely masculine raiding god, Lord of Glory and of Feud-rights; but in lands of milk and honey they succumbed to the peasant cult of the Baals and still more to the cults of the Ashtaroth, nymphs of fields and fertility and goddesses of the earth's gifts,—and the Bedaw became Fellah. So also in the classic land, when the huntsmen who had followed Apollo, the Wolf of the Skies, and his master the Sky himself, Zeus, Lord of Thunders, had come out of the steppes into the softer Mediterranean, they accepted the marriage of their arrow and bolt-wielding gods, nomads of the heavens, with the seductive *korai* and earth-mothers of the peasant-lands. Thus the Divine Lady, in the end, became mistress of their world and the daughter of Zeus, herself half Valkyrie, brought forth the olive branch. In such ways does myth record the interplay of male and female culture-moments in man's epic life.

America affords similar examples. On the Great Plains, east of the Rockies, the two types of culture met and mingled. The Pawnee and the Arikara have best title to antiquity in this region, with their kindred Caddoans; and it is precisely among these that farmer ways and farmer lore were most developed, while in their myth and ritual, more than other peoples they display that oft-repeated accommodation of huntsman and farmer of which the Old World so richly sets example. No American people, of their level, has so eloquently developed astral imagery; the stars were for them the book of life as well as being battle scouts; in constellations they sat in their nightly council chambers, while at the same time Father Heaven ruled over them, head of a veritable Olympus of star and sky deities. All this belongs to that Eastern and Northern cosmic order which derives man and his fates directly from upperworld archetypes and makes of him the heaven-descended. But in Pawnee myth there is also another strain, in the end dominant, which clearly comes from the South and from the maize-fields which had been brought thence. For among these Caddoans, although sent thither, like another Ishtar, by the helpless Sky-Father, Mother Corn descends into the underworlds, thence to lead forth mankind, and from the place of emergence to conduct the First People by journeyings to the final and fruitful abode favored among mortals. The whole image (as in an Arikara version) is extraordinarily suggestive of a period of gestation and an embryonic development—analogous to the

THE CORN MAIDENS

Pueblo tales—beginning with the descent of Mother Corn down into the foetal abodes whence the grown man is to be upraised: [15]

Before the World was we were all within the Earth.
Mother Corn caused movement. She gave life.
Life being given we moved toward the surface:
We shall stand erect as men!
The being is become human! He is a person!
To personal form is added strength;
Form and intelligence united, we are ready to come forth,—
But Mother Corn warns us that the Earth is still in flood.
Now Mother Corn proclaims that the flood is gone, and the Earth
  now green.
Mother Corn commands that the people ascend to the surface.
Mother Corn has gathered them together, they move half way to the
  surface;
Mother Corn leads them near to the surface of the Earth;
Mother Corn brings them to the surface. The first light appears!
Mother Corn leads them forth. They have emerged to the waist.
They step forth to the surface of the Earth.
Now all have come forth; and Mother Corn leads them from the East
  toward the West.
Mother Corn leads them to the place of their habitation. . . .
All is completed! All is perfect!

(In Greek vase-paintings, too, the goddess is portrayed as emerging from the Earth and the Titans of the First Age are shown waist-risen from the parturient soil: Old World and New create identic images.) The Pawnee go on to tell how when the folk are established in their Middle Place, the appropriate tasks of mankind are set. To woman Mother Corn gives in custody the seeds and the moisture to fructify them; to her also the earth lodge with its altar and holy place and fireplace; it is to her that speech is given—speech for children's teaching—and to her also the materials of the sacred pipes, the calumets of the *Hako,* which is a prayer for children and the breath of life. To man she assigns the hunter's kit and the warrior's regalia—a meager showing, save that the peril of his days forbade the warrior ever to leave from reach his accoutrements, for he was "the wall of defense" of the house of life; and the Thunderbird, levin-flashing, was his emblem.

The Thunderbird may, indeed, be taken as a symbol of a second great North American culture group, impinging from the North and the East upon the plateau cultures of the Southwest. For it is in the forests and the plains of the great continental river valleys that the Thunderers, the Sky-Warriors, approach to the zenith of the Indian pantheons. Normally the Thunderers are represented as great birds of the hawk family: their eyes and beaks send forth the arrowy lightnings, their sweeping wings beat the air into thunders, their plumes are rain-dripping, and their flight is wind-swift. The warrior paints their emblem upon his person, his shield, his pony, his "medicine"; and the priest or shaman seeks the powerful protection of this chieftain of the skies. The falcon of Egypt, the eagle of Assyria, Persia, Rome, and of the Caesar-lands of later Europe, as well as the bald American eagle, are all emblematically akin to the Thunderbird; essentially he belongs to captains and foray-bands and to all who deal sudden death and become the lords of imperial states. . . .

> The Earth behold!
> All these shall be yours!

This is a song which the horsemen of the sky, the mounted Thunderers, taught in a vision to a Sioux warrior out on the war-path. Something akin to this was taught to Thutmosis, and Shalmaneser, to Cyrus and Caesar and Charlemagne, and to all who have followed the eagle and the double-eagle. The wind-driven rout of Odin and Thor was not different, where the winged-helms swept down from the North in times past, even to the coasts of America. Indeed, if one looks for any ensign of the Old World Occident which can vie with the eagle as token of its far-winding civilization, it can only be found in the emblem derived from the Southerners, in the cross which was a Roman tree of death and becomes a Christian tree of life. Curiously enough, something similar occurs in ancient America: the eagle of the north is the warrior's Thunderbird; the foliated cross of Palenque and of many other southern lands is the tree of world-life. It is odd that the simple geometrical cruciform of the Roman pattern became eventually, even for the red men of the Plains, the symbol for the spread-winged hawk or eagle as well as for the dicotyledon of the maize plant, earth-emergent—and this natively and without any influence from Europe. Thus, in a fashion, the symbolism and cult of north and south unite.

Nevertheless, the duality of these two great Indian culture-trends is real and evident in their complexions. The tribes of the North and East are of nomad offspring, for whom the sky-guides and sky-powers are dominant; they think in terms of sky chieftains and warriors, and of masterful male force; theirs is no moth-ered, but only a sired world, into which the woman fits as any captive might. Mankind, for them, is rarely autochthonous, earth-born; he is heaven-fallen. His fathers are denizens of sky-ter-races above, of heavens that are above the heavens, where in a land of archetypes they dwell, dimly foredooming the *orbis ter-rarum,* the "runs" and "ranges" that down below are to fall to man-beings and beast-beings and to the quick and the dead. Iroquoian and Algonquian cosmogonies, although in dramatic details they differ,[16] all turn upon this one theme, of the fall, the descent. In the Plains regions, the myths are mixed, many obviously harking from the South; yet on the Plains, also, the dominant theme is of the Lucifer type, the *fall* from the star-lands, rather than ascent from underworlds. It is interesting to note that the fall is brought about through woman's frailty: it is she who breaks the tabu of the Lord of Heaven, is cast downward, and on a lower level of being gives birth to man and his mortality. The gods of the North are war-gods and hurlers, not growing things.

The meetings and mingling of these two culture-strains—hunter and farmer, heaven-sired and earth-mothered, war-wan-dering and towning—are complexly varied. Undoubtedly long ago the whole thought of the south came northward with every ex-pansion of the maize and its rituals. But art itself leaves some traces of the movement. In a far prehistoric art of shell and stone and copper discs and ornaments found from Illinois to Georgia and Louisiana, there are instructive plays upon the Thunderbird motif. Northerly he is frankly a bird of the *Falconidae.* At Etowah (Georgia) he is a hawk-nosed man who swings a trophy head and a rattle inscribed with a roman cross. All his symbolism in the

Etowah copper-plate repeats what is to be found not only in ancient Mexico but even more in the pre-Inca towns of the Peruvian coastlands: item for item, trophy head with serpent-body and bird-mask, the rattle that still today in our Southwestern corn dances symbolizes the pattering of the rain upon the leafy fields, the wings which are of the sky-being. These and other indications, ritual and material, make it hardly possible seriously to doubt some identity of provenience from Georgia to Peru. Yet the designer's style for the Etowah plaques is identical with those of the gorgets of Tennessee and Illinois, and there are transitional developments of the central symbol throughout the whole region.[17] Somehow, the Thunderbird—eagle of Ashur and Zeus—as time passes and cultures mingle, becomes also the lord of fertility and of the cross-symboled Earth. The maize is his also.

In the eagle's art-expressed neighborhood, and eventually closely associated with him, appears the serpent. The rattlesnake no doubt has many meanings: his poison and his power assure him significance. He appears in the region of the shell-discs and gorgets and on Floridian food-bowls, and with other serpents he appears in Mexico and New Mexico indubitably in close association with the maizefields. Here is a second element of symbolism: the serpent-kind, whose northern Elder-in-Potency is the rattlesnake, just as the eagle lords it in the skies. Is it possible that his place is due to the fact that tilled maizefields are favored abodes of serpents (who there make prey of the rodent corn-destroyers) or that the developed rattles bear a magical resemblance to the kerneled rows of the maize, or again that the rattling itself suggests once more the rain-rustle and the dancers' swishing gourds? All these are conceivable, though the ritual of the Snake Dance—still a corn-service among the Hopi of Arizona and once a rite of all the Pueblo peoples as of the Aztec and other tribes of Mexico—comes close to giving us the true meaning: the Serpent is of the Earth and of the Mother, and to it is entrusted that ceremonial communication of man with the *di inferi,* the Powers Below, which for Those Above, *di superi,* is mediated by the eagles and the feathered kinds, to whom prayers, often sticks, are plumed for their symbolic ascension. Old World and New World alike employ bird and serpent, plume and fang, in identical imagery: birds are the angelic messengers, while from the realms of darkness emerge the serpents. . . . Thus the language of nature becomes the speech of men's essential thought, and the breath of life and the bread of life are conjoined in imagery. From this, in final symbol, comes the Plumed Serpent as the Lord of Salvation.

V

EAGLE-BEAKED AND WINGED, fire-breathing, scaly and serpent-bodied is the Dragon of European folklore and art. Yet he does not seem native; in all his embodiments there is something of artifice and bug-a-boo unreality; he does not seem to "take" in the European environment but remains a toy of the nursery or an ornament—unconvincing from Roman to Wagnerian times. For a living dragon in the Old World, the true fire-vomiter, it is necessary to go to the Orient. Already the Serpent-of-the-Waters-Beneath appears on Sumerian tablets; but it is in the farther East, in the Sinitic empire, that the Dragon comes fully into his own. There he is a cloud-dweller, and swims, flaming, through the mists and billows of the upper skies, flashing all the hues of the prismatic universe in his broideries—azures of the East, reds of the South, blacks of the North, of the West the white which for the Chinese is the color of death and mourning, and most imperially the yellows of the Middle Kingdom's earth.[18] Further, for the Chinese geomancer, there are lakes in the four directions, and a dragon for the lake of each color and direction, and one for the Pool Beneath—all these in addition to the king-dragon of them all whose abode is the sky-realm. The whole cosmic pattern is convincingly analogous to that represented on the Mexican codices, where great serpents likewise govern the quarters and breathe cataclysmic disasters when time has counted its fates and run its courses. Among the corn-dancing villagers of New Mexico, likewise the Quarters have all their distinctive colors, and to each, as well as to the Pool Beneath and the Pool Above, whose mingling waters are the tides of growth, is assigned a magic serpent, plumed to show his kinship. To this day on embroidered kilt and painted bowl and cere-

monial altar the Avanyu (Tewa) or Koloowisi (Zuñi) or Polulukoñ (Hopi) is figured—as he was in the days when the thriving
peoples of Pueblo Bonito and Chetro Ketl and the cliff people
of Mesa Verde adorned their altars and their sacred vessels. It appears, too, that Chinese Dragon and Plumed Serpent participate
in like powers: for both are genii of the fruits of the earth and of
the fecundation of the fields, and hence ultimately of the whole
thunderous interplay of sexual strife, whence Yin and Yang engender creation. Yet this does not imply any missionizing or
chance transference from Asia to America; for when it is understood that the Plumed Serpent and the Dragon are only bird-serpent embodiments of the raincloud and of the heaven-fallen fluid
which alone to farmer folk can mean life, then the image needs
no transfer from land to land, but is self-sown wherever agriculture becomes a state's foundation. Sumer, China, Mexico, all
speak but the natural language of men who read the heavens for
their seasonal gift.

In the New World the cult and myth of the bird-serpent, in
identic or related forms, is mainly coterminous with the highland areas which define the regions of the most ancient maize cultures. It is as vivid and varied in the Pueblo Plateau as in that of
Central Mexico and again on the Yucatec peninsula and in the
Guatemalan highlands; it appears in Colombia, and southward
through Peru to Bolivia. The images of the serpent, the bird, and
the cross, everywhere recur in relation to rain and fertility. Natu-
ralistically the myth-being is associated with moisture and with
the waters of the world-regions and with seedings and fecundity,
yet always, in his greater forms, with the sky. He is not only the
"Green-Feather Snake" and the "Cloud Snake," bearded with rain,
but he is also the "Son of the Serpent" and again the "House of
Dews," and, transformed, the "Lord of the Dawn." He is, as the
myths tell, driven by the Wind God, dissolved by the Sun, or sacrificed to the Sun, and he is conquered by the supreme male-
female Master of Heaven, of whom, indeed, he is also represented
as born and whose peculiar gift of generation is abundantly his.
The Plumed Serpent is first of all the rain cloud, and in a special
right the high-terraced, silver-shining cumulus cloud of midsum-

mer (whence he is called also the "White God"), from whose black belly falls the reek of rain. These forms are attested not only by the myth and the imagery, but also by the art which in Mexico represents him as masked, now as bird, now as serpent, and in New Mexico as a serpent body whose dorsal burden is the cumulus cloud and whose tongue is the jagged levin. The Chinese Dragon, it will be recalled, swims in just such billowing cumulus.

But there is another aspect which the Plumed Serpent assumes, with qualities not derived from nature but from the dramatic course of human life. In his classic form he is the Quetzalcoatl of the Nahuatlan peoples, identical in name-meaning with the Kukulcan of the Maya and the Gucumatz of the Kiché—for all of these names have the meaning of "Green-feather Serpent." The bird known to the Aztec, and thence to us, as the quetzal (*Pharomacrus mocinno*) is distinguished by long, flowing tail plumes, brilliantly green, and treasured by the Mexican peoples as insignia of kings and gods just as the tail plumes of the macaw are for Pueblo folk symbols of the bladed glories of the maizefields, so for Aztec and Maya were the curving splendors of the quetzal feathers—the "rich plume" which, with the emerald stone, is a favorite metaphor of Nahua poetry:[19]

> My Lord, let thine emerald waters come descending!
> Now is the old tree changed to green plumage—
> The fire-snake is transformed into the quetzal!

Now this Quetzalcoatl appears in Mexican tradition no longer as a cosmic serpent, but as a man, and a man to whom historical place is assigned. In the tales he was lord of Tollan, the ancient city of the Toltec, fabled as the fountain of the glories of civilization; and in our day he is tentatively identified with the ancient pyramids of Teotihuacán, which are of the Sun, of the Moon and of the Plumed Serpent, as the sculptures show. But Tezcatlipoca, he of the mirror and of the windy roads, drove forth the ancient king; so that he departed with his arts and his precious gifts, and from the east coast sailed into the dawn, borne upon a serpent-twining raft—yet with the promise that one day he would return in the brightness of his power to reclaim and redeem his people.

How Montezuma, in terror of this fable, thought to recognize in the Spaniard the god returning, and out of dread lost his life and his city and his people's freedom is one of the epic tales of history —made vivid by the gauds of the deity sent to Cortez as the monarch's propitiatory gift, and now in the British Museum. Plausibly the story of the departure of Quetzalcoatl may record the overthrow of the elder power and perhaps of the king Topiltzin Quetzalcoatl, named for the deity, in the hour of the invasion by the eagle-guided Aztec Northerners, who built their capital where the eagle seized the serpent and gave the emblem of Mexican power and nationality. Nevertheless, found recurrently among all the more cultured peoples of ancient America, north and south, is the tale of the coming of the god, bringing with him metallurgy, law, letters, and the arts of life, and after glorious years, departing, but with promise of a redemptive return (possibly an ancient myth of the returning summer with the wealth and joy of the fields).

Into it historical events may well interweave, of which probably the latest instance is in New Mexico, where the Pueblo peoples have, since Spanish times, created a legend of Montezuma, the fabulous emperor of the South, who in olden times was their lord and who, after bringing the blessings of Indian civilization, ascended into the eastern skies upon his royal eagle, there to abide the hour of his triumphant return. In this, the old legend of the Indian Messiah is mingled with an echo of history, while back of both lies a drama of nature, as ancient in consciousness as the first maize-planting and the first rain-prayer.

Thus for the aboriginal peoples of America the domestication of the maize was the key to the whole pattern of a human civilization and the vivid coloring of a unique philosophy of life. Expanding north and south from its Middle American beginnings, this culture marginally encountered and mingled with the warrior-creeds of the braves of the Thunderbird, man-born from the Sky-Father; but within its own native centers, the whole complexion of thought had been for so many tens of centuries hued from the grain-fields that men had no imagination outbordering them. Their own flesh and blood was maize in substance and creation:

in the narrative of the *Popul Vuh,* which is the greatest surviving monument of our autochthonous literature, not alone is man maize-formed, but the images associated with the fruitful fields are archetypal of a civilization premeditated in the dusks of time, when the Seeds of Things were in cosmic generation. Like our own Semitic Genesis, the creation story of the Kiché Scripture figures the reflective thought of men for whom the momentous transformation from flesh-feeder to farmer has long since passed into an intimate understanding of nature; and like the Semitic the Indian version possesses both maturity of reflective thought and majesty of expression.[20]

Admirable is the account—so the narrative opens—admirable is the account of the time in which it came to pass that all was formed in heaven and upon earth, the quartering of their signs, their measure and alignment, and the establishment of parallels to the skies and upon the earth to the four quarters thereof, as was spoken by the Creator and Maker, the Mother, the Father of life and of all existence, that one by whom all move and breathe, father and sustainer of the peace of peoples, by whose wisdom was premeditated the excellence of all that doth exist in the heavens, upon the earth, in lake and sea.

Lo, all was in suspense, all was calm and silent; all was motionless, all was quiet, and wide was the immensity of the skies.

Lo, the first word and the first discourse. There was not yet a man, not an animal; there were no birds nor fish nor crayfish; there was no wood, no stone, no bog, no ravine, neither vegetation nor marsh; only the sky existed.

The face of the earth was not yet to be seen; only the peaceful sea and the expanse of the heavens.

Nothing was yet formed into a body; nothing was joined to another thing; naught held itself poised; there was not a rustle, not a sound beneath the sky. There was naught that stood upright; there were only the quiet waters of the sea, solitary within its bounds; for as yet naught existed.

There were only immobility and silence in the darkness and in the night. Alone was the Creator, the Maker, Tepeu, the Lord, and Gucumatz, the Plumed Serpent, those who engender, those who give being, alone upon the waters like a growing light.

They are enveloped in green and azure, whence is the name Gucumatz, and their being is great wisdom. Lo, how the sky existeth, how the Heart of the Sky existeth—for such is the name of God, as He doth name Himself!

It is then that the word came to Tepeu and to Gucumatz, in the shadows and in the night, and spake with Tepeu and with Gucumatz. And they spake and consulted and meditated, and they joined their words and their counsels.

Then light came while they consulted together; and at the moment of dawn man appeared while they planned concerning the production and increase of the groves and of the climbing vines, there in the shade and in the night, through that one who is the Heart of the Sky, whose name is Hurakan.

The Lightning is the first sign of Hurakan; the second is the Streak of Lightning; the third is the Thunderbolt which striketh; and these three are the Heart of the Sky.

Then they came to Tepeu, to Gucumatz, and held counsel touching civilized life: how seed should be formed, how light should be produced, how the sustainer and nourisher of all.

"Let it be thus done. Let the waters retire and cease to obstruct, to the end that earth exist here, that it harden itself and show its surface, to the end that it be sown, and that the light of day shine in the heavens and upon the earth; for we shall receive neither glory nor honour from all that we have created and formed until human beings exist, endowed with sentience." Thus they spake while the earth was formed by them. It is thus, veritably, that creation took place, and the earth existed. "Earth," they said, and immediately it was formed.

Like a fog or a cloud was its formation into the material state, when, like great lobsters, the mountains appeared upon the waters, and in an instant there were great mountains. Only by marvelous power could have been achieved this their resolution when the mountains and the valleys instantly appeared, with groves of cypress and pine upon them.

Then was Gucumatz filled with joy. "Thou art welcome, O Heart of the Sky, O Hurakan, O Streak of Lightning, O Thunderbolt!"

"This that we have created and shaped will have its end," they replied.

None but a mind seasoned by the centuries and acquainted with thought of human destiny could have framed this last judgment; it lifts out of myth and into philosophy, recording not merely the transient gloss of a sensuous imagination playing upon the broken surfaces of nature, but the depth-shadowed thought of a mind long matured in reflection. It is just such a maturity of thought that flashes through, from time to time, the scanty remains of the literature of the maize-raising peoples of America, giving evidence, which no archaeology is needed to corroborate, of a native development of the human spirit, centuries-seated.

CHAPTER V

Many Children

I

INDIAN RITUALS are the symbolism of the Indian understanding of
life, and viewed as a body they serve to define this understanding
from the many approaches which living experience opens. First of
all they raise up the phantasm of a structured outer world, a *cosmos* as we adjudge it after the Greeks, within which a *nature*
flourishes. Law and life are the two facets of this minted world,
not quite intelligibly adjusted to one another, and our human
part is imperiously with life: that is why we assign a mediating
rôle to nature, which is ambiguously neither law nor life, but is at
least a birth—this on the life side—and implies a destiny, which is
the lawful or cosmic facet. Perhaps the most perfect image for
nature is "breath"—which can be wind, or soul,, or breath of creation, or breath of life, as it is in the red man's (and our own)
symbolism. Secondly, the rituals turn upon a prayer for life, mediated by this breath, or its emblems of smoke and feather: a
prayer for years, for hale living, for the good, for permission for
man to continue an existence that seems so utterly at odds with
world and nature's destinies and so perilously placed where law
and life meet. And this becomes not alone a prayer for individual
protection, but far more for children and for tribal generations

and human nations. Permission that man *in his own kind* may continue to be, and after his manner flourish, this is what the ceremonies most plead for, and this also is in some universal mode the quest for God.

Of the many Indian ceremonies that play about such a meaning, none is more impressive than those which make of their central figure the human child. Infancy is curiously universalized by all peoples. Every babe is in some degree vicariously every other babe; like the Christ-child in art his semblance is of every race, but his essence is undisturbed: he is the Infant that is in a mystic mode the Savior of Men, and hence of Mankind. It is as children grow in years that they become more than hopes and prophecies and are transformed into historic lives and characters; as babes they are *life* only, human life, certainly, but persons only in a blocked-out way. Mothers, to be sure, cannot concede this, but human custom affirms it: adoptions, foundlings, changelings, and the odd practice once so common of naming the next-born after an infant dead, or among the red men of giving only a child-name until the boy or girl had won the right to be known by a name which should be descriptive and his alone. In these customs, as in sacrifices, the child is only an emblem of kind, and may be given up, devoted, protected, blessed, not for himself alone, but for all humankind and for the fortune of the race.

It is this symbolism of the child as emblem of the life of the community that lies at the heart of one of the most interesting and revealing of all American Indian ceremonies. In varying forms the ceremony is known to the greater portion of the Caddoan and Siouan tribes of the Missouri Valley, and there is reason in judging that the Calumet Ceremony observed by Père Marquette among the Illinois may have been a version of this prairie rite. By the different tribal groups it is given local names. The Pawnee refer to the *Hako,* which is the term applied to the two feathered wands borne by the priestly leaders, and which literally means the "breathing mouth of wood"; the Omaha, who apparently received the ceremony from the Pawnee, know it as the *Wawan,* "to sing for someone"; the Dakota employ a not dissimilar term, *Hunka-lowanpi,* meaning "they sing or chant for the Hunka-child"; the most descriptive name is perhaps that of the Arikara, *Piraskani*, "many children." There are indications that the rite came from the Caddoan tribes to the Siouan, and the Pawnee ritual of the *Hako*,[1] which is the most complete version that we possess, contains internal indications of the origin of the ceremony in a more southerly land than the prairies of Nebraska, which had been the Pawnee tribal seat from times anterior to the first encounters with white men. Indeed, one record of the Teton Sioux places the date of the first singing of the ceremony in that tribe as late as 1801, and there are other evidences that it is not aboriginally Siouan, although it attained to a wide dissemination among the Siouan tribes of the prairies.[2] The tribes of the prairies, even in quite recent times, have been not infrequent borrowers from one another of ritual ideas and forms, and in this borrowing there is latitude both of symbol and interpretation. The Hunka rite of the Dakota is by no means identical with the Hako of the Pawnee, although the central symbols and purport are too close to permit question as to some community of origin. In the symbolism the important rôle of Mother Corn seems definitely of Caddoan, and particularly of Pawnee, source and cult; Pawnee, too, is the philosophical universality of the symbolism of the child. Dakota groups have given to the Hunka-child a personal prestige and benefit which, while it also obtains for the symbolic child in the Hako, nevertheless is in the latter subordinate to a more broadly vicarious intent and to a more seasoned understanding of human relationships.

The whole significance of the ceremony grows directly out of the relationship of parent and child, father and son, first in a biological sense, and second in an adoptive. The symbolism springs up from the natural emotions of the parent who loves his child; but the essence of the ceremony is to give a new social benefit and spiritual protection to the child, and, even more, to bring all the elements of the good life to all of the participants and their kindred. "The principal purpose of the Hunkaloanpi," says Curtis,[3] "is to implant in the initiate the virtues of kindness, generosity, hospitality, truthfulness, fairness, honesty. At the same time it is a prayer for continued prosperity—for abundance of food, for health, strength, and moral well-being as a people." This was felt to be achieved through the spiritual guardianship and social relationship established between the symbolic Father and his Child-by-adoption in the ritual itself. Said a Teton, Looking Elk: [4] "The great result of this ceremony is that the man who performed it was regarded as a father by the child for whom he performed it. He made a solemn vow, taking that child under his protection until one or the other died. He became like a brother to the man whose children he sang over and painted with the hunka stripes. In all the great ceremonies of the Sioux there is not one that binds two men together so strongly as this." This is the personal phase of the meaning of the rite; its broader intention is voiced in the words of Tahirussawichi, the Pawnee priest who gave the rituals to Alice Fletcher.[5] Speaking of the final rite, he said: "Upon this little child we are to put the signs of the promises which Mother Corn and Kawas [the Eagle] bring, the promise of children, of increase, of long life, of plenty. The signs of these promises are put upon this little child, but they are not merely for that particular child but for its generation, that the children already born may live, grow in strength, and in their turn increase so that the family and the tribe may continue." It was the same priest who said of this ceremony in relation to its natural setting: "We take up the Hako in the spring when the birds are mating, or in the summer when the birds are nesting and caring for their young, or in the fall when the birds are flocking, but not in the winter when all things are asleep. With the Hako we are praying for the gift of life, of strength, of plenty, and of peace, so we must pray when life is stirring everywhere."

It was from the mouth of Tahirussawichi that the Pawnee ritual was recorded and it is to him that are due the illuminating expositions of its meanings which make of the *Report* that preserves them perhaps the most significant document for the understanding of Indian thinking that we possess.

II

THE CEREMONY was conducted by the priestly leader, whose native title is *Kurahus,* aided by assistants—acolytes to whom he was

imparting the rituals—while the participants for whom the ceremony was performed comprised two groups.[6] These two groups
could not belong to the same clan, and they were often of different tribes. They were called *Fathers* and *Children*. The leader of
the Fathers was called *the Father,* the leader of the Children, *the
Son;* they were men of equal standing in their respective clans;
and if they were not chiefs, they secured the attendance of chiefs
in their parties. The parties were made up of relatives of the two
leaders, and certain other persons, such as drummers and singers
and two doctors who carried their eagle-wing ensign.

The complete ceremony involved some twenty principal rituals. Seven of these were devoted to the Preparation, seven to the
Public Ceremonies, six to the Secret Ceremonies. Following these
came the dance of thanks and the interchange of gifts which usually closed a great tribal ceremonial.

The ceremony proper consisted of three parts: the Preparation,
the Public Ceremony, and the Secret Ceremony. The aims of the
Preparation were: to make and sanctify the *sacra,* the *Hako,* this
being work of the Father's party, done at their home; to notify
the Son's party of the coming of the Fathers; and, for the Fathers,
to journey to the home of the Children and be received by them.
The Public Ceremony, at the home of the Children, comprised
feasts of a sacramental character, invocations of the powers of
nature and of the visions by which the rites were supposed to
have been revealed—the history and cosmic setting of the mystery. The Secret Ceremony centered in the symbolic birth and
sanctification of a child, who figured the various aspects of the
purpose of the ceremony, namely, the establishment of a relationship between the Fathers and the Children, the promise of children and hence the perpetuity, strength and plenty to the partici-
pating clans.

The rituals open with an invocation of the powers: *Awahokshu,*
Heaven, the abode of *Tirawa atius,* the Mighty Power; *Hotoru,*
the Winds; *Shakuru,* the Sun; *H'Uraru,* Mother Earth; *Toharu,*
life-giving Vegetation; *Chaharu,* Water. The physical world as
the place of man's abode is then addressed: *Kusharu,* a Holy
Place; *H'Akaru,* House of Life; *Keharu,* Wall of Defense; *Kata-*

haru, the Fireplace; *Kekaru,* the Glowing Coals ("as we sing . . . we rub the sticks to make the sacred fire come, and we think of the lesser power that is making itself seen in the glowing wood"); *Koritu,* the Flames; and finally, *Hiwaturu,* the Entranceway, through which "man goes to and fro," so symbolizing "the days of man's life."

Analogous was the symbolism of the ceremonial objects which, with suitable songs and prayers, were prepared during the preliminary days. The most important of these objects were two wands—"feathered stems about a meter in length, made of ash wood." One of these wands was painted blue, symbolizing the sky, a lengthwise red groove being emblematic of the red passage "through which man's breath comes and goes to give him life." The stem was feathered like an arrow, symbolic of surety. A fan-shaped pendant of ten feathers from the mature brown eagle was attached to the stem, while a woodpecker's head, the head and breast of a duck, and a bunch of owl feathers were also attached close to the wood. The eagle is sacred to the Powers above and is the medium of communication between them and man. The woodpecker averts the disasters of storm and lightning. The duck is the unerring guide, familiar alike with air and water. The owl has the power to give help and protection at night. Red and white streamers representing sun and moon, day and night, and a tuft of blue down symbolizing the clear blue of the sky also adorned the wand. The second wand was like the first except that it was painted green, symbolizing the earth, and the fan-shaped pendant consisted of seven plumes of the white eagle.

The symbolic importance of the brown eagle, Kawas, in this ceremony is very great. It is worthwhile therefore to quote at length the Kurahus's description of the use of the wands:

In this ceremony the brown eagle is called *Kawas.* This eagle has been made holy by being sacrificed to Tirawa. Its feathers are tied upon the stem that has been painted blue to represent the sky.

This stem was the first one painted and decorated, because it is female and the leader. It represents the night, the moon, the north, and stands for kindness and helpfulness. It will take care of the people. It is the mother.

Throughout the ceremony the Kurahus carries this feathered stem. . . .

The white eagle is not holy; it has not been sacrificed to Tirawa. It has less power than Kawas; it is inclined to war, to hurt someone. It can not lead; it must follow. So the green stem is painted last, and all the decorations are put upon it after the other stem is completed.

This feathered green stem represents the male, the day, the sun, and the south. During the ceremony it is carried by the assistant of the Kurahus, whose place is on the right of the Kurahus, toward the south.

When we move about the lodge waving the two feathered stems to the rhythm of the song we are singing, Kawas, the brown eagle, is carried next the people, and the white eagle-stem on the farther side, away from the people, where it can do good by defending them and keeping away all harm. If it were carried next the Children it would bring them war and trouble. It is the brown eagle that is always kept near the people and is waved over their heads to bring them the gifts of plenty and of peace.

Ranking in importance with the wands, in the ceremony, is the ear of maize, symbolic of the Corn Mother, the spirit of life-giving grain. An ear with white grain is chosen, and it is fastened to a support. The top of it is painted blue, again symbolizing the sky, and down the sides are carried four blue lines emblematic of the four paths (the cardinal points) leading from heaven to earth. At the summit of the ear is fastened a white plume symbolic of the fleecy clouds above and of the breath of heaven. "The ear of corn," says the Kurahus, "represents the supernatural power that dwells in H'Uraru, the earth which brings forth the food that sustains life; so we speak of the ear of corn as h'Atira, mother breathing forth life. The power in the earth which enables it to bring forth comes from above; for that reason we paint the ear of corn with blue."

In painting the corn, blue clay is used. The clay is mixed with running water: running water represents the continuity of life from one generation to another; water from a spring or a well cannot be used in the ceremony. The mixing is done in a wooden bowl, a bowl "taken from the trees, a part of the living covering of Mother Earth, representing the power of Toharu"—i.e., the life-giving vegetation. "The bowl is round, like the dome shape of the sky, and holds the blue paint, which also represents the sky. The bowl is a vessel from which we eat when we have the sacred feast of the corn. Tirawa taught us how to get the corn." It is this bowl, or one like it, which is used in the baptismal ceremony of the Seventeenth Ritual.

There are a number of ceremonial articles, but they are rather of the nature of accessories than *sacra* in the strict sense. After the preparation of these articles, a smoke offering was made and the First Ritual brought to a close.

The Second Ritual the editor names "Prefiguring the Journey to the Son." The actual journey is to be made under the leadership of the corn symbol—Mother Corn, the spirit of the corn and of life-sustaining vegetation. The prefiguring is a spirit journey: the Fathers, stanza by stanza, sing of the journey, believing that their spirits under the leadership of the corn spirit do actually pass to the home of the Son and inform him of the place to which he is chosen.

"It is not the ear of corn [says the Kurahus] that travels through the air, nor do our bodies follow; it is the spirit of the corn that moves, and it is our spirits that follow, that travel with her to the land of the Son. . . . We must fix our minds upon Mother Corn and upon the Son, who is the object of our search. It is a very difficult thing to do. All our spirits must become united as one spirit, and as one spirit we must approach the spirit of Mother Corn. This is a very hard thing to do."

When the spirit journey is completed and the lodge of the Son is reached, "the Son does not see us as we stand there; he is sleeping. . . . We fix our minds upon Mother Corn and upon the Son; if we are in earnest he will respond to her touch. He will not waken, he will not see her, but he will see in a dream that which her touch will bring to him. . . . Then, when he awakens, he will remember his dream, and as he thinks upon it, he will know that he has been chosen to be a Son, and that all the good things that come with the ceremony which will make him a Son are now promised him."

This ritual introduces the mysticism which underlies the whole ceremony: from of old "the rites came in a vision."

The Third Ritual concerns the sending of actual messengers to the man chosen as Son. The messengers come saying, "Behold! Your father is coming!" And "as the Son hears the words of the messengers he will be reminded of his dream in which Mother Corn touched him. And as he looks at the men he will recognize the tribe from which they have come and will know who has chosen him to be the Son." If he accepts the honor, he instructs the messengers to return to the Father saying, "I am ready!"

The first event of the Fourth Ritual is the elevation of the *sacra* on a pole set up at the lodge entrance. "Here it stands where the wind of the dawn may breathe upon the Hako and the first rays of the sun strike the sacred objects and give them life. . . . It is all done in silence before the day dawns."

After this the Kurahus anoints himself, his assistants and the chief of the Fathers, and the men anointed sing a song emblematic of the leadership of the Corn Spirit. Says the Kurahus:

As we sing this song we remember that Mother Earth is very old. She is everywhere, she knows all men, she gave life to our fathers, she gives life to us, and she will give life to our children. The ear of corn represents venerable Mother Earth, and also the authority given by the powers above; . . . As we sing we think that Mother breathing forth life, who has come out of the past, has now started to lead us on the journey we are to take and to the fulfillment of our desire that children may be given us, that generations may not fail in the future, and that the tie may be strong between Father and Son.

The anointed men then take up the Hako and present it in turn to the Powers of the East, the West, the South and the North, the bearers moving in a figure which simulates the human form: "We have traced upon the earth the figure of a man. This image that we have traced is from Tirawa. It has gone around with us, and its feet are where we now stand; its feet are with our feet and will move with them as we now . . . in the presence of all the powers . . . begin our journey to the land of the Son."

The Fifth Ritual is the ritual of the journey and contains three parts.

In the first part, "Mother Corn, who led our spirits over the path we are now to travel, leads us again as we walk, in our bodies, over the land. . . . She led our fathers and she leads us now, because she was born of Mother Earth and knows all places and all people, and because she has on her the sign (the blue-paint symbol) of having been up to Tirawahut, where power was given her over all creatures."

The second part is devoted to the songs sung on the journey. There is a "Song to the Trees and Streams," a "Song When Crossing the Streams," a "Song to the Wind," a "Song to the Buffalo," another of "The Promise of the Buffalo." "We do not sing this song any more as we travel," said the Kurahus, "for now there are no buffalo herds to be seen sending the dust up to the sky as they run. We sing the song in the lodge of the Son, that we may remember the buffalo, and that our children may hear of them." Two other songs of the way, of interest as indicating that the Pawnees derived their ceremony from the West or Southwest, are the song to be sung in ascending mountains and a song to be sung in traversing mesas. Of the latter the Kurahus said:

We are told that long ago our fathers used to see the mesas. . . . This song has come down to us from that time. As we have never seen mesas, we do not sing the song on the journey; we sing it in the lodge of the Son, that we may not forget what our fathers saw when they traveled far from where we now dwell.

The third part consists of two hymns to Mother Corn sung when the village of the Son is reached.

The Sixth Ritual embraces the songs and ceremonies attended upon the reception of the Fathers by the Children. The Son's messenger is received. He is fed and clothed by the visitors—"an act which marks the care of a father for his child"—whom he then conducts to the village and "the lodge of my Son wherein he sits waiting for me."

The Seventh Ritual has to do with the consecration of the lodge prepared for the ceremony by Kawas, the Eagle, and by

Mother Corn; with the clothing of the Son in gift garments; and finally with a smoke offering to the powers.

The lodge has now been opened by Mother Corn and cleansed of all bad influences by Kawas; the Son, clothed as a child by the Father, has offered prayer and smoke to the powers above; the garments worn during this act have been removed and given away; and now everything is ready for the public ceremony to begin.

III

THE PUBLIC CEREMONY of seven rituals occupies three days and three nights. It opens with a feast in which the Fathers feed the Children with food they have brought.

Before any one can be served, the thoughts of the Fathers and of the Children must be turned toward Tirawa, the father of all things. . . . All the powers that are in the heavens and all those that are upon the earth are derived from the mighty power, Tirawa atius. He is father of all things visible and invisible. He is father of all the powers represented by the Hako. He is the father of all the lesser powers, those which can approach man. He is the father of all the people, and perpetuates the life of the tribe through the gift of children. So we sing your father, meaning the father of all people everywhere, the father of all things that we see and hear and feel.

After the songs, the Children are fed by the Fathers: for "it is the duty of a father to provide food for his child, and not to partake himself until the child is satisfied." When the Fathers are left alone, they eat their evening meal.

With the Ninth Ritual the Mystery proper may be said to begin. When the sun has set and it is dark and the stars are shining, the Hako is taken up, and the singers carrying the drum follow the Hako slowly around the lodge singing the Invocation to the Visions.

> Holy visions!
> Hither come, we pray you, come unto us,
> Bringing with you joy;
> Come, oh,.come to us, holy visions,
> Bringing with you joy.

Visions come from above, they are sent by Tirawa atius. The lesser powers come to us in visions. We receive help through the visions. All the promises which attend the Hako will be made good to us in this way. Visions can come most readily at night; spirits travel better at that time.

The visions come from their abode above, conducted by the spirits of the birds on the wands; they reach the lodge and enter.

As we walk, the visions walk; they fill all the space within the lodge; they are everywhere, all about us . . . touching the Children, touching them here and there and by their touch giving them dreams, which will bring them health, strength, happiness, and all good things. The visions touch all who are in the lodge, so it is a good thing to be there, to be touched by the visions. . . . One by one the Children go to their homes, and the dreams brought by the Visions which attend the Hako go with them to make their hearts glad.

The Tenth Ritual covers the ceremonies with which the breaking day is greeted. The Kurahus and the Chief of the Fathers have kept vigil, waiting for the dawn. "As the night draws to a close, the Kurahus orders the server to lift the skins which hang at the outer and inner doors of the long passageway of the lodge, and to go outside and watch for the first glimmer of light."

When the morning air begins to stir, the *sacra* are taken up and the Birth of the Dawn is sung. Says the Kurahus:

We call to Mother Earth, who is represented by the ear of corn. She has been asleep and resting during the night. We ask her to awake, to move, to arise, for the signs of the dawn are seen in the east and the breath of the new life is here. . . .

Mother Earth is the first to be called to awake, that she may receive the breath of the new day.

Mother Earth hears the call; she moves, she awakes, she rises, she feels the breath of the new-born Dawn. The leaves and the grass stir; all things move with the breath of the new day; everywhere life is renewed.

This is very mysterious; we are speaking of something very sacred, although it happens every day.

We call upon Kawas to awake, to move, to arise. Kawas had been sleeping and resting during the night. Kawas represents the lesser powers which dwell above, those which are sent by Tirawa atius to bring us help. All these powers must awake and arise, for the breath of the new life of the Dawn is upon them. The eagle soars where these powers dwell and can communicate with them. The new life of the new day is felt by these powers above as well as by Mother Earth below.

Kawas hears the call and awakes. Now all the powers above wake and stir, and all things below wake and stir; the breath of new life is everywhere. With the signs in the east has come this new life.

Kawas, the brown eagle, the messenger of the powers above, now stands within the lodge and speaks. The Kurahus hears her voice as she tells him what the signs in the east mean. . . .

The Kurahus answers Kawas. He tells her that he understands the words she spoke to him when standing there in the lodge, that now he knows the meaning of the signs in the east; that Night is the mother of Day, that it is by the power of Tirawa atius moving on Darkness that she gives birth to the Dawn. The Dawn is the child of Tirawa atius. It gives the blessing of life; it comes to awaken man, to awake Mother Earth and all living things that may receive the life, the breath of the Dawn which is born of the Night by the power of Tirawa atius.

The words, adds the Kurahus, do not tell all that the song means; the meaning has been handed down from our fathers and may be taught to any serious-minded person who is sincerely desirous to learn.

With the rising of the Morning Star, for which a server has been on the watch, the second song is sung—"slowly, with reverent feeling, for we are singing of very sacred things."

The Morning Star is like a man; he is painted red all over; that is the color of life. He is clad in leggings and a robe is wrapped about him. On his head is a soft downy eagle's feather, painted red. This feather represents the soft, light cloud that is high in the heavens, and the red is the touch of the ray of the coming sun. The soft downy feather is the symbol of breath and life.

The star comes from a great distance, too far away for us to see the place where it starts. At first we can hardly see it; we lose sight of it, it is so far off; then we see it again, for it is coming steadily toward us all the time. We watch it approach; it comes nearer and nearer; its light grows brighter and brighter. . . .

The Morning Star comes still nearer and now we see him standing there in the heavens, a strong man shining brighter and brighter. The soft plume in his hair moves with the breath of the new day, and the ray of the sun touches it with color. As he stands there so bright, he is bringing us strength and new life.

As we look upon him he grows less bright; he is receding, going back to his dwelling place whence he came. We watch him vanishing, passing out of our sight. He has left with us the gift of life which Tirawa atius sent him to bestow. . . .

The day is close behind, advancing along the path of the Morning Star and the Dawn. . . .

The next song is a paean to the Daylight.

We sing this song with loud voices; we are glad. We shout, "Daylight has come! Day is here!" The light is over the earth. . . . We call to the Children; we bid them awake. . . . We tell the Children that all the animals are awake. They come forth from their places where they have been sleeping. The deer leads them. She comes from her cover, bringing her young into the light of day. Our hearts are glad as we sing, "Daylight has come! The light of day is here!"

The sun has not as yet appeared above the horizon. In the last part of the Tenth Ritual messengers are sent to awaken all the Children that they may be assembled to greet the rising sun.

The second day of the Public Ceremony is devoted to an invocation of the male element in nature typified by the sun. The course of the sun is followed throughout the day, special songs celebrating its several stations.

Whoever is touched by the first rays of the sun in the morning receives new life and strength which have been brought straight from the power above. The first rays of the sun are like a young man, they have not yet spent their force or grown old. . . . We think of the sun, which comes direct from Tirawa atius, the father of life, and his ray (hukawi) as the bearer of this life. (You have seen this ray as it comes through a little hole or crack.) While we sing, this ray enters the door of the lodge to bring strength and power to all within. . . .

As the sun rises higher the ray, which is its messenger, alights upon the edge of the central opening in the roof of the lodge, right over the fireplace. We see the spot(ta), the sign of its touch, and we know that the ray is there. The fire holds an important place in the lodge. . . . Father Sun is sending life by his messenger to this central place in the lodge. . . .

As the sun rises higher . . . the ray is now climbing down into the lodge. We watch the spot where it has alighted. It moves over the edge of the opening above the fireplace and descends into the lodge, and we sing that life from our father the Sun will come to us by his messenger, the ray. . . .

Now the spot is walking here and there within the lodge, touching different places. We know that the ray will bring strength and power from our father the Sun as it walks within the lodge. Our hearts are glad and thankful as we sing. . . .

When the spot has reached the floor we stop singing and do not begin until the afternoon, so that our song can accompany the ray as it leaves the lodge, touches the hills, and finally returns to the sun. . . .

In the afternoon . . . we observe that the spot has moved around the lodge, as the sun has passed over the heavens. . . . After a little time we see the spot leave the floor of the lodge and climb up toward the opening over the fireplace, where it had entered in the morning. . . . Later, when the sun is sinking in the west, the land is in shadow, only on the top of the hills toward the east can the spot, the sign of the ray's touch, be seen. . . . The ray of Father Sun, who breathes forth life, is standing on the edge of the hills. We remember that in the morning it stood on the edge of the opening in the roof of the lodge over the fireplace; now it stands on the edge of the hills that, like the walls of a lodge, inclose the land where the people dwell. . . .

When the spot, the sign of the ray, the messenger of our father the Sun, has left the tops of the hills and passed from our sight . . . we know that the ray which was sent to bring us strength has now gone back to the place whence it came. We are thankful to our father the Sun for that which he has sent us by his ray.

There are a number of incidental songs that belong to this day between the morning and afternoon chants to the sun.

MANY CHILDREN

On the evening of the second day of the Public Ceremony, in the Twelfth Ritual, the origin of the rites in vision is told in song. The Kurahus states:

We have been taught that in a vision our fathers were told how to make the feathered stems, how to use them, how to sway them to the songs, so that they should move like the wings of a bird in its flight. It was in a vision that our fathers were told how they could cause a man who was not their bodily offspring to become a Son, to be bound to them by a tie as strong as the natural tie between father and son.

Visions, he tells later, come in the night, for spirits can travel better by night than by day. Visions come from Katasha, the place where they dwell. This place is up in the sky, just below where Tirawa atius appointed the dwelling place of the lesser powers. Katasha, the place where the Visions dwell, is near the dwelling place of the lesser powers, so they can summon any vision they wish to send us. When a vision is sent by the powers, it descends and goes to the person designated, who sees the vision and hears what it has to say; then, as day approaches, the vision ascends to its dwelling place, Katasha, and there it lies at rest, until it is called again.

The songs given in Ritual Twelve of the Hako are brief reminiscences, hardly more than mnemonic suggestions, of various revelations that had come to inspired men. One of these may serve as illustration. The Kurahus tells the story:

The next song is about a man to whom Mother Corn came in a dream; it happened very long ago. The song and the story are very old and have come down to us from our fathers, who knew this ceremony. Mother Corn spoke to this man in his dream. We are not told what she said to him, but when he awoke he started out to find the man in whose keeping was a shrine containing the ear of corn. As he walked he met a man and asked him, "Is it far to the lodge where the corn is?" The man pointed to a lodge some distance off and said, "It is within." Then the man who had had the dream walked toward the place. As he entered the lodge he saw a shrine hanging on one of the poles and he asked the keeper if it contained the sacred ear of corn, and he was told that it did. Then he took his pipe and offered smoke and prayer in the presence of the corn; because Mother Corn had appeared to him in a dream and had spoken to him he came to offer her reverence.

The song connected with this story is rendered by Miss Fletcher:

> As I lay sleeping, as I lay dreaming,
> Out of the distance came one advancing,
> One whom I ne'er had seen before, but when her voice
>   addressed me, straightway I knew her—
> Lo! 'Twas our Mother, she whom we know.
> I rose from sleeping, my dream rememb'ring;
> Her words I pondered, words of our mother.
> Then I asked of each one I met, Tell me, how far
>   may her shrine be? When I found it
> Sweet smoke I offered unto our Mother.

The morning songs of the second day led on to the invocation of the male element, the Sun Father; on the third day these same songs serve as an introduction to the invocation of the female element, typified by Mother Earth.

The invocation is preceded by a sacramental feast of corn, prepared by the Children after the manner of their forefathers. Hymns to Tirawa are then sung, "remembering that he is the father of the Sun which sends its ray, and of the Earth which brings forth." Then follows the song to the Earth, beginning: "Behold! Here lies Mother Earth, for a truth she lies here to bring forth, and we give thanks that it is so."

The gifts of the Earth are remembered, stanza by stanza. First the fields, "where seed is put in Mother Earth, and she brings forth corn"; then the trees and forests from which come "shelter and fire"; and lastly the water—springs, streams, rivers—which symbolize the continuity of life.

After this song the Kurahus addresses the Children: "My Children, your fathers are listening to what I have to say. Yesterday we remembered our father the Sun, today we remember our mother the Earth, and today Tirawa has appointed that we should learn of those things which have been handed down to us. Tirawa is now to smoke from the brown-eagle stem, Kawas, the mother, and you are to smoke from it also."

The smoke offering is then made, after which each of the Children smokes from the pipe. "This is a holy act and gives long life to the people."

On this day, though at no fixed time—save that "the song of the owl must be sung toward night"—come the songs of the birds.

The songs about the birds begin with the egg, so the song of the bird's nest where the eggs are lying is the first to be sung. Then comes the song of the wren, the smallest of the birds. After that we sing about the birds that are with the Hako from the smallest to the largest. These songs are to teach the people to care for their children, even before they are born. They also teach the people to be happy and thankful. They also explain how the birds came to be upon the feathered stems and why they are able to help the people.

The Song of the Bird's Nest commemorates the story of a man who came upon a bird's nest in the grass.

He paused to look at the little nest tucked away so snug and warm, and noted that it held six eggs and that a peeping sound came from some of them. While he watched, one moved and soon a tiny bill pushed through the shell, uttering a shrill cry. At once the parent birds answered and he looked up to see where they were. They were not far off; they were flying about in search of food, chirping the while to each other and now and then calling to the little one in the nest. . . . After many days he desired to see the nest again. So he went to the place where he had found it, and there it was as safe as when he had left it. But a change had taken place. It was now full to overflowing with little birds, who were stretching their wings, balancing on their little legs and making ready to fly, while the parents with encouraging calls were coaxing the fledglings to venture forth. "Ah!" said the man, "if my people would only learn of the birds, and, like them, care for their young and provide for their future, homes would be full and happy, and our tribe be strong and prosperous."

The Song of the Wren was made by a priest who noted that the wren, the smallest and least powerful of the birds, excelled them all in the fervor of its song. "Here," he thought, "is a teaching for my people. Everyone can be happy; even the most insignificant can have his song of thanks."

The Song of the Woodpecker and the Turkey tells how, long ago, the feathers of the turkey, the most prolific of birds, held the place of the eagle feathers on the feathered stems used in the Hako. The woodpecker challenges the turkey's right. The turkey defends, saying: ". . . in my division of life there is great power of productiveness. I have more tail feathers than any other bird and I have more eggs. Wherever I go my young cover the ground." "True," replied the woodpecker, "but you build your nest on the ground, so that your eggs are in constant danger of being devoured by serpents, and when the eggs hatch the young become a prey to the wolves, the foxes, the weasels; therefore, your number is continually being reduced. Security is the only thing that can insure the continuation of life. . . . I build my nest in the heart of the tall oak, where my eggs and my young are safe from the creatures that prey upon birds. While I have fewer eggs they hatch in security and the birds live until they die of old age. It is my place to be a protector of the life of men." The turkey was deposed; and though the eagle was put in his place, the woodpecker was given an important position on the stem, where it presides over the red path along which travels the help that comes from the Hako.

The Song of the Duck and the Song of the Owl tell how each of these two birds in visions revealed to a holy man their dominions, the duck's over the pathways of water and air, the owl's over the night. "So the people are guided by the duck and kept awake by the owl." The ritual closes with a song of thanks for the Hako.

The final ritual of the Public Ceremony, falling on the evening of the third day, is a chant accompanied by symbolic action, sung in remembrance of the coming of the revelation to the fathers. "We remember the visions of our fathers, the holy men to whom was taught this ceremony."

> Oh, come hither,
> Holy dreams—Our fathers knew them—
> Hither come to us!
> Thanks we give unto them. They our message will hear,
> Calling them to come.

IV

THE SIX RITUALS of the Secret Ceremony, occupying a night and a day, begin on the evening of the fourth day.

At sunset the Fathers call the Children to the lodge. When all have been seated, the Children on the south side, the Fathers on the north, the Kurahus, who sits at the west, back of the holy place where the Hako are at rest, addresses the Children in the name of the Fathers. He explains the meaning of the ceremony about to take place, for on this last night and the following morning everything that is done refers to the nest and to the direct promise of Children to the Son, who is also to be bound by a symbolic tie to the Father.

The Fifteenth Ritual is the symbolic Flocking of the Birds, carrying on the bird symbolism which the songs of the preceding day have presented. The Kurahus says:

In the early spring the birds lay their eggs in their nests, in the summer they rear their young, in the fall all the young ones are grown, the nests are deserted and the birds fly in flocks over the country. One can hear the fluttering of a startled flock, the birds suddenly rise and their wings make a noise like distant thunder. Everywhere the flocks are flying. In the fall it seems as though new life were put into the people as well as into the birds; there is much activity in coming and going.

This song tells of the flocking of birds. We do not use the drum as we sing it, but we blow the whistle. The whistle is made from the wing bone of an eagle. In this song we are singing of the eagle and the other birds, so we use the whistle.

When the eggs are hatched and the young are grown, the birds flock; the promise of young has been fulfilled. In this song which we sing toward the close of the ceremony, we are thinking of the fulfilling of the promise given by the Hako, that children will be granted to the people, so that they may be many and strong, and we sing that the great flocks are coming. . . .

As we sing . . . we are thinking of the great flocks of birds. The noise of their wings is a mighty noise. As they fly from one tree to another they shake the branches as they alight, and the tree quivers as they rise. The flocks are many and powerful; so, through the promises of the Hako, the people will become many and powerful.

After the symbolism of the flocking birds there follow sixteen circuits of the lodge accompanying hymns to the Powers. The first songs are to the Corn Spirit, during four circuits. Then follow songs to the messenger of the powers above, Kawas, the brown eagle, during the second four. Of the first of these songs to the eagle, the Kurahus says:

One day a man was walking on the prairie; he was thinking, and his eyes were upon the ground. Suddenly he became aware of a shadow flitting over the grass, moving in circles that inclosed his feet. He stood still, wondering what this could mean; then he looked up and beheld a brown eagle flying round and round over his head. As he gazed the bird paused, looked down at him, then flapped its wings and flew away. Again the man was walking and thinking, when he caught sight of a tall tree about which a great white eagle was flying, around and around as if it were watching over something. As it flew it screamed, making a great noise. It was the father bird guarding its nest. The brown eagle was Kawas, and she flew [as told in the second song] straight to her nest, to her young, who cried out with joy as she came near.

The next songs are to the Powers above: first in doubting hope —"I know not if my prayers are heard or if they will be answered"; afterwards in assurance—"Tirawa atius hears us pray . . . and will answer our prayers."

We have now made four times four circuits of the lodge. In the first four we remembered Mother Earth through the corn. In the second four we sang of the eagles, which are the messengers of the powers above. In the third four we spoke of the prayers we send to Tirawa through this ceremony. In the last four we lifted our voices to the powers themselves, the mighty power above and all those which are with the Hako.

Four times four means completeness. Now all the forces above and below, male and female, have been remembered and called upon to be with us in the sacred ceremonies which will take place at the dawn.

The night is nearly over when the last circuit is completed; then the Children rise and go home.

On the morning of the fifth and last day occur the final ceremonies, which are the heart of the mystery.

At the first sign of dawn the Fathers rise and, preceded by the Kurahus with the feathered stems, the chief with the corn, . . . the doctors with their eagle wings, and the singers with the drum, go forth to the lodge where the family of the Son is living. As they march they sing . . . ; the words mean that the Father is now seeking his child.

The child referred to is usually a little son or daughter of the Son, the man who has received the Hako party. Upon this little child we are to put the signs of the promises which Mother Corn and Kawas bring, the promise of children, of increase, of long life, of plenty. The signs of these promises are put upon this little child, but they are not merely for that particular child but for its generation, that the children already born may live, grow in strength, and in their turn increase so that the family and the tribe may continue.

The Sixteenth Ritual is divided into three parts: The Seeking of the Child by the Fathers, Passing in Processional to the Lodge of the Son; the Symbolic Summoning of the Powers to the Child, in which the *sacra* are brought near the Child in the Son's lodge; and the Symbolization of the Progress of Life, in the return to the ceremonial lodge.

In the first of these parts, the procession sets forth singing, "I go seeking my child."

In the second part, first the ear of corn, representing the fruitful union of Heaven and Earth, is held above the child; then the Kurahus "wraps the white-eagle feathered stem within the feathers of the brown-eagle stem [male and female conjoined] and, holding with both hands the bundle, he stands before the little child, and, while the . . . song is sung, he points the stems toward it. This movement means that the breath of life is turned toward the child. The breath passes through the stem."

In the third part, first is sung, "Come and fear not, my child;

all is well"; then, the child takes four steps forward, representing the progress of life, and they sing, "I am ready; come, my child; have no fear!" And finally, as they return with the child, they sing, "Behold your father walking with the child!"

The Seventeenth Ritual contains four parts, each concerned with a phase of the ceremonial preparation of the child, which takes place concealed from the view of the warriors by an inner group closely surrounding the child.

In the first part, an old man, "chosen because of his long life, and his having received many favors from the powers above, in order that similar gifts might be imparted to the child," touches the child with water from the symbolic bowl, "shaped like the dome of the sky, because water comes from Tirawa atius. The little child is to be cleansed and prepared for its future life by the water—sustained and made strong by the water." Afterwards, he touches the child with grass representing Toharu, the living covering of Mother Earth, which gives food to men and animals.

In the second part, the old man anoints the child with an ointment made of red clay and the fat of a sacrificed animal—"the first animal killed on a hunt belongs to Tirawa. . . . This is in recognition that the life which has been sustained and nourished is now consecrated to Tirawa atius, the father above, who gives life to all things." In the third part, the old man paints the child's face. First, with red paint, symbolizing the coming of the new day, the rising sun, the vigor of life, and, as the paint is spread entirely over the face, the full radiance of the sun with all its power, giving to the child its life vigor. Next, with blue paint, drawn in an arch about the forehead, down each cheek and down the bridge of the nose, so symbolizing the arch of heaven and the paths from earth to sky: "In these lines we see the face of Tirawa atius, the giver of life and power to all things."

There is a group of stars overhead which forms a circle (Corona Borealis). This is a circle of chiefs. Tirawa atius placed them there and directed them to paint their faces with the same lines we have put upon the child, and all who are to be leaders must be so painted. From this circle of stars came a society called Raristesharu. . . . The members of the society . . . are chiefs, and these men are permitted by the star

MANY CHILDREN

chiefs to paint their faces with the blue lines and to wear the downy
feather on the head. The members of this society do not dance and
sing; they talk quietly and try to be like the stars. I was told that it
was from this society that permission was given to paint the child with
the blue lines and to put the downy feather upon it.

In the fourth part, the old man fastens the featherdown in the
child's hair. "The down is taken from under the wings of the
white eagle. The white eagle is the mate of the brown eagle, and
the child is the child of Kawas, the brown eagle. The down grew
close to the heart of the eagle and moved as the eagle breathed.
It represents the breath and life of the white eagle, the father of
the child." The white down also represents the fleecy clouds of
the sky and the life of heaven: "ever moving as if it were breathing," it represents "Tirawa atius, who dwells beyond the blue
sky, which is above the soft, white clouds."

When the child is fully adorned it is told to look into the bowl
of water and behold its face. The running water symbolizes the
passing on of generations, one following another. The little child
looks on the water and sees its own likeness, as it will see that
likeness in its children and children's children. The face of
Tirawa atius is there also, giving promise that the life of the child
shall go on, as the waters flow over the land.

A black covering is now put over the child's head . . . that no one
may look on the holy symbols. Only Tirawa looks on them and knows
all that they mean. We do not look on them, for they are holy.

In the Eighteenth Ritual the Kurahus marks off a symbolic
nest. He does this with his toe, "because the eagle builds its nest
with its claws."

Although we are imitating the bird making its nest, there is another
meaning to the action; we are thinking of Tirawa making the world
for the people to live in. If you go on a high hill and look around,
you will see the sky touching the earth on every side, and within this
circular inclosure the people live. So the circles we have made are
not only nests, but they also represent the circle Tirawa atius has
made for the dwelling place of all the people.

Over the symbolic nest the child is held so that its feet rest within the circle. A chief puts his hand under the robe which conceals the child's legs and drops there an oriole's nest so that the child's feet rest upon it. "The oriole's nest is used because Tirawa made this bird build its nest so that no harm could come to it. It hangs high, is skilfully made, and is secure. An eagle's nest may be torn away by a storm, but the oriole's nest sways in the wind and is not hurt." Tobacco and bits of fat representing "the droppings that mark the trail made by the hunters as they carry meat home from the field" are placed in the nest. "No one but the chief and the Kurahus know what is being done beneath the robe."

The child represents the young generation, the continuation of life, and when it is put in the circle it typifies the bird laying its eggs. The child is covered up, for no one knows when a bird lays its eggs or when a new birth takes place; only Tirawa can know when life is given. The putting of the child's feet . . . upon the oriole's nest means promised security to the new life, the fat is a promise of plenty of food, and the tobacco is an offering in recognition that all things come from Tirawa. The entire act means that the clan or tribe of the Son shall increase, that there shall be peace and security, and that the land shall be covered with fatness. This is the promise of Tirawa through the Hako.

The ritual closes with a thank offering of sweet smoke.

The Nineteenth Ritual contains the songs sung during the dance of thanks which follow the mystery. This is performed before the lodge and is accompanied by the giving of gifts, the recounting of exploits, and other social features. At its close the prominent members of the two parties return to the ceremonial lodge for the final rites.

In Miss Fletcher's rendering the excitement of the songs that accompany the dance of thanks is vividly indicated:

Harken! List! We are calling you. Come! Come! Children, come!
Come! We're ready and waiting, your Father's waiting. Come!
    Children, come!
Hear us calling, calling you! Children, come!

MANY CHILDREN

Children, come! Come hither!
Harken! List as we call you, call to the Children to come. . . .
Look, where they come, see them, see them, young ones and old ones!
Look! Here they come, this way, that way, flocking together.
Hither they come, shouting like eagles, shouting come.
Joyous, happy, gladly come they, gaily coming, coming hither.
See where they come, flocking like birds, shouting like eagles
As they come to the Fathers.

In the Twentieth Ritual, before the child is unveiled and dismissed to his play, a song of blessing is eight times sung over the child:

> Breathe on him!
> Breathe on him!
> Life thou alone canst give to him.
> Long life, we pray, Oh Father, give unto him!

The song means:

All that I have been doing to you, little child, has been a prayer to call down the breath of Tirawa atius to give you long life and strength and to teach you that you belong to him—that you are his child and not mine.

When I sing this song I pray to Tirawa to come down and touch with his breath the symbol of his face and all the other symbols on the little child. I pray with all my spirit that Tirawa atius will let the child grow up and become strong and find favor in its life.

This is a very solemn act, because we believe that Tirawa atius, although not seen by us, sends down his breath as we pray, calling on him to come.

As I sing this song with you I cannot help shedding tears. I have never sung it before except as I stood looking upon the little child and praying for it in my heart. There is no little child here, but you are here writing all these things down that they may not be lost and that our children may know what their fathers believed and practiced in this ceremony. So, as I sing, I am calling to Tirawa atius to send down his breath upon you, to give you strength and long life. I am praying for you with all my spirit.

V

IT IS PERHAPS not too much to say that the ceremony which has thus been described, chiefly in the words of an intelligent and reverential custodian of the mystery, is the most complete and perfect extant example of a type of religious rite worldwide in its development.

The essentials of the rite are a mystic representation of the union of Father Heaven and Mother Earth and the resultant birth of a Spirit of Life, primarily a Vegetation Spirit, vegetation being the basis of animal life. This fundamental cosmical event gathers additional meaning: (1) as an account of creation, as a cosmogonic or theogonic myth; (2) as a forthfiguring and in some sense an explanation of animal procreation and of human parenthood; (3) as a symbol of the perpetuity of life, tribal and individual; and (4) in the highest developments, as a symbol of rebirth in a life to come.

Thus the rite stands at the center of the primitive conception of the world and of man's life; it stands at the center of what used to be called "natural religion"—the attitude of the mind without revelation to the divine powers encompassing mortal ways. It is wholly to be expected, therefore, that such a rite would assimilate to itself, as we find that it does, many of the more incidental elements of early mythologies, so that in various centers it would appear in varying forms and with changing accessories.

In the New World, the rite or its near analogy appears not only in North America, but also in ancient Mexico and Peru—wherever, in fact, agriculture had gained a sure foothold. In the Old World we have reason to suppose that it was spread over primitive Europe, while the whole series of Mediterranean mysteries—Isis and Osiris in Egypt, Ishtar and Tammuz in Babylon, Venus and Adonis in Syria, Cybele and Attis in Asia Minor, Demeter and Persephone in Greece—center about the birth of Corn from Mother Earth.

How remarkable the analogies in two utterly remote localities may be is beautifully illustrated by a comparison of the Pawnee Ceremony with the Eleusinian Mysteries of ancient Attica. The Hako represents the mystery in its primitive and pure form, with a minimum of mythic addition. The Mysteries of Eleusis present us with a highly complex version, and one, moreover, in which the highest promise of religion, that of human immortality, had come to be the paramount meaning. Nevertheless, the two are astonishingly similar.

The likeness extends even to the externals. The Mysteries of Eleusis open with the bringing of the *sacra* from Eleusis to Athens and with ceremonial purifications of the initiates in the latter city. This corresponds closely enough with the Pawnee preparation of the *sacra* (Hako) at the home of the Fathers and the attendant purification of the participants. The correspondence might be still closer were we to take into account the fact recorded by Miss Fletcher that the Indian *sacra* were often carried from one tribe to another, being preserved through many ceremonies, and that this transmission was the symbol of the establishment of a bond between diverse peoples; this, as scholars agree, is precisely what happened between Eleusis and Athens, for the participation of the Athenians in the Mysteries was a part of the covenant of agreement between the two cities, originally hostile.

The return of the *sacra* from Athens to Eleusis was made in the company of the party of candidates for initiation led by a "genius of the mysteries," Iacchos, who was at once a vegetation-god, and, as Sophocles hails him, "dispenser of men's fate." Also, we recall, the party sang songs by the way. This is surely a striking parallel to the reverential journey of the Fathers to the home of the Sons, under the leadership of Mother Corn, singing the Songs of the Way. Speaking of the journey with the Hako, Miss Fletcher says: "If from some distant vantage a war party should descry the procession, the leader would silently turn his men that they might not meet the Hako party, for the feathered stems are mightier than the warrior; before them he must lay down his weapon, forget his anger, and be at peace." And in Greece the period of the mysteries was a period for truce in war.

THE WORLD'S RIM

As the Pawnee ceremony, at the village of the Son, comprised public and private rites, so at Eleusis the rites were public and private. The public rites at Eleusis consisted of sacrifices to the gods and a torch-light dance in honor of Iacchos. Fasting was observed by both the Indian and the Greek initiates, and both observe a kind of sacramental feast in honor of the Earth Mother. The Indians prepare the corn "in the manner of our fathers"; they pound dried corn in a wooden mortar and boil the coarse meal. The Greeks drank from the *kykeon,* the sacramental cup, and partook of cereal cakes, also from sacred vessels.

In the Eleusinian Mysteries it is supposed that the myth of the rape of Persephone was dramatically presented to the *mystae,* or initiates of the first degree. With this there is no parallel in the Hako, though curiously enough the Algonquian myth of Manabozho and Chibiabos offers a striking duplication of the main elements in the story of Demeter and Persephone—as has been pointed out by Andrew Lang (who wrongly attributes the story to the Pawnees). This Algonquian myth, too, was made the subject of a mystery.

But there was yet another mystic drama at Eleusis, that which seems to have been reserved for the *epoptae,* or initiates of the second degree. This second degree was identical in meaning with the central mystery of the Hako: the Holy Marriage of Heaven and Earth and the Birth of a Sacred Child. At Eleusis it was Zeus and Demeter; among the Pawnees it was Tirawa atius and H'Uraru: but the two pairs of terms carry an identical meaning, Father Sky and Mother Earth. The Child was in each case a symbolic child, typifying at once the fruitfulness of the earth and the promise of continuing life.

A part of the ancient ritual of Eleusis is preserved. The initiates looked up to the Heaven and cried, "Rain!" They looked down to the Earth and cried, "Conceive!" And we know that the Corn was the Child that was brought forth, for the symbol that was displayed was an ear of corn fresh reaped. Said the Kurahus: "The life of man depends upon the Earth, the Mother. Tirawa atius works through it. The kernel is planted within Mother

[128]

Earth and she brings forth the ear of corn, even as children are begotten and born of women."

The union of Heaven and Earth is symbolized over and over again in the Pawnee ceremony. Each of the principal *sacra* typifies it: the feminine ear of corn is capped with the blue of the masculine sky; so, too, the feminine brown-plumed wand is painted blue, while the masculine white-plumed mate to it is painted the green of Mother Earth. Finally, in the Sixteenth Ritual, the Kurahus wraps the feathers of the two stems together, male with female, and holds them with his two hands over the child, pointing the stem towards it, and this movement, he says, "means that the breath of life is turned toward the child." Surely here is a parallel to the union symbolized in the Greek mystery.

There are a number of minor parallelisms. The sacred child, Triptolemos, in his winged chariot, bearing the cereal gift of the goddesses, Mother Earth and Daughter Corn, to bless and succor mankind, is a parallel to the Hako child and perhaps also to the winged messenger who plays so great a rôle in the Indian ceremony. Another child whose rôle in the Eleusinian festival recalls that of the Hako child was the boy, or girl, who (as Farnell interprets) "comes to the mysteries from the city's hearth, the hearth in the Prytaneum," and "by proceeding thence was representing the future hope of the state of Athens, and by his initiation was supposed to specially guarantee the favor of the goddesses to the younger generation of the community." [7] So, it will be recalled, the Hako child comes from the sacred hearth-altar of the ceremonial lodge adorned with the signs of the promises which Mother Corn and Kawas bring, signs, says the Kurahus, "not merely for that particular child but for its generation, that the children already born may live, grow in strength, and in their turn increase so that the family and the tribe may continue."

Of course the Pawnee Ceremony lacks the great and central aim of the Mysteries of Eleusis in their classical development, namely, the promise of happiness in a future life. Possibly the Pawnee's faith in such future stood in less need of mystic revelation than the Greek's; and in all probability the Greek mystery in prehistoric days conveyed no more of this than does the

Pawnee ceremony—for it is the briefest step from the symbolism of birth and the perpetuation of life to symbolism of re-birth and immortality. But it is worth noting that even without this great promise the ceremony brought to the Indian a joy wholly comparable to that rapture of the Eleusinian initiates which has proved so puzzling to moderns. "Happy those men living upon Earth who have seen the Mysteries," says the Homeric hymn—words reechoed while Paganism endured. Miss Fletcher says of the Hako symbols: "I have seen manifested among the tribes not only reverence toward these sacred symbols, but an affection that was not displayed toward any other objects. Few persons ever spoke to me of them without a brightening of the eyes. 'They make us happy,' was a common saying." And Tahirussawichi, in giving the ceremony, said to her: "Just before I came to Washington I performed this ceremony, and now as I sit here and tell you about the meaning of this song, I can hear the happy shouts of the people as I heard them some weeks ago. Their voices seemed to come from everywhere! Their hearts were joyful. I am glad as I remember that day. We are always happy when we are with the Hako."

VI

THE CEREMONY of the Hako is throughout symbolic, but the symbolism employed is so elemental that it must seem the very portrait of truth as truth appears to the mind untaught in science. Further, it is a symbolism that is not merely Pawnee, not merely American Indian, but in its main features it is world-wide. Hardly a hint is required to make it intelligible to any human being who has breathed the free air of the open country, who has looked up to the blue sky, to sun and moon and stars and moving clouds, who has looked about him at the green earth and glowing fields. Indeed, we may fairly say that the Pawnee conception of the frame and governance of the world is nearer to the ordinary thinking of even educated men than is the conception which the science of astronomy presents. For however honestly we may believe astronomical doctrines, they are still doctrines that must be intellectually mastered and held: they are not instinctive in human experience. Our senses tell us each day that the blue heavens are above and the green earth below and that the sun and stars in their daily courses journey through the arc of the skies. And our senses are powerfully fortified in their interpretation by language and literature—the props and stays of our ideas—in which are preserved the conceptions of sense as they have come to expression throughout the course of human history.

In the Cratylus Plato makes Socrates say: [8] "I suspect that the sun, moon, earth, stars, and heaven, which are still the gods of many barbarians, were the only gods known to the aboriginal Hellenes." When we reflect that primitive man's revelation of divinity must be through nature, we can clearly see how every early pantheon must be headed by the Sun, the Moon and the Stars, under the leadership of Earth and the shining Sky. But it is not only to primitive men that this is so—or perhaps I should say that even the most civilized and the best instructed of men, in all ordinary experience of the world, are primitive in their ways of thinking.

The simplicity and truth to sense of the Indian conception is beautifully shown in the words of the Kurahus:

If you go on a high hill and look around, you will see the sky touching the earth on every side, and within this circular inclosure the people live. So the circles we have made . . . represent the circle Tirawa atius has made for the dwelling place of all the people.

The conception of the heavens as a roof, standing, as the Kurahus elsewhere says, "on the edge of the hills that, like the walls of a lodge, inclose the land where the people dwell," and of the earth below as a floor, a fold—this conception is as ancient as thought and as inevitable as sense. Caedmon expresses it in his dream hymn:

He, the Eternal, established a world:
First for Earth's children reared as a roof
The high dome of Heaven—Holy Creator!
Made, then, the Mid-Earth—Warder of Men,
Lord Everlasting! Thereafter the land,
A fold for us fitted—Father Almighty!

And centuries before Caedmon, in that literature which was his inspiration, Isaiah calls:

Who hath measured the waters in the hollow of his hand, and meted out heaven with the span, and comprehended the dust of the earth in a measure, and weighed the mountains in scales and the hills in a balance? . . .

He that sitteth upon the circle of the earth, and the inhabitants thereof are as grasshoppers; that stretcheth out the heavens as a curtain, and spreadeth them out as a tent to dwell in! [9]

The analogies between the Pawnee conception of the universe and the Hebrew are not limited to this general framework. Heaven is the abode of the Father. Men are His children. But in each case there is intermediation through the winged beings that pass to and fro between the Upper and the Lower Worlds. Kawas and the visions that dwell in Katasha, the Lower Heaven, are surely analogous to the Angel and Vision Messengers of the Old Testament. When the Heavens were opened to Ezekiel, so that he saw "visions of God," among the four faces of the winged creatures one face was that of the eagle, while the author of Revelation, also gazing into Heaven, beheld among the four beasts before the throne one "like a flying eagle."

Nor is there want of resemblance between the Pawnee conception of Tirawa atius and the Hebrew idea of the Lord of Heaven. "The white man," said the Kurahus, "speaks of a heavenly Father; we say Tirawa atius, the Father above, but we do not think of Tirawa as a person. We think of Tirawa as in everything, as the Power which has arranged and thrown down from above everything that man needs. What the Power above, Tirawa atius, is like, no one knows; no one has been there."

When Kawas explains to the Kurahus the meaning of the signs in the East, "she tells him that Tirawa atius there moves upon Darkness, the Night, and causes her to bring forth the Dawn. It is the breath of the new-born Dawn, the child of Night and Tirawa atius, which is felt by all the powers and all things above and below and which gives them new life for the new day. . . ."

Is not this a Genesis in the making?

In the beginning God created the heaven and the earth.

And the earth was without form, and void; and darkness was upon the face of the deep. And the Spirit of God moved upon the face of the waters.

And God said, Let there be light: and there was light.

And God saw the light, that it was good: and God divided the light from the darkness.

And God called the light Day, and the darkness He called Night. And the evening and the morning were the first day.[10]

The conception of the earth as the Great Mother to whom the Sky Father or the Sun Father is united for the bringing forth of life is, of course, not prominent in a monotheistic religion like the Hebrew. Nevertheless, this idea, too, underlies many Old Testament passages, showing clearly enough that it was as familiar to Israelite as to pagan. In the Sixty-fifth Psalm we read:

. . . Thou makest the outgoings of the morning and evening to rejoice.

Thou visitest the earth and waterest it: thou greatly enrichest it with the river of God, which is full of water: thou preparest them corn, when thou hast so provided for it.

Thou waterest the ridges thereof abundantly: thou settlest the furrows thereof: thou makest it soft with showers: thou blessest the springing thereof.

Thou crownest the year with thy goodness; and thy paths drop fatness.

Paths dropping fatness is a sign of plenty to the Indian as well as to the Psalmist. The bits of fat used in the Hako represent, says the Kurahus, "the droppings that mark the trail made by the hunters as they carry the meat home from the field. This trail is called the path dropping fatness, and means plenty."

Again in the Nineteenth Psalm: "The heavens declare the glory of God . . . In them hath he set a tabernacle for the sun, which is as a bridegroom coming out of his chamber." [11] Here we get the image of the nuptials of Earth and Sun which is the most ancient and universal figure of the generation of life, represented as perfectly as anywhere in the one prayer of the pagan Saxons which has been preserved to us: "Hail be thou, Earth, Mother of Men, wax fertile in the embrace of God, fulfilled with fruit for the use of man!" So the Eleusinian mystics called upon Heaven to rain, Earth to conceive. So Ezekiel makes the Lord say: "I will cause the shower to come down in his season; . . . and the earth shall yield her increase." So the Zuñi prays the Earth Mother to invoke the Sun Father's embrace to warm her children into being. And so the Pawnee gives thanks to Tirawa atius, who "causes Mother Earth to lie here and bring forth."

In passing, it may be noted that much of the Pawnee symbolism lends itself beautifully to a yet nobler meaning. For surely in the search for a Son, who is at once the Child of the Father of Heaven and the promise of Life unto Men, whose heralds are the Morning Star and the Winged Messenger of Heaven, whose coming is with gift of Peace and Joy and widening human Fellowship—surely in all this we have a shining image, not of the Old, but of the Christian dispensation.

VII

THERE IS ONE more speech of Tahirussawichi that should here be repeated, words spoken to Miss Fletcher after the complete ceremony had been recorded and his explanations set down: [12]

During the days I have been talking with you I have been carried back in thought to the time when Estamaza came to the Chaui. I met him in this ceremony; he was the Father, and as I have worked here day and night, my heart has gone out to you. . . . I never thought that I, of all my people, should be the one to give this ancient ceremony to be preserved, and I wonder over it as I sit here. I think over my long life with its many experiences; of the great number of Pawnees who have been with me in war, nearly all of whom have been killed in battle. I have been severely wounded many times—see this scar over my eye. I was with those who went to the Rocky Mountains to the Cheyenne, when so many soldiers were slain that their dead bodies lying there looked like a great blue blanket spread over the ground. When I think of all the people of my own tribe who have died during my lifetime and then of those in other tribes who have fallen by our hands, they are so many they make a vast cover over Mother Earth. I once walked with these prostrate forms. I did not fall but I passed on, wounded sometimes but not to death, until I am here today doing this thing, singing these sacred songs into that great pipe [the graphophone] and telling you of these ancient rites of my people. It must be that I have been preserved for this purpose, otherwise I should be lying back there among the dead.

CHAPTER VI

The Sun Dance

I

Two CEREMONIALS of the Indians of North America, more than any others, have attracted a world-wide attention. These are the Sun Dance of the Plains tribes and the Snake Dance of the Pueblo Indians. Beyond doubt, what has given to these rituals their flair is the sensational element attached to each of them and open to the most superficial eyes: the bloody self-tortures associated with the Sun Dance, for the one, and for the other the plaza performance in which living and venomous serpents are carried in the hands or by the teeth of the dancers—both yielding images which have registered on the public imagination just where that imagination dallies most preciously with the gruesome. Actually this element is mainly adventitious in each rite, and it is not at all for this that the ceremonials are deservedly notable, and profoundly symptomatic of Indian culture.

For each of these ceremonies is key to a whole interpretation of life and to an entire cultural development; and the two, in a dramatic fashion, excellently serve as initials and illuminations of social and human diversities as essential as any that hold between groups that are primarily hunters and warriors and those which are primarily farmer-folk. With the rituals of the farming tribes are phantasmically associated flutes and butterflies, rainbows, pools, feather-prayers and pollen; and there is needful only a wraith of hearing into their songs for the growth and the sap-succor issuing from the Underworld to clear away from their snake-dancing all that is miasmic and serpent-hating in our own vision. Then we see instead of the prisoner-serpent in each un-dulating form, some clean Hermes, message-carrying to the Gods of Increase; we see behind the serpent and the whole dance the intense, hoe-grown musculature of an earth-cult long since rooted into the maize hills of ancient America. For that is what the Snake Dance means when we view it as a sacred thing, and with the conviction which guides the caciques; the word "reptile" has never entered their vocabulary, but *messenger* and *minister* and *magic* are autochthonous, and the charm of the Corn Maiden and the charm of the Serpent are of the same flowing field. It is a whole civilization, *ab origine* of the table-lands of America, which is evoked in image by the spectacle of the Snake Dance.[1]

In a similar fashion, the Sun Dance of the Plains tribes [2] is also the index of an entire culture, not merely in a material sense but especially with respect to the whole pattern of life, social and ideal, which guided into its development the particular genius of the hunters and warriors of the prairies. It is not that dances or ceremonials, honoring the sun-power, are peculiar in America to the peoples of the great grasslands: far from it. In Pueblo and in Southwestern culture generally, the Sun Priest is (as he must be among calendar-noting farmers) the guidesman of the people's ceremonial life; and in art and rite the Solar Disc is as much in evidence as in old Egypt. There survive here not only titular Sun Dances, but it is probable that other of their dances (such as the Eagle Dance) are fragments of the more elab-orated sun rituals of other days; certainly, what we know of the cognate cultures of Mexico and Peru would lead to this infer-ence. Again the Eastern and the Gulf State Indians, as our earliest relations attest, were likewise so devoted to the cult of the sun-god that certain of them (the Natchez) were early characterized as sun-worshippers—although today we recognize that their sun-cult was, among all of these tribes, only incidental to a much broader conception of nature powers than the early observers conceived. For these American tribes recognized as divine their Zeus and Demeter, and all the hosts of Heaven and Earth, along with the Sun, which for them, as for the Greeks, was little more than another lordly Phoebus. Close in its analogies with Plains custom is the Sun ritual of the Floridian Indians, as noted in the sixteenth century,[3] whose Sun Dance—in that southern land vernal rather than solstitial in its association with returning life—was celebrated by the erection of a pole at the summit of which was mounted the skin of a deer, taken from an animal ceremonially captured, stuffed into life-form with plants, and adorned with suspended fruits or vegetation. This image was oriented to the rising sun, and around it was held the dance, with prayers for a fruitful season; and, like the sacred cedar of the Arikara, the pole with its effigy was then left standing until another springtime should call for its renewal. Anyone will be at once struck with the likeness of this ceremony to the sun-pole and its buffalo effigy, with the suspended bundle of sweet-grass, which mark the Plains ceremony; nor is it unreasonable to surmise in the two rituals the same group of associations—of fresh-sprung vegetation and animal food and renewed procreation throughout all nature, as attendant upon the returning sun. But for that matter, the maypole of our own tradition is an instance of like associations leading to analogous expression, long familiar in other continents.

Certainly there are elements in the Sun Dance rituals of the peoples of the Great Plains which are familiar in other and analogous rites in North America, and which may indicate some remote community of foundation. Yet it is not to these that we look when seeking the central significance of this most famous expression of Plainsfolk genius. Rather our concern is with the distinctive thought which has incorporated itself into the great summer ceremonial in a fashion that indicates at once the social spirit and the moral and natural philosophy of the red man of the prairies, as the centuries have impressed it upon his consciousness and transferred it into his moulded life. The Sun Dance, as known to the Dakota and Arapahoe and Cheyenne, and to their neighboring nations of the prairies who share largely the same culture and ideals, is essentially an interpretation of life, of the meaning of nature for man, and of man's sense of his own human significance in the midst of nature—in short, of that which we call a philosophy of life. And it is just such an interpretation which by its force and vividness has challenged powerfully the imagination of the white race. The world which all men know cannot reveal itself in full to any one man or to any one people; for each thinking life and each manful people gain something of its meaning which is revealed to none other, so that a full human understanding must be collectively built up from the best experiences of all men and all peoples. From their first contacts with the red men of North America the white races have recognized that in the Indian's temper of mind there is something commanding, some deep-run human value, which the white man's own philosophy has mainly missed; and this something, rather than any likeness of complexion or any community of custom, is what has given to the red races their unity, making them all "Indian" even in the midst of their tribal variations and the regional developments of their native civilizations. It is this something, this "Indian" character, that finds in the Sun Dance of the Plains tribes its certain expression; and it is for this, an understanding rather than a spectacle, that the Sun Dance should be known.

II

THE CEREMONY known as the Sun Dance, in forms of varying complexity, was familiar to some twenty or more tribes of the Indians of the Great Plains. These tribes represent five or six linguistic stocks, although a greater number of them are of Siouan than of any other language group. Nevertheless, not all Siouan tribes have practised the rite, and this is likewise true of the Western Algonquian and other groups of linguistically related tribes who have known the ceremony. The Sun Dance is peculiar to no language division of the Indians, but is rather a cultural trait of local development and regional significance, distinctive, as we have suggested, of the life and ideals of the peoples of the Great Plains.

Here again, however, there is some distinction to be made, for it was by no means common to all Plains tribes. The more sedentary and agricultural Indians of the river-banks of the Missouri and its tributaries knew the Sun Dance, if at all, only in modified forms; at the full, it flourished with the nomadic and scattering tribes of the western grasslands, who followed the great treks of the buffalo herds, their prime subsistence, and for whom agriculture was unpracticed or wholly incidental. It was, in fact, a buffalo-hunter's rite, as most of the myths of its origin indicate, and the main axis of its spread followed the feeding-grounds east of the Rocky Mountains from Northern Texas to Manitoba, from Kiowa to Cree. Within this area, as indicated by the studies of Spier and of Wissler,[4] the Sun Dance shows greatest complexity of organization among the Arapahoe, Cheyenne and Dakota, especially the Oglala Dakota, and it is to one of these tribes that its origin, or at least its elaboration from some more primitive form, is plausibly to be ascribed. As the older tribal traditions themselves give only tales of native and supernatural transmission of the rite, no inference may be drawn from them, beyond the fact that these tales normally associate the Sun Dance with plentiful bison. It is altogether probable that the rite grew up slowly, through centuries, assimilating to itself many elements from earlier rituals and gradually crystallizing the moral and religious factors associated with the gifts of nature, as the hunting tribes knew them.

Native names for the ceremony vary widely, and in the majority of cases do not contain any direct reference to the sun. Indeed, more frequent is the reference to the ceremonial lodge or its symbol ("Dance of the Offerings-Lodge" is the Arapahoe name), but prayers to the Sun and solar symbolism are so intrinsic to the rite that it is certainly best designated by the title implied in the Dakota name *Wi wan' yank Waci'pi*, "Gazing-at-the-Sun Dance," a name referring to the dancers' turning their faces ever towards the sun in the last gruelling performance. It is from the Dakota, too, that the fullest descriptions of the ritual are preserved; and it is with this people that the philosophic and religious ideas animating it are expressed in a manner indicating long-seasoned thought and a depth of reflection which of itself should justify our regarding the Sun Dance as theirs in a peculiarly intimate sense. It is the Dakota form, therefore, which we may regard as exemplary.

As in the case of other great festivals of the Plains peoples, the Sun Dance was normally undertaken in fulfillment of a vow made by an individual, man or woman, in an hour of peril or in a plea for aid in carrying through the enterprise of war or vengeance. With the maker of the vow others might associate themselves, each to join in the performance in his own fashion and according to his own measures; for instance, it is known that a group of warriors, about to enter battle, have delegated one of their number, known to be worthy, to lead with a vow to the Sun that in case of the success of their expedition the ceremony should be observed through their mutual initiative and responsibility. Thus there was at the foundation of the rite a factor, not of tribal pressure but of personal initiative—that direct and unshared reliance upon his own manhood and his own powers (aided only by the Medicine Powers which each man felt to be in some revealed fashion his own). This self-reliance was the proud mark of the Indian warrior, and it distinguishes the Plains culture from that of the more collective-minded societies of the farmer nations. The Plainsman was first of all, in his own stature, an individual, and it was this that gave him pride of carriage among men.

The performance of the dance, of course, itself demanded tribal participation and cooperation,[5] and the ritual was wholly regulated by tradition. The season for its celebration was mid-summer, especially at the time when vegetation was flourishing and the buffalo abundant, and preparatory to it prayers were said and songs sung soliciting clear skies and shining weather—the favor of the Sun. Preparations, perhaps of months' duration, had been necessary for accumulating stores of food and Indian wealth which could provide for the feasting and the giving. He who gave the vow, and those who joined with him, were under the tutelage of the priest or leader who was to take charge of the ceremony and conduct the rituals. It was necessary to engage relatives and friends in these tasks of preparation, but such association constituted an honor which was not readily relinquished. The whole people felt the seriousness and importance of a rite which became virtually annual, even while its undertaking depended upon personal initiative; and when the time of the performance had been announced, and word sent abroad, the scattered bands drew together, gathering upon the prairies at the designated spot, and erecting their tipi groups in the circles which denoted the assemblage of the kindred peoples.

The period of the ceremony is eight days. The first four days are primarily days of ceremonial preparation, while the second four are devoted to the important elements of the performance. On the first of the preparatory days the priestly leader is chosen, and in council with those who have made the vow of the dance and with their mentors, after the ritual of smoking which opens all such rites, the criers and marshals and all officers of the ceremony are chosen and given their insignia. On the second day, the day of the Feast of the Bear God, those who aspire to be the lesser participants in the dance present themselves—mothers who wish to have the ears of their babes pierced, children who may join the procession of the sacred tree, maidens who are to be the attendants of the dancers, and those who are to have the honor of felling the tree. The third preparatory day opens with the appointment of those who are to select and erect the tree that is to become the Sun Pole: the hunter who is to find and mark it, the digger of the hole into which it is to be set, the escort of warriors, the musicians. The painting and ornamenting of the buffalo skull, facing the Sun in the Council Lodge, also takes place on this day; and finally there is the Feast of the Buffalo, the last feast in which the devotees may take part. It is a feast in which the tongue of the animal plays a peculiar part; each participant should receive at least a morsel of buffalo tongue, while to each of the dancers is allotted the entire tongue of an animal— a festal symbolism known to other rites than the Sun Dance and to other tribes than those practising it.[6] The fourth day is the day of the Feast of the Maidens, its essential business being the formal naming and face-painting of the women who are to share in the ceremonies. The most important of these are four women who are to fell the tree, women known for their Indian virtues of hospitality and industry, and for the esteem in which they are held.

After this the maidens of the tribe who are to be attendants upon the dancers are named by the priestly leader, and as each girl's name is announced she must stand forth and attest her virginity. This is open to challenge by any man present, but if in answer she repeat her oath and set her teeth into a snake-skin or the effigy of a serpent, then she is esteemed innocent unless he do likewise, in which case the truth is left for the Serpent to decide, for the one who has sworn falsely will surely be bitten. The feast follows, given by the kindred of the maidens named, and after it, when the Sun is near his setting, comes the Women's Dance, each woman choosing her own male partner. . . .

The four days of preparation close with an impressive smoke-offering to the declining Sun—just as the opening of the first day smoke-offering was to the rising Sun. Now the priest and mentors gather upon an elevation and pray to the Four Winds and to the Above for blue days for the ceremony, and as the Sun sinks from sight they extend to him the mouthpiece of the pipe, asking his favor upon the ceremony. This night the camp is quiet with the dusk, and none are abroad but the marshals—save only those whose faces are painted black, mourners for their dead, who may go beyond the camp circle there to wail their songs of sorrow.

The second four-day period must be days of high summer, and sun-clear. On any day should the sky be clouded and the sun veiled, then the ceremony is held in abeyance: on such a day symbolic war is made against the malevolent beings who may have invaded the camp, the priests with their medicine exorcise the evil influences, and if any man is judged to be unworthy he is expelled from the camp, for perchance he is the cause of the Sun's displeasure. Thus, while the ceremony proper lasts four days, only blue days are ceremonially active, and such must be awaited.

The rites of the First Sacred Day have to do with the establishment of the hallowed site for the Sun Pole Lodge, with the erection of the Sacred Lodge and with the formation of the camp circle as the major enclosure of these; on this day, too, the chosen hunter must scout for the devoted tree, which is to be felled to become the Sun Pole. The day opens with a prayer to the Sun, and afterwards with a symbolic battle, the warriors charging the site upon which the sun's symbol is to be erected, to cleanse it of evil and to drive thence all ill-willed and mischievous beings. Afterwards the sacred spot is located, to be the actual center of the camp and the locus of the Sun Pole, and there a smoke is raised propitiating the Buffalo—all this with a procession and assembly of the people, who forthwith proceed to form the ceremonial camp in a great circle with an eastern entrance. Sixteen paces eastward from the locus of the Sun Pole is placed the entrance of the Sacred Lodge, opening southward. The Sacred Lodge is forthwith erected, and into it are inducted those who are to be the dancers, each being seated upon a bed of sage and each with his mentor; the Leader of the Dance is first to enter and is seated in the place of honor. Thereafter, the men within the lodge are tabu to all except their mentors and attendants. It is while this is going on that the hunter is sent to scout for the enemy; and after he has found and marked with a circle of red paint a suitable tree (which should be a growing cottonwood, straight and strong), he returns and notifies the priest in charge that he has discovered the foe. During this period, also, after they have set up their tipis, the people erect the arbor or shade which in horse-shoe form encircles the dancing space about the site for the Sun Pole, designed to afford shelter to participants and spectators. Finally there is held a Buffalo Feast, wherein the buffalo dance is performed, and the Buffalo Itself and the Whirlwind, as lords and patrons of plenty and fruitfulness, are sung and lauded. On this day food and other gifts are rendered to the old and the poor; the young men and maidens meet at their trystings, so that the sound of the lover's flute is heard; the old women burn incense of cottonwood twigs, which is protective of women's honor, the old men shake their rattles, while the priests with their medicines drive forth all evil. Thus the ceremonial camp is set.

The Second Sacred Day opens with the cry of the red herald who speaks for Anpeo, the Dakota Aurora, the spirit of the dawn; and during this day takes place the capture and bringing in of the sacred tree and the erection of the Sun Pole. The Bear is honored as was the Buffalo on the day preceding, and after a procession in his honor the warriors scout for the reported enemy, and having been thrice unsuccessful, at a fourth trial they discover the devoted tree, strike it, and with taunts and jeers bind it as if it were an enemy; afterwards they return with victorious shouts and the people sing of war and triumph. Whereupon a procession of the people is sent forth to bring in the captive; and after four warriors, men of renown, have struck the tree and recounted the deeds which make them men of name, the four women who have been previously chosen fell the tree, the last blow being struck by her who is foremost in repute. It must be so struck that the tree shall fall southwards—whereupon the people again utter shouts of joy and also the peculiar keening cry, falsetto in timbre, which for the Indian is expression of tense emotion. After the tree is felled it is stripped of bark up to the fork which is left at the top, with above this, perhaps, a panache of foliage; and then men carry it in, as if bringing in a captive, and from time to time give the wolf howl which is the warning of warriors returning with captives. Meantime, the young men race to the camp for the honor of being first messengers, and he who wins is entitled to carry a red coup-stick or a feather banner. Within the dancing-lodge the pole is painted longitudinally red and blue and green and yellow, for the west and north and east and south, up to the fork, and images of buffalo hide are made, one in man's form and one in that of a buffalo bull. These are bound and fastened securely, for it is supposed that the spirit of licentiousness is within them, and they must not be abroad this night. Feasting and dancing may follow, at the whim of the several societies; but with the night the camp is once more sedate, and only the marshals are abroad.

The Third Sacred Day of the ritual is marked by the erection of the Sun Pole, and, in a symbolic sense, by the final effort to expel evil from the tribe—in brief, by a tribal purification. A processional, in which children have no part, is ordered, and it four times encircles the camp, with the women preceding the men; the women chant songs to the Earth Spirit and to the Female Power, while the men invoke the Sky and the Winds, each sex calling for the aid of its kindred element.

Thence they proceed on the Sun Trail, which leads from the

Sacred Lodge where the devotees await their hour into the arbor of the Sun Pole, there to observe the erection of the pole. Prepared for it are the bundle of sweetgrass and sage and also of shed buffalo hair which is to swing from the fork of the pole, and the red sun banner is placed at the summit or just under the crown of foliage. These are bound securely to the pole and less securely tied are the black images of the buffalo bull and of the man, for the latter, as symbolizing impurity or at least license, are to be brought down with arrows. The pole is then erected, with four pauses, and songs are sung: [7]

> At the center of the Earth
> Stand looking around you!
> Recognizing the tribe
> Stand looking around you!

Strangely, after this there ensues a period of free action and free tongue, in which men and women jest and taunt about sexual affairs, and are familiar in fashion . . .

Until, when the Priest-Leader determines, he summons the warriors in full panoply. The warriors dance the war dance, and then assail the black symbols of indecency upon the Sun Pole, shooting and striking until they fall, whereupon they trample them underfoot and sing songs of victory—for thus are the licentious spirits expelled from the tribe, that for another year it may be clean of them. It is after this that the Sacred Place is prepared: the drum is set up and the rattles for the musicians; the ceremonial calumet is set with its stem sunwards; and the altar-space, dug into the substance of earth, beneath the sods, is marked with a cross of glittering mica dust upon a ground of vermilion face-paint, while tobacco and eagle-down designate its prayer symbolism. Thus the Lodge is prepared for the final ritual, the Sun Dance itself, and the day closes with a feast on the part of priests and people. But the men who are to be the morrow's dancers receive no food, only the final instructions of their mentors.

The Fourth Sacred Day is devoted to the climax of the ceremony. On this day the people assemble in gala dress, adorned with insignia and tokens of rank or prowess, and the priests and medicine men open the day with invocations of the Sun and Sky, whereafter all assemble beside the Sun Trail leading from the Sacred Lodge to the Sun Pole. The dancers who have been keeping vigil within the lodge are now painted and adorned; hands and feet are red; then totems and tokens of their ordeal are painted upon their bodies; the hair hangs loose and the head is bound with a wreath of sage; only an apron or kirtle of red cloth or of deerskin, an otterskin cape, and armlets and anklets of buffalo hair and rabbit fur form the costume. Then the Leader takes up the buffalo cranium which has reposed with them within the lodge, making of it the symbolic guide of the procession which now forms, following the Sun Trail. There are pauses from station to station along this trail, and the people offer gifts to the Sun, which may be appropriated by anyone who feels need of them. Thus they proceed into the arbored area centered by the Sun Pole, and as they go, the lodge of the vigil is torn down behind them, that none may desecrate it by profane use. Prayers and wailings mark this processional.

Within the dancing area the buffalo cranium is deposited upon the earth-altar and while the pipe is being smoked the attendants also make a fire of buffalo chips, with incense of sweet grass, after which each dancer is given a whistle upon which he must blow from time to time during the ordeal and which in some intimate sense is the essential symbol of his supplication. Such whistles are made from the ulnae of eagles and to each is attached a waving plume of the sky-bird; the whistle also may have been ornamented with quill embroidery or other decoration dictated by the fancy or affection of the woman who prepared it. When these have been received, the candidates, standing, are addressed by the officiating priest in regard to their duties: how each must dance facing the Sun and from time to time sounding his whistle, and the meaning of the action, and its gifts. With this instruction the function of the mentors ceases, and the dances are now in charge of the Leader.

The essential dances are two, the Buffalo Dance and the Sun-gazing Dance, or Sun Dance proper. The Buffalo Dance, which is four times repeated, is the opening performance and is ordered about the cranium of the buffalo, at which each dancer must gaze as later he gazes at the sun. The dance is in imitation of the defiant or enraged buffalo bull, and the dancer who undeviatingly carries through his part becomes thenceforth a Buffalo Man and may expect a direct communication, or vision, from the Sun. Following this dance comes the ceremony of piercing the ears of children—a feature of similar tribal rituals—the significance of which seems to be a kind of consecration of the child to the duties and ideals of the tribe. He who is chosen by the parents to perform this rite (for which he receives valuable gifts) is expected to recount the deeds performed or honors won which justify this selection—and he is in a sense the godfather or fosterer of the child's virtues. The rite may be simultaneous for numbers of children, so that with the cries of the children, harangues of the piercers, songs of the musicians, and shouts of the people the enthusiasm rapidly mounts.

Following this first offering of tribal blood comes the last and culminating drama of the ritual—the Dance Gazing-at-the-Sun, which fulfills the vows of the devotees and constitutes the central mystery of the whole ceremony. There are four acts in this final drama: the Capture, the Torture, the Captivity and the Release —all reflecting the perils and chances of a warrior's life. Possibly, in a more mystical sense, here is shown the drama of all embodied human life—for more than one religion and philosophy, from the ancients onward, have depicted man as snared in the flesh, there to suffer and endure, and if by the prowess of his spirit enduring to the end, escaped and triumphant in a newer and more spiritual vision. Assuredly there is here an elemental coincidence between the essential elements of Indian and Neo-Platonic or even Christian thinking. . . . The first act of this drama is the feigning of capture. Certain of the Buffalo Men, or other warriors chosen for the rôle, with cries of war, rush upon the dancers, wrestle with them and throw them, and announce the capture of an enemy; whereafter the dramatic victors confer together as to the fate of their prisoners. This is the Capture, accompanied by songs of grief and desolation on the part of the women and the choir. Thereafter comes the Torture. The Sun Dance ordeal was formerly of four orders (the United States Government having now prohibited the three blood-letting forms), of which the first was simply a dance of endurance for the prolonged and trying period of the dancing. The others involved the piercing of the flesh of the dancer in one of three fashions, according to his vow. If he were to dance dragging buffalo crania, then incisions were made beneath his shoulder blades; if he were to be attached to the Sun Pole or suspended therefrom, incisions were made in the flesh of his breasts, or sometimes, for suspension by the back, again under the shoulder blades; if he were to dance with thongs attached to four posts, incisions were both on breasts and under shoulders. Within these incisions, which must pierce beneath muscular fibre, skewers of wood were inserted, to which stout thongs were attached, binding the dancer in captivity to the pole or to the weights which he must drag until the strands of flesh should be broken through. The ordeal began when the captors performed the act of torture, piercing the flesh and inserting the skewers into the bodies of their prone victims. Songs encouraging fortitude during suffering were sung during this act, and the dancer was expected to smile with indifference or to retort with songs of defiance to his captor.

The third act, the Captivity, begins with the binding of the captive by the leather thongs. If he is to be suspended from the Sun Pole, the suspension is arranged so that he can be drawn up or lowered from the fork of the pole. The sun-gazing dance itself follows, and it must be repeated at least four times before any dancer may free himself from his bonds. Between each dance period there is a rest in which the participants are allowed to repose and the blood may be wiped away by the women attendants; but it is only with the fourth period that the dancer may struggle to break free, tearing through the flesh or sundering the bindings. During his struggles, in this or succeeding repetitions of the dance, the people sing songs of the captivity and of encouragement to the captive, but when he succeeds in gaining his freedom there is a paean of victory and a song of rejoicing. A simple sundering of the bonds as result of the dancer's unaided struggles was the most successful form of release; if he were to faint in the struggle, he might be cut free at the Leader's command; or he might be aided to his liberation by adding the weight of his own shield and weapons to his body's pull, or by a friend's clasping him by the waist and forcing the flesh to part. It is of record that dancers have been held in their captivity all through the night, only to be released, at priestly command, when the sun rises to a new day.

With the coming of another day the Sun Dance is ended. The camp is broken and the Lodge of the Sun Pole is destroyed, only the pole itself, with its emblems, being left to stand until the Powers of storm and wind should fell it. But for each dancer there should have come either a vision vouchsafed by the Sun or the right to expect in good time such a revelation—his in an intimate and untransmitted sense. It might be through the tuition of a Medicine Man, one learned in nature's symbolisms, that he should master the meaning of his vision, or it might be that his own life and deeds would make it clear to him: but in any case he was thenceforth a man of new endowment, won by the gift of his own body's strength, so that he should thereafter be accepted into the company of men who through fortitude have proven themselves as fitted to walk erect mid nature and to converse with her more manly Powers.

III

THE SYMBOLISM underlying and taking form in the Sun Dance is manifold. Many of the elements such as the use of tobacco, sweetgrass, sage, the fat of animals, furs, the colors of the world quarters, and the like, are accessories of numerous Plains Indian ceremonies, and are customary in their ritual generally rather than distinctive of the Sun Dance. The Sun Pole, too, belongs clearly in a class of tree and pole emblems having a wide and ancient American distribution, and without much question leading back to some common and primitive imagery of vegetation and life—back to the Tree of Life and the foliage of the greening year. With this, almost universally, is found associated the notion and emblem of animal life, which shares with the emblem of vegetation the imagery of the vital glorification of the height of the year—whether it be of birds, as in the Aztec tree, of the deer, as in the rite of the Florida Indians, or of the bison, as with the Indians of the Plains, for whom this animal was prime subsistence. Such images are not at all peculiar to America but come naturally into form the world over, wherever men follow the seasons for their food and their life.

Undoubtedly the bison symbolism is one that is deeply rooted in the Sun Dance ceremonial, as it must have been in the major ceremonials of all the Plains tribes since hunting began. The animal was not only of first importance as their source of food; but its hide, tendons, horns, greases entered so variously into their material equipment—blankets, coverings, ropes, utensils, crafts— that their whole way of life might well from this foundation be termed the "buffalo culture." Certainly there is no difficulty in accounting for the Buffalo as a Medicine Power of the first order —as was the Sacred Bull in the Egyptian, Semitic and Classic worlds of antiquity: the bison was not domesticated, as were its Old World cousins, but its natural herds fell little short of their kindred bovids of the Eastern Hemisphere in honors rendered or in men's sense of proprietorship. For the Indian tribes of the Plains the buffalo were their "cattle" not less truly than the bulls and steers, cows and dogies of the cowboy period were the cattle of the white men; and ritually they belonged to the Indians with sanctions only to be compared to those which for the white man's ancestors attached to the sacrificial bullock, to the bucranium, and to the "horns of the altar."

The origin of the Sun Dance, in Cheyenne mythology,[8] is ascribed to a certain medicine man, known from his buffalo headdress as Erect Horns, who in a time of famine finds his way into the interior of a mountain, the Medicine Lodge of the Manitos, where from the gods themselves he learns the rites which will restore the buffalo and other game so that the people may have food. This release of the animals from a great cavern in order that the food supply may be replenished is a repeated theme of Indian myth, and it is obvious that it is seasonal in intent, the cavern being the hollow hill of Winter whence the Sun hero releases the spring-renewed animal life as (for example, in the Pueblo legends of Montezuma) he returns from the South and mounts to his zenith, leaving his blessings with mankind. Thus the association is the simple and natural one of the summer sun and the springing life of nature, with herds prolific and supplies abundant; and it may well be that the Sun Pole and the Buffalo effigy originally bore no more than this significance, and that for many tribes they retained little more.

The Cheyenne are a branch of the important group of Plains peoples of Algonquian stock which includes also the Arapaho, the Crow, the Gros Ventre (or Atsina), and the Blackfoot peoples, all of them tribes of moment. That their ancestors issued from the lake and forest regions which were the great center of Algonquian population, seems to lie beyond doubt; but it is not less evident, from their complete acculturation to Plainsfolk modes of life, that their separation from kindred Eastern tribes is of long standing. In part this is implied in the animal symbolism which enters into the Arapaho version of the great dance, for the buffalo robes which are there worn by the impersonators of the Creator and the First Mother are painted with the image of a rabbit and decorated with strips of the fur of a rabbit which has been suffocated in the robe itself. The Great Hare is for the Algonquian peoples widely a mythical demiurge of such importance as is best to be explained on the supposition that the tribes of this stock are descended from dwellers in the regions north of the bison ranges, for whom the rabbit was of prime importance for food and clothing. He is thus an "ancestor" of the nation, antedating the bison, and perhaps also the deer which appears among the Forest Nations as a symbol of the dawn and of life's fecundity. It is certain that this symbolism is continued among the Plains Peoples with a transfer to the buffalo of significances which had formerly pertained to these other food-game animals.

Food and fecundity are naturally associated not only with the returning sun in the season of plenty and of the multiplying and breeding of young among the animals, but also with the conception of the tribal life of men. Tribal life can only be preserved by food-getting and procreation, whence the pursuit of game and the rearing of children are the two most anxious concerns of hunting tribes. In the great tribal ceremonies therefore, celebrated at the height of the life of the year, not only is the symbolism devoted to the most prolific food-animal, which thus becomes in a sacramental sense a "Forefather" of the tribe, but also there enter symbolisms of the sex and generation of mankind itself, in which the feminine powers of earth are no less significant than are the creative deities of the skies or their avatars, the food animals. In the Cheyenne myth referred to, Erect Horns takes with him to the mountain lodge a woman of the tribe, strong and virtuous, who brings her digging-stick as he his hunting-knife. And in the complex Arapaho ritual one of the most significant features is the symbolical marriage of the Father and the Mother of creation, impersonated by a priest and a consecrated woman, as she, nude, throws her body upon the earth beneath the night sky, and he, standing above, but with face to sky places between her lips a bit of root symbolizing the Seed of Life. The meaning of this rite is expressed in the prayer by which the sacred woman is consecrated as she is about to undertake the rôle of the Mother: [9]

My Father, have pity upon us! Remember that we are your children since the time you created the heavens and the earth, with a man and woman!

Our Grandfather, the Central-Moving-Body, who gives light, watch us in the painting of the belt which our Father directed, as it is before us! Now speak to your servant who is to wear the belt! Look at her with good gifts, and may she do this for the benefit of the new people (children), so that this tribe shall have strength and power in the future! . . .

We cannot cease praying to you, my Father, Man-Above, for we desire to live on this earth, which we are now about to paint on this occasion. We have given this belt to the sweet smoke for our purity hereafter. May our thoughts reach to the sky where there is holiness. Give us good water and an abundance of food!

"We desire to live on this earth!" This is the essential prayer, sustained by the symbolism of food and of procreation, emblem of which is the painted zone (as her zone was emblem of the Great

Mother of the Old World's ancient East, whose sacred marriage,
likewise, was enacted by priestess and hierophant). The "new
people" referred to in the prayer are the children which are to
be born into the nation, maintaining the tribal continuity upon
the soil of the Fathers and thereby carrying forward the stream
of life which, irrespective of the fates and accidents which befall
individuals, is the tribe's true being. For to the Indian a people,
not less than an animal kind, possesses its spirit, its Elder of Being,
somehow intimately designed at the creation of all things "with
a man and a woman." It is a Platonic world into which we enter,
and in it the presiding Forms are the primal man and the primal
woman, the Adam and the Eve who were with the Creator from
before the beginning.

From this angle it is easy to grasp the significance of the ceremonial emphases upon chastity and virginity which characterize
the Sun Dance. In the Arapaho ritual the sacred woman is called
"the Virgin," and the conception of sexual cleanliness is throughout stressed. In the Oglala ritual, as has been seen, the expulsion
of the Obscene Powers, first dramatically impersonated in a period
of licentious expression, is preliminary to the climactic ceremony,
while the Feast of the Maidens calls for the avowal of virginity by
the young women who are to take part in the rite; for it is evident that the whole ceremony, charged as it is with a petition to
the Life Givers for their favor and blessing, must in the Indian's
thought be purged from all sense of impurity or stain: it must
issue from a clean heart, or be as naught.

Thus there is a profoundly moral element in the fundamental
meanings of the Sun Dance, surcharging and intensifying its
more primitive, physical intentions. In its inculcation of ideals
of conduct this moral teaching extends far beyond problems of
sex. It stresses the sanctioned virtues of both men and women, of
man as the protector and of woman as the conserver of the tribal
life, and it defines for men and women and children their essential duties. Further, in the stress which falls upon inner sense,
the clean mind, and the sincere heart, it indicates, too, that for
the Indian no less than for the white man the inner life is intrinsic in morality; the cleanliness that is sought may be symbol-

ized by ritual acts, but in its essence it is to be found only in the purified spirit and upright character; wanting these the ceremony is futile. For those who have thought that a sense of inward truth and of spiritual fidelity are but late and sporadic attainments of man's nature, examination of the Sun Dance should suggest other interpretations: in this religion, as in Christian teaching, it is the pure in heart who shall see the vision.

These broader moral implications, both on the individual and the communal scales, are perhaps best shown in the Dakota legend of the origin of the Sun Dance. The tale is preserved in a number of recorded versions, but all agree in portraying how the essential institutions of mankind are derived from the teachings of the White Buffalo Woman, whose coming mythically records eventful changes in the life of the Dakota people. The date of the event is traditionally set at nearly a thousand years ago, and the tale may well commemorate an occurrence of such antiquity. Two young men, in time of famine, were scouting for game upon the prairies. They encounter a beautiful woman, solitary. One of the young men, being lascivious in thought of her, is enveloped in a cloud, which, lifting, leaves only his bones. The other, reverent in heart, is instructed to hasten to the tribe and prepare them for the reception of the stranger. The Medicine Lodge is erected, and at sunrise on the following day to the awaiting tribesmen the mysterious maiden appears, bearing with her a sacred calumet. This she bestows, as something very precious, to the tribal custodians, at the same time charging the members of the tribe with their duties to one another. The version of Lone Man, a Teton, gives most fully the essential teaching. His narrative is recorded by Frances Densmore: [10]

Braided sweet grass was dipped into a buffalo horn containing rain water and was offered to the Maiden. The chief said, "Sister, we are now ready to hear the good message you have brought." The pipe, which was in the hands of the Maiden, was lowered and placed on the rack. Then the Maiden sipped the water from the sweet grass.

Then, taking up the pipe again, she arose and said: "My relatives, brothers and sisters: Wakantanka has looked down, and smiles upon us this day because we have met as belonging to one family. The best thing in a family is good feeling toward every member of the family. I am proud to become a member of your family—a sister to you all. The sun is your grandfather, and he is the same to me. Your tribe has the distinction of being always very faithful to promises, and of possessing great respect and reverence toward sacred things. It is known also that nothing but good feeling prevails in the tribe, and that whenever any member has been found guilty of committing any wrong, that member has been cast out and not allowed to mingle with the other members of the tribe. For all these good qualities in the tribe you have been chosen as worthy and deserving of all good gifts. I represent the Buffalo tribe, who have sent you this pipe. You are to receive this pipe in the name of all the common people [Indians]. Take it, and use it according to my directions. The bowl of the pipe is red stone—a stone not very common and found only at a certain place. This pipe shall be used as a peacemaker. The time will come when you shall cease hostilities against other nations. Whenever peace is agreed upon between two tribes or parties this pipe shall be a binding instrument. By this pipe the medicine-men shall be called to administer help to the sick."

Turning to the women, she said:

"My dear sisters, the women: You have a hard life to live in this world, yet without you this life would not be what it is. Wakantanka intends that you shall bear much sorrow—comfort others in time of sorrow. By your hands the family moves. You have been given the knowledge of making clothing and of feeding the family. Wakantanka is with you in your sorrows and joins you in your griefs. He has given you the great gift of kindness toward every living creature on earth. You he has chosen to have a feeling for the dead who are gone. He knows that you remember the dead longer than do the men. He knows that you love your children dearly."

Then turning to the children:

"My little brothers and sisters: Your parents were once little children like you, but in the course of time they became men and women. All living creatures were once small, but if no one took care of them they would never grow up. Your parents love you and have made many sacrifices for your sake in order that Wakantanka may listen to them, and that nothing but good may come to you as you grow up. I have brought this pipe for them, and you shall reap some benefit from it. Learn to respect and reverence this pipe, and above all, lead pure lives. Wakantanka is your great grandfather."

Turning to the men:

"Now my dear brothers: In giving you this pipe you are expected to use it for nothing but good purposes. The tribe as a whole shall depend upon it for their necessary needs. You realize that all your necessities of life come from the earth below, the sky above, and the four winds. Whenever you do anything wrong against these elements they will always take some revenge upon you. You should reverence them. Offer sacrifices through this pipe. When you are in need of buffalo meat, smoke this pipe and ask for what you need and it shall be granted you. On you it depends to be a strong help to the women in the raising of children. Share the women's sorrow. Wakantanka smiles on the man who has a kind feeling for a woman, because the woman is weak. Take this pipe, and offer it to Wakantanka daily. Be good and kind to the little children."

Turning to the chief:

"My older brother: You have been chosen by these people to receive this pipe in the name of the whole Sioux tribe. Wakantanka is pleased and glad this day because you have done what it is required and expected that every good leader should do. By this pipe the tribe shall live. It is your duty to see that this pipe is respected and reverenced. I am proud to be called a sister. May Wakantanka look down on us and take pity on us and provide us with what we need. Now we shall smoke the pipe."

Then she took the buffalo chip which lay on the ground, lighted the pipe, and pointing to the sky with the stem of the pipe, she said, "I offer this to Wakantanka for all the good that comes from above." (Pointing to the earth:) "I offer this to the earth, whence come all good gifts." (Pointing to the cardinal points:) "I offer this to the four winds, whence come all good things." Then she took a puff of the pipe, passed it to the chief, and said, "Now my dear brothers and sisters, I have done the work for which I was sent here and now I will go, but I do not wish any escort. I only ask that the way be cleared before me."

Then, rising, she started, leaving the pipe with the chief, who ordered that the people be quiet until their sister was out of sight. She came out of the tent on the left side, walking very slowly; as soon as she was outside the entrance she turned into a white buffalo calf.

The calumet which is brought in the Sacred Maiden's hands is unquestionably of major importance in the symbolism of the ritual.

In the ceremony itself, among virtually all the tribes, such a calumet is placed on the altar in association with the bison cranium, and is so arranged as to suggest the passage of the breath of life from above to the cranium. In the Yankton band of the Teton it is said that the man who originally received and kept in charge the pipe from the Buffalo Maiden was named Buffalo-Stands-Upward, and also that the keepers of this pipe had each lived nearly a hundred years. The stem of the pipe was made to resemble the windpipe of a calf,[11] and when it was smoked the pipe was passed to the left, this being the direction taken by the Maiden upon her departure. The pipe was named "the White Buffalo Calf pipe." Similar symbolism is to be found in the Algonquian Sun Dance rituals, and the interpretation that in these it represents the Ancient Above, the Creator, is wholly reasonable—just as the cranium is certainly symbolic of the life sustained upon the earth beneath. The juxtaposition of the pipe and the cranium at the altar may therefore be regarded as again typifying the sacred marriage, the union of the life of heaven and of the life of Earth. But here in the thought underlying the Sun Dance, the symbolism of this union enters with a broader and a more philosophical significance than is to be found in any one mythic act or event: back of it, indeed, lies an entire interpretation of nature, a theory of God and Man, as the Indian mind conceives it. To this we shall recur.

IV

THERE YET REMAINS for consideration that feature of the Sun Dance ritual which most gives it fame, the ordeal or self-torture. This feature is not present among all the tribes that perform the ceremony, nor is it an essential rite, at least not in the forms involving laceration and bloodshed. Furthermore, it is not at all evident that self-torture had originally any part in the ceremony, or by any primary right belongs to it. The practice is found in other ceremonies of the Plains peoples, and belongs rather to the spirit of a warlike culture than to one of devotional mutilation; the sense of sacrifice and propitiation are present, but more im-

portant is that of self-proof, of ordeal, and of the power to endure suffering with fortitude. In the Dakota version, where the
ordeal is of greatest significance, another motive enters, namely
the need of carrying through the drama in the full sense of
petition or religious rite: the dancers are in a way *priests;* they
undergo rather than perform or render the rite; their action is
in the nature of symbolism but at the same time the symbol is
made real in the highest mode possible. Here lies the distinction
between the purely histrionic and the religious drama; the latter
is a sacrament, not alone a representation, and while in emblem
it reveals a meaning behind the action, at the same time it con-
veys a power and a good to the participant which gives it both
ritual and spiritual reality. In this fashion the religious rite
differs from the allegorical drama: both are mimetic, but only
the first is sacramental, although between them the line of dif-
ferentiation may be wavering. The drama of the Christian Mass
and the Passion Play of Oberammergau, or the Bayreuth Parsifal, if only in degree, share the reality that attaches to the
sacred and the sacramental and hence become rite; in another
dimension of experience lies the merely lay dramatic performance. Similarly in Indian ritual, the heart of which is a drama,
the *action* is not merely symbolic; it partakes of that spiritual
reality which enters into every religious ceremonial, making it
sacred: hence the demand for the clean mind and the pure
heart, and hence also the sacramental and the sacrificial character
of the ordeal and of the suffering flesh. To the onlooker there
is barbarous and brutal blood-letting; to the participant the
dramatic sacrifice, rendered not in mime but in lifeblood, is a
progress on the way unto illumination, and to an illumination
which for him is to be inward, first as a Sun-given vision and
after as a quality of his manhood and an endowment of his life.
The most vivid picture that has come to us of the Sun Dance
tortures is that given by Catlin of the ceremony witnessed by
him in the Mandan villages in 1833, and it is this account more
than any other that has spread the fame of the rite. Catlin speaks
of the festival as the "Mandan religious ceremony," and he says
that it has three objects.[12] First, it commemorates a cosmogonical

myth of the "subsiding of the Flood," and with this, of course, incorporates the religious thought of the Mandan tribe, which, along with purely Siouan elements, includes others of South-western affinities. Secondly, the Bull, or Buffalo, Dance is celebrated (as with the other tribes) to insure plentiful game. But the third purpose is that "of conducting all the young men of the tribe, as they annually arrive at the age of manhood, through an ordeal of privation and torture, which, while it is supposed to harden their muscles and prepare them for extreme endurance, enables the chiefs who are spectators to the scene, to decide upon their comparative bodily strength and ability to endure the extreme privations and sufferings that often fall to the lots of Indian warriors; and that they may decide who is the most hardy and best able to lead a war party in case of extreme exigency."

Some question has been raised as to whether the Mandan ceremony is genuinely a form of the Sun Dance, but there can be no doubt that its general features as described by Catlin are essentially akin to the rituals of the Dakota and constitute little more than a variant upon the great Plains ritual. At the same time it may well be that the use of the ordeal as a manhood initiation represents the true, if remote, origin of the tortures—which among the Mandan and certain other tribes included the sacrifice of the little finger, and sometimes the index of the left hand, leaving only the two fingers necessary for supporting the bow. Initiation ordeals are a not infrequent feature of Indian tribal life, and in a number of cases are associated with the great summer festival, where (in the Busk, for example) the young men dance a dance of endurance, keenly watched by their elders for display of the least sign of weakness, which forthwith disqualifies them from entering into manhood's estate. Nevertheless, although this may have been the origin of the ordeal, it is by no means the conscious motive or understanding of it entertained by the Indians of today, or by those of the recent past. For to these it is entirely clear that the Sun Dance is in full sense a religious ceremony, and that the Drama of the Captivity and the Passion has a far more spiritual meaning than is involved in the mere test of manhood. The virtues of courage and endurance are certainly under test, and so felt to be; but along with the test there are the elements of supplication and sacrifice, and the quest of "medicine" powers, and of what might be called a *vis spiritalis,* which lift the ritual to a religious plane. The man is not only proved, he becomes endowed.

No interpretation of this deeper meaning of the rite of ordeal can be more telling than are the words of Chased-by-Bears, a Yankton Sioux, as recorded by Miss Densmore.[13] He said:

The Sun dance is so sacred to us that we do not talk of it often. Before talking of holy things we prepare ourselves by offerings. If only two are to talk together, one will fill his pipe and hand it to the other, who will light it and offer it to the sky and the earth. Then they will smoke together, and after smoking they will be ready to talk of holy things.

The cutting of the bodies in fulfillment of a Sun dance vow is different from the cutting of the flesh when people are in sorrow. A man's body is his own, and when he gives his body or his flesh he is giving the only thing which really belongs to him. We know that all the creatures on the earth were placed here by Wakantanka. Thus, if a man says he will give a horse to Wakantanka, he is only giving to Wakantanka that which already belongs to him. I might give tobacco or other articles in the Sun dance, but if I gave these and kept back the best no one would believe that I was in earnest. I must give something that I really value to show that my whole being goes with the lesser gifts; therefore I promise to give my body.

A child believes that only the action of some one who is unfriendly can cause pain, but in the Sun dance we acknowledge first the goodness of Wakantanka, and then we suffer pain because of what he has done for us. To this day I have never joined a Christian Church. The old belief which I have always held is still with me.

When a *man* does a piece of work which is admired by all we say that it is wonderful; but when we see the changes of day and night, the sun, moon, and stars in the sky, and the changing seasons upon the earth, with their ripening fruits, anyone must realize that it is the work of some one more powerful than man. Greatest of all is the sun, without which we could not live. The birds and the beasts, the trees and the rocks, are the work of some great power. Sometimes men say that they can understand the meaning of the songs of birds. I can believe this is true. They say that they can understand the call and cry of the animals, and I can believe this also is true, for these creatures and man are alike the work of a great power. We often wish for things to come, as the rain or the snow. They do not always come when we wish, but they are sure to come in time, for they are under the control of a power that is greater than man.

It is right that men should repent when they make or fulfill a vow to Wakantanka. No matter how good a man may appear to others, there are always things he has done for which he ought to be sorry, and he will feel better if he repents of them. Men often weep in the Sun dance and cry aloud. They are asking something of Wakantanka, and are like children who wish to show their sorrow, and who also know that a request is more readily granted to a child who cries.

We talk to Wakantanka and are sure that he hears us, and yet it is hard to explain what we believe about this. It is the general belief of the Indians that after a man dies his spirit is somewhere on the earth or in the sky, we do not know exactly where, but we are sure that his spirit still lives. Sometimes people have agreed together that if it were found possible for spirits to speak to men, they would make themselves known to their friends after they died, but they never came to speak to us again, unless, perhaps, in our sleeping dreams. So it is with Wakantanka. We believe that he is everywhere, yet he is to us as the spirits of our friends, whose voices we can not hear.

"I must give something that I really value, to show that my whole being goes with the lesser gifts; *therefore I promise to give my body.*" The spirit and faith which in the end enter into the Sun Dance and make of it a ritual to which the Indian is profoundly attached by a sense of devotion is here expressed in a manner which can leave no doubt that back of the ritual itself there lies in his mind a philosophy of life and of conduct, at once religious and thoughtful. It is no mere pride of prowess, much less cruelty or blood-lust, that prompts the ordeals of the Sun Dance, but deeply it is a quest of understanding. In Miss Densmore's study, when Red Weasel came to sing the four songs which he had received from Dreamer-of-the-Sun, the phonograph caught this prayer: [14] "Wakantanka, hear me. This day I am to tell your word. But without sin I shall speak. The tribe shall live. Behold me, for I am humble. From above watch me. You are always the truth, listen to me. My friends and relatives, sitting here, and I shall be at peace. May our voices be heard at the future goal you have prepared for us."

The culmination of the Sun Dance was the dream or vision which came to the dancer, in which frequently some Animal Power or other attribute of Wakantanka (though it could not be a vision of the Sun himself, for the Sun is the giver of the vision), revealed itself as the man's helper or as testimony of his inner relation to the divine power. The vision might come in the midst of the dance, to the Sun-gazer or it might befall at any time subsequent to the actual performance, yet before the onset of winter. That the bodily torture was felt to be conducive to the coming of the vision seems beyond doubt; but when the vision came this was as testimony to the suppliant's earnestness and sincerity rather than a consequence of mere suffering; nor does it appear that any greater virtue attached to a vision won in the midst of the dance than to one later vouchsafed. The dream vision might be prophetic or didactic, but its essential significance was as attestation of the candidate's having been received favorably by the Powers of nature, by Wakantanka, whose visible embodiments these Powers are: it came as evidence of his having fought the good fight and having run the course. Animating his action was a faith, which was itself his interpretation of nature and of God and the support of his moral life and its ideals. Only with an understanding of these ideals, and of the red man's philosophy of life, can we hope to comprehend the motives of his rituals.

V

COMPARATIVELY LITTLE attention has been directed to the speculative backgrounds of Indian ceremonial life and mythic thought. Yet it is abundantly clear that patterns of life and interpretations of nature are here developed not less than among other peoples with seasoned cultural backgrounds. The Plains Indians, certainly, are in a distinct sense thinkers, and it is of more than passing interest that among their tribes were associations of men of mature mind who were devoted to reflection upon the meaning of nature and to the transmission of wisdom from generation to generation: there were conclaves of initiates; there were esoteric teachings of a metaphysical character, and exoteric instruction chiefly of a moral kind; and there were developed not only cryptic symbols but also cryptic tongues, with peculiar meanings attached to words, or words which themselves did not belong to the common speech. It is customary to refer to the members of such groups as shamans, and shamanistic functions are indeed in their practice, yet the truer analogy would seem to lie with the Druidic orders of the ancient Celtic peoples, wherein were combined mystical, priestly and secular offices, with ascription of powers to the Druids themselves entirely similar to the "medicine" powers of the Indian sages. Nor is it without point to note that, from the little which we know of Druidic teaching, its pantheistic philosophy was directly akin to the genius of Indian thought. Not a little that comes to us in the utterances of the Celtic bards would be near to the Indian's comprehension, while, in reverse, a study of the red man's thought should make more vivid to the modern mind what must have been the Druidic thinking of two thousand years ago.

From the metaphysical viewpoint the most extraordinary system as yet recorded for the tribes north of Mexico is that of the Dakota, as reported by J. R. Walker in his study of the Sun Dance of the Oglala.[15]

The key to this metaphysic, as an organized system, is to be found in the number four, conceived as a principle of organization, and in some sense as a potency. The symbolism of this number is, of course, almost universal among the aborigines of America; both their art and their lore attest its long domicile in the native mind. But nowhere else have we such evidence of a sense for its significance consciously worked out as in this Siouan tribe. Every group of human beings has evolved in its life and thought some chart of a world order or mode which is capable of being presented as a philosophy, but in most cases such philosophies represent mainly the bent of mind of a people, to be deduced from the study of ideas not deliberately organized but representing an habitual manner of thought more or less adventitiously evolved in tradition. In the case of the Oglala, however, as of other tribes with related ideas, the systemic character of the thinking can hardly be accounted for in this manner; it represents such plan and system as only long deliberation and studied reflection, thoroughly conscious and designed, can explain: it is, in brief, philosophic thought. The fact that this thought shapes itself upon a symbol more or less obviously derived from the anatomical structure of man does not detract from its metaphysical character; for in the interpretation of nature framed by these Indians, the symbol has become in fact a principle, a law, similar in function to our own charts and projections of physical nature. And the fact that within this projection (phenomenal, we might call it) the Dakota recognize, no less than do we, an inner and pervading power, a domain of energies variously manifested, does not lessen the analogy which the metaphysics of the red man offers to the natural philosophy of the white.

There are four divisions of the terrestrial world, says the Indian, and this quartering of the planisphere is his organization of Space. Likewise there are four dividers of Time, the day and the night and the moon and the year. Of plants there are four parts, the root and stem and flower and fruit, and the kinds of animals are four, crawling and flying, and four-feet walking and two-feet walking (quadruped and biped). Of celestial beings the four are sky and sun and moon and stars, and four are the winds "walking about the rim of the world." In the pattern of human life infancy, youth, maturity and old age form "the four hills" that mark its years; and as with the classic peoples, so with the Dakota there are four cardinal virtues, which are in proof in the Sun Dance and display the man's quality, and these are courage, fortitude, generosity, fidelity—to which for the woman correspond her own virtues of industry, hospitality, faithfulness, fruitfulness. Finally, all actions are to be performed in a fourfold manner, and in the ceremonies each subdivision of the sacred rites, from the pauses in a ceremonial march to the modes of suffering, is into the groups of four. Such are some of the many analogies which represent the hold which the number-symbol maintains upon the Indian mind, like that other tetrad yielding the root-form of all nature.

But it is in the conception of the Great Mystery, Wakantanka, which is at once a One and a Many, outward embodiment and inward power, that the tetrad becomes most purely a principle of metaphysical order. Wakantanka is a Quaternity, four persons in one in a fashion wholly theological. The four are the God-Chief, the God-Spirit, the God-Creator and the God-Executive. But these four Divine Persons are themselves each a quaternity, each having its superior and its inferior dyad, for the four are not persons of equal weight. Thus the superior dyad of the God-Chief comprises the Sun, who is par excellence the Chieftain of the Gods, and his associate, the Moon; his inferior dyad is formed of the Buffalo God, or Spirit Elder of the buffalo kind, and the Soul, which is in every creature. The superior dyad of the God-Spirit, or Great Spirit, *Skan*, the Sky, is the visible Sky and his associate the Wind; while the inferior dyad completing this quaternity is composed of the Bear God, or Spirit Elder of the bear kind, and of the Ghost. The God-Creator similarly subdivides into Earth and her associate the Female Genius, the Four Winds, which range the earth, and the Spirit, which is like a wind. The God-Executive comprises in his fourfold nature the dyad of the Rock, which was before earth's creation as eldest of material things, and the Winged Ones, as Thunders associated with the great rocks of the mountains; and the dyad of the Tornado, half giant-monster, half magical jinni, and that Medicine, or magic, which in some degree is possessed by all beings. It is thus to be seen that in each of the four greater Persons whose sum or union is the Great Mystery, the Quaternity of the Indian's theology, there are four beings or natures each of which in separation may be regarded as a deity, thus giving a pantheon of sixteen major divinities. Viewed as a group these fall into an hierarchical order: dyads of superior and inferior orders, each dyad composed of a superior and his associate, or of a higher inferior and his like or cognate. But viewed as the animating powers of the visible and invisible world they form a single being,

Wakantanka, which, like the Christian Trinity, is a Mystery of many persons in one.

EVERY object in the world has a spirit and that spirit is *wakan*. Thus the spirit of the tree or things of that kind, while not like the spirit of man, are also *wakan*. *Wakan* comes from the *wakan* beings. These *wakan* beings are greater than mankind in the same way that mankind is greater than animals. They are never born and never die. They can do many things that mankind cannot do. Mankind can pray to the *wakan* beings for help. There are many of these beings but all are of four kinds. The word *Wakan Tanka* means all of the *wakan* beings because they are all as if one. *Wakan Tanka Kin* signifies the chief or leading *Wakan* being which is the Sun. However, the most powerful of the *Wakan* beings is *Nagi Tanka*, the Great Spirit who is also *Taku Skanskan*. *Taku Skanskan* signifies the Blue, in other words, the Sky. . . . Mankind is permitted to pray to the *Wakan* beings. If their prayer is directed to all the good *Wakan* beings, they should pray to *Wakan Tanka;* but if the prayer is offered to only one of these beings, then the one addressed should be named. . . . *Wakan Tanka* is like sixteen different persons; but each person is *kan*. Therefore, they are all only the same as one.

These are words of Sword, an Oglala, as recorded by Walker.[16] Clearly they indicate a conception not of many gods but of one being or power expressing itself in many forms—a pantheism, if one choose so to name it. The elaborate organization into the system of a four of fours represents the Indian's theology, the metaphysical side of his thought, especially in its outward, or manifestational, form. But innerly the sixteen are one because they partake of one power or energy, which pervades all. This power, also, may assume varying guises as it is directed to varying ends; and the gods, indeed, are these guises; they are the activities of Wakantanka directed to distinct or specialized purposes, so that each is solicited by name when mankind shares its purpose. But innerly and ultimately they are all components of one being, or avatars of one godhead, their parent and source, and the most profound prayers were addressed to this godhead. "A man from the earth I am, I have sung concerning an event, for which have

compassion on me, whoever from above, you the supreme ruler."
This is another of those prayers caught by chance upon the recording cylinder.[17] It is enough of itself to show the reverence
for the Powers Above which inspires the Indian, and at the
same time his dramatic personification of them into a single
divine being. It is thus that Zeus, also, was petitioned now as a
Soter, now as Philios, now as Meilichios, now as Strategos, now
as Keraunios, now as Nikephoros, or by other names and lord-
ships, even while his devout follower could still utter, "though
I sink my plummet into all depths, yet I find only Zeus." Many
in expression, one in being, are the gods of all peoples.

Such, then, in broad lines, is the religious philosophy of the
Dakota, and in kind that of all the Plains peoples. In this Dakota
form it first suggests to us the speculations of the Pythagoreans,
with their profound reliance upon the significance of number in
explaining both the physical and the moral cosmos. For the
followers of Pythagoras, too, made of the tetrad the key to a
number symbolism which could give frame to a world-order; and
though for them its development was into the decad rather than
the hekkaidecad, the sixteen-in-one, of the Dakota, yet in principle the two represent a similar type of mathematical abstrac-
tion, such that in the Dakota schema we can see, as it were, a
New World Pythagoreanism in formation. And it is pertinent to
note that the *Golden Verses* of the Pythagorean societies inculcate a moral discipline having many features in common with
Indian modes: there is the period of fasting and abstinence; there
is testing of self-control through obedience and restraint; and there
is the insistence upon meditation and a final inward enlighten-
ment. In all these modes Indian and Ionian meet.

But the nearer analogies to the Sun Dance are to be found in
the mysteries of Mithras and of *Sol Invictus,* the Unconquered
Sun, which became the profoundest creed of the Roman legion-
aries in the later centuries of Rome's greatness, and the one important rival of Christianity. Risen in Persia, and incorporating
the military *hauteur* of the dualistic philosophy of that land,
with its primary conception of the war of Good and Evil as being
the world's essence, with its doctrine of the descent and incarna-

tion of the divine Son of the Sun, and with its ritual baptism in the blood of the slain bull, symbol of the divine bull that is to be offered up for the salvation of all mankind—the Mithraic religion held within itself that appeal to the warrior which in another hemisphere was to give form to the highest religious expression of the militant peoples of the Plains. And as in spirit, so in ritual the analogies are striking. The Mithraic rite, like the Sun Dance, centered about a symbolic trial and captivity, a liberation by the sword, and an acquisition which, no doubt, in primitive days was no more than of the physical strength of the sacrificed bull, but in later times became a renovation of the worshiper's soul. The driving out of evil, militantly, was a feature common to both, and common also was the sense of vision as final gift and fulfillment; for the Indian devotee could repeat the Mithraic's exaltation: "I have seen the Sun scintillating with a pure light! I have approached the gods below and the gods above! I have worshiped them face to face!"

CHAPTER VII

Life as Ordeal

I

THE SUN DANCE of the tribes of the Great Plains goes directly to the heart of the red man's conception of the meaning of life. Essentially this conception has to do neither with length of years nor with accumulations of outer goods nor of sensory satisfactions, but rather with the attainment of a certain quality which is the Indian's idea of manliness. This quality has a background of social loyalty, intense in its devotion to the tribe, and of a profound reverence for the nourishing earth and the fostering universe which so fatefully determine any life's chances; and it is because of the depth and pervasiveness of this sense of the interdependences of man with his fellows and of man with the powers of nature that many students have been led to ascribe to the Indian a predominant, or indeed a tyrannous, social consciousness, with little or no feeling for individual values. This, however, is far from the truth. Even in the Pueblo culture, which in its patent particulars is the most absorbedly social of all, the central polity is democratic and the primary spirit is that of men who cultivate their individual fields and invent their own songs, and in the great dances themselves, where every beat is a throb of the mass, may yet enter in guests and volunteers.[1] As for the warrior tribes, the tribal and cosmic backgrounds are far more a permission for free-born life than any constriction of it: the man must show his quality; beyond this, destiny does not greatly lead.

Indian records are starred with the names of men who have won their way by force of personal character and individual prowess, and in Indian societies those who have been the shapers and leaders have always been orators and elective chieftains, shamans, seers and prophets, men whose following has been created by powers of persuasion and the proved quality of the man. Especially the brave, the warrior, must be self-reliant and a volunteer. Indian warriors have spoken with contempt of white soldiers, as men without true courage, since they fight only in bodies and under command. Their own war-parties were volunteer and their leaders champions. Indeed, more than one native battle has opened with a duel of champions, watched by the braves of both sides, quite as in the knightly encounters that sometimes prefaced medieval battles, and their warlike traditions contain tales of women as well as men who have won for themselves the plume of valor by individual courage and enterprise. Again in social leadership, everywhere it is the seer, the man of vision, who becomes notable. Many are the Indian prophets, innovators of religion; and Indian tradition abounds in tales of vision-seekers, men who have gone into the wilderness to meditate, seeking new light upon the problems of life and bringing new revelations to their people. Indeed, the outstanding feature of Indian character is reliance upon individual visions as fundamental guides in the path of life. The red man is primarily a mystic, and to a degree elsewhere exemplified only in Christian and Oriental ascetics. Life is to him peculiarly personal and inward, with no persistent reliance upon any social sanctions. Even the transmission of ritual is not regarded as a matter of primary moment; each guards his vision as his own, jealously, and to be imparted only as impulse prompts. He is reticent not only in the presence of the white man, but among his own people also, and his pertinaceous secretiveness, above all where things sacred are concerned, has been the source of more than one tragedy of the native life. One indeed gains the impression at times that the Indian possesses only the power of meditation, not at all that of communication; and for this meditation his ritual makes abundant provision.[2] Even when his mystic experience finds expression in song and rite these are not wholly public. The song is regarded as a personal and private possession pertaining only to the song-maker until he is willing to give or sell it, and the rite may be transmitted only to approved candidates whose assimilation of it is attested to each initiate by an individual vision whose full secret is his own. Societies of "Dreamers," or visionaries, are common among the tribes, in which the essential tie is some analogy of visionary experience rather than any traditional observance or dogmatic teaching: as with the Quakers, the brotherhood is based upon the quiet sympathy of friends, each of whom speaks but as the spirit prompts—certainly the most individualist of religions. Finally, I would mention the strain of romanticism which is to be found in tribal legend. Romance, whether of the sexes or of friends, is justly regarded as evidence of the individualization of human life, and a most potent antagonist of the *mores gentium,* even if, in the forms of chivalry, it may form into custom. Loose observers have said that chivalry and romance have no place in the spirit of the red man, but this is abundantly refuted by the number and poignancy of the tales of love and war which adorn every Indian record, often recalling historic incidents. In the European tradition the lover and the madman are regarded as phantasmally akin, and it is significant that the red man, also, recognizes that right to other-world vision which these dislocations of the spirit seem to attest.

Saliently the Indian's philosophy of life is indicated in the great rituals which have been sketched. The Calumet Ceremony defines the cosmos and is a petition that man may thrive and his affairs prosper, in his place and in his time. Tribal rituals, such as those of the Cedar Tree and of the baptismal Hako are petitions for the life and welfare of the social group, although in each case the prayer for the public weal is instituted from individual need and by an individual's vow, so that this giver's personal blessing is made emblem for the whole community's gain. Even in the great food-winning ceremonies, such as the game and corn dances, while these are cosmically timed and set by nature, nevertheless in their mythic backgrounds is invariably recognized some personal adventure or sacrifice: some seer adventuring the wilderness that he may bring thence the secret teachings of the gods that will lure forth the food-animals, some hero striving with Mondawmin or giving himself as immolation that grain may find increase. Finally, in a third elevation of the ceremonial spirit, the ritual is only the outer and incidental setting for the man's self-proof and inward vision. Throughout, the central conception is dualistic and dramatic; the natural world and the social provide the scene and the spectacle, but in the man's soul is the action. This action may be brief and fateful, or it may be for the wearing through of the allotted years of our humankind, but in every case it is the true drama of reality, and at its core is the test of the quality of the man.

The Christian world well understands such a conception of life. For with all its emphases upon the Church as an *Ecclesia* or an Assembly of Saints, still at its center Christianity also considers human life as a trial and ordeal, the purpose of which is to prove the individual human soul; and its most sacred rites are the series of sacraments which limn and sanction the career of the individual through life. Indeed, life is called a Way and the embodied man a Wayfarer (Viator), whose course is marked by Baptism and Confirmation, by the rite of Marriage, by Vigil and Consecration at the undertaking of those Crusades which form the man's career, and finally by the Viaticum with which each soul departs for its further journey into the realms of spirits. Such sacraments symbolize Christian philosophy; they represent that valuation of the individual soul for its own sake which is the prime distinction of the Christian faith; and they open our understanding to the world's reality, as Christians conceive, in those elements of Grace and Inner Illumination which the sacraments convey.

In their own modes the Indians of America have developed a similar charting of life and symbolism of the progress of the human spirit. Virtually all primitive peoples have age-rites and rituals of initiation and of the laying of ghosts, but these are by no means invariably accompanied by that sense of inner and individual meaning which characterizes the North American rituals. For, not less than ourselves, the Indian consciously visualizes the pattern of human life and indeed frequently maps and diagrams its prospective course. Biography no less than history is recorded in pictographic charts, and the Way of Life itself is shown in emblem in more than one of the great medicine societies. Thus an Ojibwa chart, of Midé wiwin origin, depicts human life with nine turns, and after seven of these, representing the years of discretion and activity, are symbolized besetting trials or "temptations," touching some virtue such as respect for elders, obedience, purity, faithfulness. "The seventh temptation is said to be the hardest of all, and if a man can endure it he will live to the allotted age of man." [3] The Midé wiwin lodges, or degrees, are typically four, and again are symbolized as a progress; and not less typical is the Plains Indian conception of a man's life as the surmounting of the "four hills" of Infancy, Youth, Maturity and Old Age, each with its perils. If the last of these is attained, then indeed is the man to be honored, not so much for his personal wisdom as for the power of a "medicine," his tutelary, which has brought him to the full of the dangerous course. For Indian honor for old age is apparently mainly bound up with the conviction that an elder, by his mere power to endure to the end the ordeal of his human years, has thereby demonstrated a spiritual superiority. Among the most affecting and significant of North American customs are the rituals which mark the four prime moments of an individual's years—the infant's Reception into Life, the youth's solitary Vigil and Quest of Vision, the man or woman's Self-Proof and Recognition, often accompanied by a new naming, and finally the old man's ritual Memory and Passing, or for any man his Last Singing. In each of these, from the prayer for the babe to the final hush, there is something intimate and personal, with an inward and spiritual relation at the heart of it.

II

The first of the four hills, that of Infancy, is for Indians as for all peoples the most perilous, although rather with the uninvited fates of nature than with the conscious testings which later life chooses and meets. This first stage is, then, felt to be pursued by the express permission of those Powers which have created human life and enable it to be. Such, certainly, is the implication of the beautiful rite of the Reception of the Child as practiced by Siouan peoples. Among the Omaha only priests of a certain clan possessed the right to present the new-born child to the world in which it must move. A few days after the birth a priest of this clan was summoned to the lodge of the parents of the infant, and there, taking it in his hands, he stood facing the East, the morning of days and years, and with upraised palm chanted his prayer:

Ho! ye Sun, Moon, Stars, all ye that move in the heavens, I bid you
 hear me!
Into your midst has come a new life! Consent ye, I implore!
Make smooth its path that it may reach the brow of the first hill!

Ho! ye Winds, Clouds, Rain, Mist, all ye that move in the air, I bid
 you hear me!
Into your midst has come a new life! Consent ye, I implore!
Make smooth its path that it may reach the brow of the second hill!

Ho! ye Hills, Valleys, Rivers, Lakes, Trees, Grasses, all ye of the earth,
 I bid you hear me!
Into your midst has come a new life! Consent ye, I implore!
Make smooth its path that it may reach the brow of the third hill!

Ho! Ye Birds great and small that fly in the air,
Ho! Ye Animals great and small that dwell in the forest,
Ho! Ye Insects that creep among the grasses and burrow in the
 ground—
 I bid you hear me!
Into your midst has come a new life! Consent ye, I implore!
Make its path smooth that it may reach the brow of the fourth hill!

Ho! all ye of the heavens, all ye of the air, all ye of the earth:
 I bid you all to hear me!
Into your midst has come a new life! Consent ye, consent ye all,
 I implore!
Make its path smooth—then shall it travel beyond the four hills! [4]

Like the final prayer and the anointing of the emblematic Child in the Hako Ceremony, such a rite is definitely analogous, both in form and in meaning, to the Christian rite of baptism; it is definitely priestly, and is both a petition in behalf of the child and a consecration of its life. Other types of ritual involve ear-piercing and naming, the blood from the ear being a form of dedication, or perhaps of propitiation, and the naming being the token of the taking on of a responsible personality and a soul, such that the babe or child is, as it were, no longer an accident of life but has become a member of the tribal community. In many groups the infant name of the child is only probationary; when deeds have proved him, and he is, so to speak, reborn into man's estate, the Indian receives a new and more descriptive name, consonant with his dignity and tribally recognized, but even famous warriors have been known to retain their childhood nam-ing throughout life—as is said to have been the case with the Dakota chieftain Spotted Tail, whose name was suggested by his infant glee over the striped tail of a raccoon. Often, as here, there is no ceremony at the child's first naming, for nature itself is his christener: an Apache mother, whose son was born with the first reddening of the Eastern dawn, named him Pathway of Morning. And among the Tewa of New Mexico mother and godmother stand upon the housetop at break of dawn, and the mother throws a live coal and the godmother scatters sacred meal—symbols of life—as the godmother speaks:

> My Sun!
> My Morning Star!
> Help this child to become a man.
> I name him
> Rain-dew Falling!
> I name him
> Star Mountain! [5]

For a child may have more than one name, even native—to which will be added white man's names at the church christening or with registration in the Government school. But it is the native names that are the most intimate as they are the most poetical, and it is interesting that among the Pueblo peoples there still survives, from times anterior to the coming of the church, a sacred dance in which on a plaza decked with evergreen the parents advance with their infant to the receiving priest who is to make the ceremonial presentation of the infant. On one side the men, on the other the women, form an aisle, and all are clothed with gala gaiety, with birds and butterflies and winged dragonflies flaunting above the colored headbands of the men—just such symbols as the women paint upon their water and food jars, pictured prayers for the bread of life and the living waters. It will be recalled that the Hako child, at the last sacred moment of the mystery, is asked to look upon the reflection of his own face in a bowl hewn from a living tree and filled with water from a running stream. It is not strange that the first Christian missionaries to the Indians of Mexico were struck with the analogy to Christian baptism of the Aztec ritual for the new-born, when the priest at its ceremonial bathing addressed the goddess of the flowing waters with a prayer which strangely reflects the sense of mystery and of fate wherewith all men face the miracle of the birth of life: "Merciful Lady Chalchiuhtlicue, thy servant here present is come into this world, sent by our father and mother, Ometecutli and Omeciuatl, who reside at the ninth heaven. We know not what gifts he bringeth; we know not what hath been assigned to him from before the beginning of the world, nor with what lot he cometh enveloped. We know not if this lot be good or bad, or to what end he will be followed by ill fortune. We know not what faults or defects he may inherit from his father or mother. Behold him between thy hands! Wash him and deliver him from impurities as thou knowest should be, for he is confided to thy power. Cleanse him of the contamination he hath received from his parents; let the water take away the soil and the stain, and let him be freed from all taint. May it please thee, O Goddess, that his heart and his life be purified, that he may dwell in this world in peace and wisdom. May this water take away all ills, for which this babe is put into thy hands, thou who art mother and sister of the gods, and who alone art worthy to possess it and to give it, to wash from him the evils which he beareth from before the beginning of the world. Deign to do this that we ask, now that the child is in thy presence." [6]

III

ESPECIALLY AMONG the tribesmen of the Eastern Forests and of the Great Plains there prevailed *ab origine* the rite of the Youth's Vigil, which marked the beginning of the second age or period of the Indian's life. The essence of the rite was a solitary fast and prayer undertaken in the wilderness. The usage varied as to time, some groups set four days, others made it indefinite. Though predominantly a male observance, there are stories also of girls following the custom. The age at which it was undertaken also varied, from seven or eight years to sixteen or seventeen. But the essential meaning was always the same, the quest of a visionary revelation, as a dream, a token, a spontaneous song, some natural portent, which might serve to indicate to the youth the presence and character of that Power or Being which thenceforth should serve as his *totem* [7] or personal tutelary.

In certain tribes the keeper of the vigil is expected to make a kind of altar by removing from the earth all vegetation and litter, and touching with his naked body that mothering soil from which his life is sprung as he makes his supplication; amongst others he wanders at will in quest of a sign, which might be no more than the passage of an animal thereafter to be his guardian or the discovery of an object suggesting a fetish form, though in the majority of cases it is the vision—dream or hallucination—and the drama and song which accompany it that indicates the spiritual guide. When this has been attained, the faster returns to his camp, which he may enter singing his song (thenceforth a personal property) or otherwise indicating his success. He is not, however, questioned in regard to his revelation, and he does not speak of it even to a priest until after a purification and a lapse of time. Then his recourse to priestly wisdom is rather for information as to the full meaning of his vision and the proper method of preparing his symbolic medicine than for any publicity. He may indeed paint the symbol of his totemic animal or spirit upon his tipi or wear it upon his person, but its final meaning is his own to preserve or transmit as he sees fit, and it is seldom communicated

until after its efficacy has been proved by achievement, or, if it be
the emblem of some established society, where it may indicate
eligibility to membership in that group.

Many extraordinary and many beautiful tales are preserved in
Indian folklore touching the discovery and significance of these
visionary totems. The description of the fasting of Hiawatha in
Longfellow's poem [8] is based upon the genuine form of Algonquian custom, even if the materials are mythical, having to do
with the advent of maize-culture among the northern tribes; and
it is typical of a whole class of such tales in which the fasting of
the individual leads on to a tribal benefaction. In other cases
both motive and result are intensely personal. Mejakigijig,
chief of the White Earth Chippewa, said that

when he was a little boy his father was killed by the Sioux. He well
remembered trying every night to dream of something which should
enable him, a boy of seven years, to kill a Sioux. The older people told
him to "go to sleep and be good," but his young mind was filled with
thoughts of war. He refused food, not going away from home to fast,
after the custom of the older boys, but remaining in the lodge. At
length he dreamed that he shot a Sioux. Again he dreamed that his
hair was gray, and, pointing to his flowing locks slightly streaked with
gray, the old chief said that his dream had come true, for he was at-
taining the allotted age of man. In the following spring he went
away from home to fast. The birds were just beginning to come when
he took his way to the wilderness. Selecting a large tree he built in it
a nest for himself, in which he remained without food day after day.
At last, on the fifth night of his fast, he dreamed that he held three
scalps in his hand. Then he was sure of himself and of his career.
With confidence he joined the warriors, and his faith in his dream
remained unshaken, and at last the day came when he held aloft
three Sioux scalps.[9]

War careers were often indicated by the visions of ambitious
boys, and it was not infrequent for the youth to adopt his vigil
song as his personal war song, to be chanted in battle, or even at
the last as a death song. Sometimes such ambition was sardonically
thwarted by the vision itself. A youth in vigil beheld approaching

him a Manito being who offered him his choice of bow or battle-axe, telling him that his career would be determined by his choice. Desirous of becoming a great warrior and regarding the battle-axe as the symbol of the greater valor, the youth chose this, only to find to his horror, as he joyously approached his village, that the axe had been transformed into a hoe, thus condemning him to the labors of agriculture, a woman's employment. Observers have frequently noted the presence of men in Indian tribes wearing the dress and following the customs of women; a man so changed might marry and raise a family, and on occasion even go on the warpath, but his "medicine" is feminine and all his life he must dance women's dances and follow women's ways. Occasionally the reverse happened: a woman in vision took on the dress and the weapons of the warrior, and if in action later she was successful in war she might even be admitted to the council of warriors. Such cases are of later life, induced by the desperate desire to take revenge for the slaughter of husband or son. Transformations of life in other modes were also intimated by vision. Among the Oglala the vision of any creature associated with the Winged God, or Thunderbird, implies that the individual shall in his conduct follow the inverse of his natural promptings: he must jest at suffering, play the clown, laugh at sacred things, speak invertedly, saying the opposite of what he means or of what his action shows—a curious type of contradictoriness which is found among widely separate Indian peoples, and always with ritual implications.

For most of the Forest and Plains Indians the Thunderers are "great birds in the sky, enwrapped in clouds: the lightning is the flash of their eye and the thunder is the sound of their terrible song." They are associated with war and valor and sudden death-dealing, and a dream of them is a token of the gift of power. It is thus that the youth sent forth by the Omaha, in their hour of tribal stress, beheld the branches of the sacred tree filled with the flashing and resonant with the turmoil of Thunderbirds, sign of its prowess.[10] Lone Man, a Teton Sioux, while on the warpath fell asleep and dreamed: "My face was toward the West," he said, "and I heard thunder in that direction. There was a sound of hoofs, and I saw nine riders coming toward me in a cloud, each man on a horse of a different color. Then I heard a sound in the north and saw nine riders coming toward me from that direction, each on a white horse. They joined the riders from the west and came toward me. One of them spoke to me, and said that they had appointed me to make the first attack upon the enemy. He said the man to be attacked was painted red . . . and if I could conquer that man I would gain something which would be useful to me all the rest of my life. Then a voice from among the company of riders said that, having been appointed to make this attack, I would be considered part of their company and could always call on them for help in time of need." These apocalyptic riders then bore him up into the sky and commanded him to look down upon the earth and observe everything on land and water, and to consider them all as his own; and they taught him this song—

> The Earth, behold!
> All these will be yours!
> The Earth, behold!
> All these are yours!

And they gave him as a charm the swallow, the swift, flight-changing bird whose flying precedes the thunderstorm and is, as a warrior's horse should be, swift in charging and veering, and they taught him the song of the swallow—"My horse as a swallow, flying, running!" Thereafter he fastened the skin of a swallow upon his head when he sang the song, and, he said, "When I found myself in danger I remembered my dream of the riders in the clouds and their promise to give me help. Therefore I painted my horse with streaks of lighting." [11] The Chippewa of Lac du Flambeau have the custom of erecting an ornamented pole beside a man's house, not genealogical like the carved "totem poles" of the Northwest Coast, but with its trophies recording the man's own career. The custom originated many generations ago, it is said, when a young man blackened his face and went away to fast according to the custom of his tribe. He dreamed that he saw Thunderbirds and the tall tree upon which they lived. So he set such a pole before his door and upon a piece of deerskin pictured the birds he had seen in his dream and fastened this at the top of the pole. Thereafter the men of the tribe, after the day of their youthful vision, sang its song for the first time as they entered the warpath—a song of the warbirds, of the sun, of the stars—and if their deed sustained them, then upon their return they erected such a pole beside their lodges. But in latter times men go no more upon the warpath. The song is never sung. Still, that which once was dreamed is remembered; the sign seen in vision is painted and swung from the pole; and because of the vision the man may be esteemed as a doctor and a healer. To one who understands its symbolism, says Miss Densmore,[12] the pole beside the house seems to say: "Here lives a man who dreamed a dream and the mysterious strength of his vision is in him. He never used it against human foe, but more than other men he has power against the greater enemy—death."

As the examples should indicate, the youth's first vigil is but the beginning of a visionary life which is profoundly influential upon his active career. It is the point, so to speak, when he first comes actually into touch with the Beings that are to aid him in the framing of his destiny, and in a sense it is as a Confirmation or a first Communion. But the vision-seeking and the fasting in quest of spiritual aid is not at all confined to the days of youth. In any stress of life the Indian, man or woman, may undertake to secure such a mystic communion with the Powers which shape his world. The seeker goes forth solitary, if a man, carrying his pipe and with an offering of tobacco, and there in the wilderness, alone, he chants his song and utters his prayer while he waits, fasting, such revelation as the Powers may grant. Perhaps as evidence of the intensity of his need he sacrifices a dear possession or offers the blood of his own body that the Ministers of the Great Spirit may the more readily respond. The Indian prophets, men such as Tecumseh, Keokuk, Smohalla, Wovoka, have almost invariably secured their revelations in this manner; and Indian tradition is filled with tales of men and women who have undertaken the sojourn in solitude, their days in the wilderness, not alone for their individual need but for the welfare of the whole

people. It is from such as these that most of the mystery ceremonies and native religions draw their forms and transmit their
meanings; and incorporated into these mystery-ceremonies (as
has been indicated for the Rite of the Sacred Tree, for the Hako,
for the Sun Dance) there is always to be found first the purification and the fast of the Feast-Giver, commemorative of its found-
ing, and second that blessing, best tokened by vision, which is the
sign of acceptance and of the giver's participation.

IV

THE THIRD HILL in the Indian's chart of life is the Hill of Maturity. This is the period which represents the man's career, or the
woman's, to be marked by whatever fate may permit in the way of
realization of the normal ambitions of the race. These ambitions
are typified in the tale, already referred to,[13] of the seekers of
gifts from Manabozho: skill as hunter and warrior, success in love,
the power of healing, each of these is asked and given; but when
one demands eternal life, this is granted in the only form in
which even the gods may give it, and the asker is transformed into
stone—for the Indian, with the Greek, holds to the Pindaric
maxim, "the things of mortals befit mortality." Skill as hunter
is asked first, for the red race is historically near to the age-old dependence upon the seasonal life of the hunting-ground for its
subsistence; and that hard law of nature which makes of life a
perpetual war of wits between hunter and hunted, in order that
life at all may be, is always close to the forefront of consciousness.
The Indian knows no herdsmen, and his agriculture is in the
main a remembered benefaction. From childhood onward the
huntsman's crafts are instilled, and the vast lore of the wisdom
of animals which creates so predominating a part of his imaginative instruction, ritual and fictional, is his essential schooling.
Indeed, his sincerest vital prejudice is for a kind of sympathy with
wild life itself, which, while he slays for need, is nonetheless cher-
ished and felt even in its humblest forms to be participant with
man in nature's rights. He will not rob the bee of all its honey;
with the field mouse he traffics maize for the rodent's store of

beans, being careful to leave the kernels in the nest whence the store of prized wild beans has been accumulated; and he erects tabus against the slaughter of animals with young, or the needless diminution of the herd. The white hunter, to the Indian, who slays for sport and beyond any food need, is a criminal against nature, and blasphemous of the meaning of life. His own world can know no indifference to the preservation of the animal kinds, and even toward the beasts upon which he must prey if he is to survive he directs a cult and a reverence, recognizing that man may only share in, never monopolize, the privileges of existence. In the Indian's consciousness there is always an element of uncertainty in the interpretation of man's place in nature; he feels himself, along with other creatures, to exist by the sufferance of powers not all of whom are human in form or spirit, and to deserve to live he must show his quality. If, to be a man, the hunter must take life, yet it is with a deeply underlying sense that all life is itself sacramental, and a sharing, not to be maintained or destroyed at man's lordly whim, but only to be held for an allotted span by petition and proof.

The accumulation of property as an end in itself, which bulks so huge in the white man's economy, hardly finds place in the Indian consciousness. There is Indian wealth—food, ponies, blankets, accoutrements and ornaments—but its meaning was natively not in itself, but in uses and meanings; capital wealth, in our understanding, and therefore our notions of thrift and of canny providence, hardly exist for the red man. In the main, food was seasonally stored, and was regarded as the right of the hungry, the women its dispensers, or, if in surplus, as provision for feasting. Ponies and blankets, while counted as riches, were frequently accumulated only as preparation for potlatch or give-away festivals, at which the owner impoverished himself. Utensils, arms, ornaments were peculiarly personal possessions, often heraldic in significance, and buried or destroyed at the passing of their owner. Indeed, many Indian customs other than festal givings involved rather the destruction of property than its creation. This was extensively the case where rites for the dead called for the burning, burial or breaking of personal possessions and the abandonment of houses in which death had occurred; but there were also public occasions, such as the annual kindling of the new fire by the tribes of the Southeast, when utensils were destroyed, and as far as possible the economic life was begun anew. For the Indian, material goods represented use, and it was mainly ceremonial bundles, and relics valuable because of sacred associations and medicine powers, that were piously transmitted. In these lay man's most genuine wealth, resident in the world of meanings rather than in that of things.

With the red race what largely replaces the motive of material acquisition is the cult and pursuit of wisdom, both of the body and of the mind. The Indian is eager for personal prowess, which in his understanding is not dissociated from power of thought and order of knowledge; physical and mental are, as it were, one breadth of being, magical in its action, so that at the core of every potency, whether of muscular skill or of sagacious conduct, there is a single essential force. This is what is termed "medicine" power in relation to Indian usage, and it is to the quest of such medicine that a great portion of the life-career of the Indian was devoted. The reason for the term is that men of great attainments in this medicine were often professional healers, their learning varying from actual empirical skills in the treatment of the sick or the injured to therapeutic suggestion, and indeed to arts of divination. But the meaning of "medicine" extends far beyond the practices of the Indian doctor or healer. Within most of the Indian groups, in addition to the social organization of clan and tribe and the civic forms of government, there are numerous secret societies, also called "medicine societies," entry into which is an important episode in the individual's life, while to its activities often long years are devoted. These societies form a structure within the tribal structure; they are tribally recognized and play important rôles in the greater tribal festivals, yet at the same time they have their own initiations and teachings, and each performs a special function in the total tribal economy: of surgeons, of rain-priests, of clowns, of guardians of seed-corn or devotees of cult-objects. Each of these societies will possess its own "medicine bundle," which is to the group what the individual's "medicine

bag" is to him—guardian of his life and fate—and with each such
bundle there is a body of transmitted learning, in part practical
instruction, in part tradition, in part song and ritual, which in
sum embodies its wisdom. It is this wisdom—of conduct, lore,
ritual song and dance—which is the treasure of life as the Indian
understands it, transmitted by the great mysteries which are at
the center of his attainment, and for which he pays with his labors
and their fruits, his accumulations of food, pelts, ponies, blankets,
ornaments, all forms of his native wealth. Often, certainly, underlying the quest of this wisdom there are nobler motives than the
mere personal ambition for prestige and power. There are few
histories that can show more frequently than does the Indian the
rise of prophets whose life is in essence a devotion to the better-
ment of a people, and the native legend abounds in tales of men
who have sought wisdom that their fellows may be benefited.
But even apart from these, a main concern of the Indian's life is
the pursuit of this medicine wisdom, sought as we seek truths of
science or philosophy.

The pursuit of wisdom in the Indian's life is intimately associated with the quest of songs, and these with the two great enter-
prises of love and war. One cannot too strongly emphasize the
fact that for the red man the discourse of song is in itself a magical, or indeed a spiritual thing. His music is his most certain
means of impressing his sense of need upon the Powers, and of
bringing them into communion with himself. His singing is not
at all primarily for his companions in the world of men, but
for the spirit beings that envelop the human realm. Ceremonies
are of greater efficacy if the songs are repeated at greater length,
and in many rites there is a pandemonium of noise brought on
by the fact that the several societies or even individuals are singing songs sacred to themselves, simultaneously with, but irrespective of, the others. Their music is addressed to the Unseen, not
to one another, and in that unseen world each Power is receiving
only that music which is of its own kind or teaching. Songs, too,
are intensely personal; it is profanation to sing them out of season, or without acquiring the right—"Great Grandfather, again
one of your songs I shall sing; listen to me. These you required

me to sing each day, and now, this day, I shall recall one." This is one of several similar prayers preparatory to singing recorded by Miss Densmore,[14] and it testifies to the sanctities which sustain the red man's sense of song. Perhaps, too, a like testimony lies in the fact that after death the voice of the departed may linger as his ghost; for there is more than one Indian tale of the Undying Voice still haunting the spot where the warrior, singing his death song, had met a valorous or tragic death.

In his Youth's Vigil, in Lover's Wooings, and in War the utterance of a song, whether chant or wordless melody, marks the intensities of the Indian's sense of time's consequence. From his vigil comes a personal song, sacred to his medicine and a part of it. As a young man, if he would woo, he composes a melody for the lover's flute, to be played beside the tipi of his beloved or at the pool where the maidens go for water; and if she composes a response in words, recognizing the melody, this is a token of favor. Perhaps in later life this very song may become a chant of death—for with the Indians as with other peoples the themes of love and war are interbound. A dramatic Omaha tale [15] recounts the rivalry of two young warriors. In the stress of battle the unsuccessful rival cuts the bowstring of the accepted lover, and the latter is captured by the enemy. The rival brings the bow with its severed string to camp, as evidence of the death of the lover. But the girl, sharp-eyed, observes that the string is not broken but cut; she accuses the rival of his treachery, and herself, alone, sets out for the land of the enemy. Lingering near their camp, in the gloaming, she hears from the tipi where the prisoner is bound the strains of his love-song, now sung as a death-song; and in the night, stealthily making her way to the prisoner, she succeeds in freeing him and in escaping in his company. In Indian romance are many such tales, often with more than a fictional foundation.

But it is not on the romantic side that the red man's stress falls heavily. He demands marriage and the rearing of children as a tribal obligation, but his full career is a thing yet more important. Unless it be in the knighthood of medieval Europe or among the Samurai of Japan, there is hardly an example among men in which warfare is so constantly ritualized as it was among the

Plains Indians. Furthermore, it is to the Knight Errant rather than, let us say, to the Crusading Orders that we must look for the close analogy to the Indian conception. The whole life of the mature man, and the central sanctions of the tribe, centered in the old days about the career of the warrior. One of the most curious phenomena of history is the attitude of the Aztecs of old Mexico toward their neighbors and kinsmen of Tlascala. The Tlascalans formed a small independent state in the very heart of the Aztec empire, yet there was no genuine effort to conquer it. On the contrary, its independence was recognized, although every year the two peoples engaged in what they euphemistically called their War of Flowers, the purpose of which, on both sides, was the capture of prisoners to be sacrificed upon the altars of the gods. It appears that the Aztecs, originally a wandering, warlike tribe, deliberately refrained from conquering this most warlike of their neighbors in order that they might have, as it were, a whet for their own military ardor and a sharpener of their fighting prowess. As time passed, this War of Flowers became virtually a tribal rite.

Not dissimilar was the military spirit as it developed among the peoples of the Great Plains and the Forests. Every youth looked forward to his acceptance among the warriors, and he not infrequently took to the warpath while yet a boy. His object was not conquest but trophies; and there developed an elaborate heraldry of military symbolism. The warrior's eagle-plumed headdress—one of the most magnificent of all the ornaments of costume devised by mankind—his painted robe, his ceremonial emblems, all proclaimed his feats of arms; and in every great tribal ceremony those who had earned the right were expected to stand forth and publicly "count coup," that is, recount their notable deeds. Rarely was this merely a boasting of personal prowess; all that he had attained in the way of achievement the warrior attributed to the potency of that "medicine" which had come to him with his totem; he celebrated the favor of the Sun or of the Thunders or of the Elders of the Kinds that had come to befriend him in consequence of fastings and ordeals undergone, not the strength of his own arm in overthrowing the foe. Conversely, a warrior mortally wounded might compose as his death-song a reproof to the Power that had failed him: Gawitayac, a Chippewa whose manito animal was the large bear, as he was borne dying on a litter from the field of conflict died singing, "Large Bear deceives me."

Life, as has been stated, is conceived by the Indian as an ordeal, a proving, and above all a proving of courage and patience and endurance on the warpath. As in other phases of his living, so this also found its expression in song. Indian war songs form an extensive genre in the native music, and it is not difficult to reconstruct from these songs cycles which illustrate not only the steps of the warpath, but lyrically the philosophy which underlies the military ideal. In general, war songs fall into four classes: there are those sung in the dances which mark the initiation of the war party; there are songs used by the warriors in the field, especially in the face of danger or imminent death or while enduring fatigue, and among these are found both the songs associated with the totems of the individual warriors and the songs of the medicine societies of which they are initiates; again, songs are sung by the women at home in behalf of departed warriors; and finally there are the songs of triumph celebrating the return of a successful party. Thus, from the music of the Teton Sioux, as recorded by Frances Densmore,[16] the cycle of war may be begun with the words of the song of a young man who is thinking of the warpath:

> Friends!
> In ordinary life the customs are many.
> Friends!
> These do not interest me!
> I have said it.

Next come the songs of endurance, frequently centering about the image of the wolf, which the Plains Indians regard as an emblem of the man upon the warpath:

> A Lone Wolf I am . . .
> I roam in many places . . .
> I am weary.

Or again:

> A Wolf I thought myself to be . . .
> But the Owls hoot at me, the Owls hoot at me!
> The Night I fear!

When the enemy is near or the charge is to be made, the battle song is sung:

> Clear the way!
> In a sacred manner I come!
> The Earth is mine!
> I come!

Or perhaps the warrior likens himself to the supernatural being which is his totem:

> These * may you behold!
> My horse, like the Thunderbird!
> These may you behold!

In not a few cases the warrior is desperate; for example, because of disappointed love, and he chooses death in battle as his solace. Then it may be that his song is a farewell which his comrades should bear to the heartless maiden:

> When you reach home
> Tell her that long ere then
> I shall have finished.

Most impressive of all are the songs sung in the face of almost certain death, when the enemy is too strong and the last charge is to be made:

> The old men say,
> Earth only endures . . .
> Ye spake truly,
> Ye spake well!

A successful return is celebrated with songs referring to plunder or scalps taken or to the rejoicing of those who greet the warriors with triumph:

* Painted horse and herbs.

> Friends,
> The war party returns!
> Friends,
> Whenever you say this
> That woman stands smiling!

The women's songs reflect a similar cycle. The maiden sends her lover to win for himself a warrior's name:

> You may go on the warpath!
> When I hear your name
> Then I will marry you!

And when he is gone the lover may remember her song:

> The one I was going to marry
> Is again on the warpath . . .
> It is I whom she meant by this.

Honors won and age approaching, perhaps the woman will sing her advice that the career of war be closed:

> You should give up the warpath,
> You should desire to settle down,
> You should stop for good!

Other songs commemorate, at times with a moving simplicity, those who never return. In this final example the woman is pictured as watching the returning band, seeking in vain for the form of one who has gone forth but who is never to return:

> As the young men go by
> I was looking for him . . .
> It surprises me anew that he is gone . . .
> Something
> To which I cannot be reconciled.

Such are the cycles of war as commemorated in Indian songs. Clearly they reflect the central sanctions of the martial ideal. The virtues which they inspire are the hardy virtues of valor, endurance, self-reliance, contempt for death. Their most beautiful and deepest expression appears in the death songs sung by warriors facing certain destruction or by captives preparing to meet their fate; even at the stake the captured brave undertook to chant his song of defiance. There are numerous anecdotes describing this singing of the death song. In 1827, when Red Bird, chief of the Winnebago, surrendered to Government troops in order to save his tribe, beautifully clothed in white buckskin and carrying ceremonial pipes he advanced toward Major Whistler singing his death song: "I am ready," he said. "I do not wish to be put in irons. Let me be free. I have given away my life—it is gone like that!" And stooping he took a pinch of dust and blew it to the winds. "I would not take it back. It is gone." [17] Half a century later, when the Kiowa chieftain, Setangya, was being conveyed to a Government prison, he called in his native tongue to a fellow Indian: "Tell my people that I am dead. I died the first day out, and my bones will be lying at the side of the road. I wish my people to gather them up and take them home." And saying to his companion prisoners that he was a chief and a warrior and too old to be treated as a little child, he began to sing the death song of his clan:

O sun, you remain forever, but we Kaitse'nko must die!
O earth, you remain forever, but we Kaitse'nko must die!

He worked his hands loose from the irons, tearing the skin from them, seized a knife which he had concealed in his garments and leaped upon his guards in a desperate effort to kill one more man before he himself fell. Bullets from the guns of surrounding soldiers killed him.[18] Again, in 1863, after numbers of settlers had been murdered, thirty-eight captured Indians of the Santee Sioux were condemned to hang. "As they ascended the steps [of the scaffold]," wrote General Howard, "the death song was started, and when they had got upon the platform the noise of their deep swelling voices was truly hideous." [19] Had the white man understood the meaning of the songs, or been able to grasp their melodies, they would not have seemed hideous; for today our most competent composers turn eagerly to Indian themes for their musical inspirations, and our widened understanding shows in them much that is beautiful in sentiment as well as in philosophy.

An interesting Crow legend, handed on for more than a century, tells of a council just before the moment of attack upon a Sioux encampment.[20] The chief said: "This is a fine day. Your mother must have been waiting for you, thinking you were going to bring a Dakota scalp. When a woman gives birth, it takes her a long time and she does not know whether she will live or not. . . . Mount your horses and go. . . . You will either be killed or will kill an enemy." A certain warrior named Wants-to-Die answered: "Let us all mount our horses. When I am old, I shall die. I will die at any time; I want to find out how it is. It is like going up over a divide." And he sang:

> Sky and Earth are everlasting!
> Old age is a thing of evil!
> Charge!

This is the red man's equivalent of our "over the top." And in the Crow chieftain's comparison we are reminded not only of the great verse of Euripides—"Better to enter battle thrice than to bear one child!"—but also of the Aztec belief that of all those who die only warriors fallen in battle or offered up on the sacrificial stone are joined with women perishing in childbirth in ascending to become companions of the Shining Sun.

I would cite two more examples of Omaha death songs.[21] The first is very simple in form, yet rich in associations. The warrior, about to meet his fate, sings words roughly translatable:

> Have they not said,
> Have they not said,—
> *Hin!* My brother! Here lies a man!

The exclamation *hin* is a feminine cry of joy; "my brother" is a cry of recognition; "here lies a man" refers to the elder sister's delight when she beholds the new-born baby brother lying in the tipi. To the warrior about to finish his career the image recalls not only the tender thought of his loved ones, but their satisfaction, even in grief, when they picture him meeting the end with the valor of a man. Birth and death are here united in one image. The second example is from this same tribe, and it rings like a fragment out of Greek tragedy and more than any other native poem gives the Indian's measure of human life:

> There is no evading death . . .
> The old men have not told that any has found a way
>   to pass beyond it . . .
> The career of a Leader is difficult of accomplishment.

There are Aztec rituals filled with this spirit, and indeed it seems as if it were the very genius of their thought, as the chants recorded by Sahagun pictures it. It is also deep at the heart of the entire American Indian philosophy of life.

V

BUT NOT EVERY MAN dies in battle. Birth and infancy represent the first of the hills of life; the visions of youth mark the second; the third is the divide which the warrior must surmount. But if he succeed, by the strength of his "medicine," there is still a fourth hill, the reflective and meditative life of the old man, which has its values and its poetry.

The rites which I have heretofore cited in illustration of the Indian's image of life are drawn largely from Siouan sources, Omaha and Dakota. I would return to these Indians of the Plains for the final image—a typical ritual of the meditative soul of old age.[22] On the northern prairies there grows a flower of the anemone type (*pulsatilla patens*), called by the whites the "pasque flower" because it is the first flower of the springtime and in a way the embodiment of Easter. This flower pushes its way up before the snow is gone, and its purplish blossoms appear on the brown hills while these are still showing patches of white left by winter drifts. By the time the other prairie flowers, the "flower nations," are in bloom, the pasque has changed; its hairy stem and its seed-head, plumose and white, now suggest the image of an old man, grayed and ancient. The Dakota have a song for this flower:

> I wish to encourage the children of other flower nations
> Which are now appearing over all the land;
> So, while they waken from sleep and rise from the bosom
> Of Mother Earth, I stand here, old and gray-headed.

The affinity of this plant with old age is felt to be such that in the springtime the old men go forth seeking the flower, walking with bare feet and carrying tobacco. When the elder finds a blossom, he seats himself upon the earth beside it, takes his pipe, and after saluting the Four Quarters, the Above and the Below, he offers smoke to the blossom. As he smokes he meditates the course of his lifetime: the joy of those who hailed his birth, "A man lies here!"; the vigils and vision of youth; his feats of arms; and his attainment of the fourth hill, after so many of his comrades had long since fallen. When he has finished his pipe, he reverently empties the ashes upon the bosom of earth, near the plant. Then he plucks the flower, and returning to his lodge he enters singing the song of the pasque blossom, which he now teaches to his grandchildren, at the same time commending the virtues of courage and endurance and faithfulness to the end, which the blossom typifies. Thus the form of a man's days is defined and the ritual cycle of his life made complete.

There remain but the rites for the dead, with their songs of mourning and their feasts of laying the dead or of sending on his ghost with ceremonial tuition, and naturally also such hopes of union or of return as all human beings share; for to the Indian, as to the white or the brown man, beyond the grave there are dimly blazed trails leading into the Unknown. Many a ritual undertakes to give instruction for the journey of the soul into the Hereafter, and it has been the object of more than one Indian prophet to chart for their followers this journey, which, they are convinced, their own spirits have traversed during the trance-death of their bodies. To the Indian it seems certain that the demarcation between life and death, body and soul, is by no means so sharp as it is for us. His belief in "medicine" is a belief in personal contact with an invisible world of half-magical powers; his song is direct communication with this world; and as to the visible things of this earth he has an utterly Heraclitean conviction that their outer aspects and their inner potencies are wholly incommensurate. The world of sense is a world of shape-shiftings and of illusion, behind which move the inevitable forces of the Great Mystery.

This wavering view of reality may well be illustrated by the Indian's attitude toward a scalped man. If the victim be dead, his soul is still doomed to hover restlessly in the ghostly limbo of the unhappy dead, from which it may be freed only by the piaculum of a scalp taken in revenge. But men have survived scalping, stunned but not slain. To the Indian this was in a sense incomprehensible. The man who has lost his scalp seemed no longer fully a man; he belonged neither to the dead nor to the living, and in the old days he was condemned to live in solitude, approached only by a shaman familiar with the ways of the other world. Those ways were conceived to be somehow the inverse of ours. Our summer is their winter, and it is for this reason that the great festivals honoring the dead are most appropriate to the winter season, when their world is at zenith. On the other hand, when man is at his height of power, he must not forget the blessings bestowed by Those Below, partners in his fate. A curious story was recently related by a Pueblo cacique [23] about the coming of Christianity to his people and the celebration of Easter. A certain young man, hostile to the new festival brought by the white man, fled to the solitude of a sacred cave. There he was visited by spirits rising from underworld waters. Said the Spirits: "Follow the new religion and its feasts. It is good and will help you even as we help you, whom you must not forget." And then they added: "For you must know that we help one another, the living and the dead, and together hold up the world. We worship you even as you worship us, and we depend upon you for life as you depend upon us."

Life and death are not separate but confluent in Indian lore; and it may be for the very reason that the old man has traversed the ascents of life, and has mastered the meanings of joy and sorrow, that he is felt also to have a clearer insight into that land of the dead which he is nearing, and is consequently conversant with spiritual meanings. At any rate, in more than one mythic account, the Grandsire and the Grandmother who sit above the arc of the heavens are not only responsible for the miracle of birth and the creation of life, but also it is they who in the beginning of things decreed death for their children. That a wisdom of love underlay this myth is evidenced by the simple version which the Blackfoot teachers tell.[24] In the beginning Old Man and Old Woman debated whether people should die. "People will never die," said Old Man. "Oh," said Old Woman, "that will never do; . . . if people live always there will be too many people in the world." "Well," said Old Man, "we do not want to die forever. We shall die for four days, and then come to life again." "Oh, no!" said Old Woman, "it will be better to die forever, so that we shall be sorry for each other."

CHAPTER VIII

The Last Trail

I

DEATH LIKE LIFE is a mystery and must have its origin and meaning. Both are natural, but in naming them "natural" merely their fact is stated; neither is explained. They are interbound in meaning. Before the world was, in the creative intent, they were predestined, as dual aspects of one meaning, which might be that of the world itself as well as of any individual man, for First Things and Last Things are of one creation, and cosmogony and eschatology are but the beginning and ending of a single narrative. "This that we have created and shaped will have its end," is the terse comment which greets the ejaculations of joy and pride when the first mountains are uplifted from the cosmic waters by the Kiché creators,[1] and for the animal kinds birth is the prediction of death; their fabric is single.

With little exception Indian cosmogonical myths contain in their cycles, along with episodes of the creation of life, other episodes which recount the coming of death into the world. For death, also, must be created, and usually, as it appears, not as a wounding but as a fulfillment of the world's meaning. From the Eskimo of the farthest north, where the year is a brief day and a long night, comes the parable of the elders of creation debating, when as yet there was no sun and as yet no death. Said the one,

"Let us do without light, if so we can be without death"; but the other answered, "Nay, let us have light and death!" The Tlinkit, of Alaska, tell how the Creator undertook to form men out of a rock and a leaf, but the rock was slow and the leaf quick, wherefore human beings came from the latter. Then the Creator showed a leaf to the new race, and said: "See this leaf. You are to be like it. When it falls off the branch and rots there is nothing left of it." It is Indians of the Northwest again who tell how the ancestral beings descended from heaven, wishing to endow man with eternal life. But a little bird, of a kind accustomed to nest in the burial scaffolds of these people, cried out: "Where shall I dwell if ye always live? I would build my nest in your graves, and warm me!" [2]

In such tales the sense of fate and the sense of beauty commingle to yield that poetry of understanding which at the last is the only reason that can satisfy our human quest of insight into what is final in our world. And more perhaps than any other such tale the Wintun tale of Olelbis and the Brothers Hus [3] makes explicit this meaning: Olelbis, about to create men, sends the two brothers Hus (buzzards) to build a stone ladder from earth to heaven. At the summit are to be two pools for bathing and drinking, and when a man or a woman grows old, by climbing to Olelpanti and there bathing and drinking in the waters of life, youth will be restored. But as the brothers build, Coyote, the tempter, comes saying in effect, "I am wise; let us reason. Suppose an old man and an old woman go up, go alone, one after the other, and come back alone, young. They will be alone as before, and will grow old a second time, and go up again and come back again young, but they will be alone just the same as at first. They will have nothing on earth whereat to rejoice. They will never have any friends, any children; they will never have anything to do, but to go up this road old and come back again young. Joy at birth and grief for the dead is better."

Of eschatology in the fuller sense, as world fate, there is little trace in the myths of the tribes north of Mexico. But the astral and calendric lore of Aztec and Maya had brought into these southern civilizations a fateful sense of impending cataclysms which should end this our Sun of Time as in the past other Suns had moved to cataclysmic dooms—the strange obsession of destinies inbound with cosmic numbers which even in our own day holds the human mind beleaguered. Among the northern peoples, however, at least the Pawnee felt such an influence, and gave to it mythic form. These Indians, probably of southern origin, associate both the creation and the end of the world with the stars. Their creation myth is dramatic and splendid, with the Council of the Stars as its key, and their eschatological myth is based upon a close observation of the heavens—to which was devoted the society of the Raristesharu, men who sat in a circle after the image of Corona Borealis and in their conduct aimed to imitate the dignity and beauty of the stars. In the Northern Heavens, they say, about the Star-that-Never-Moves four Doctors bear the litter of the Sick-Man-of-the-North, while three Doctors follow it singing (image of Ursa Major). But in the Southern Heavens there is the Spirit Star which rises and sets. As time progresses its rising is higher and higher in the skies, and on that day when it shall rise to the Zenith, the Sick-Man-of-the-North will perish, and his soul together with the souls of all living beings will hasten over the Pathway of Souls (the Galaxy) from North to South, following the trail of the spirits of the generations of the dead who have taken this trail before them; thereafter, life will be no more. . . . This is the philosophy of an invalid world moving to its doom, and it at once calls to mind the not dissimilar beliefs of the pessimistic and world-weary sages of the declining nations of the South. But in one particular it is deeply of the North: for from the forests of Atlantic regions to the arid plateaux of the Far West almost universal was the Indian conviction that the Milky Way is the Pathway of Souls, patterned by the myriad footfalls of spirit beings and leading into the Beyond. Death has its origin but also its meaning, and for the Indian, as for other races of mankind, this meaning was not exhausted by the physical manifestation: its secret is deep in the fibre of the world and is interbound in the fabric of all things.

II

To be sure, not by all Indian peoples was the pathway of souls conceived as following the *celestial way* that leads athwart the heavens; rather, for many of the red men death meant a descent *ad infernos,* via the Way Perilous whose gates are granite and the clang of whose closing is the last echo of mortality. When among the Aztecs a mortal died the "straw death," before the corpse the priest uttered these words: [4] "Our son, thou art finished with the sufferings and fatigues of this life. It hath pleased our Lord to take thee hence, for thou hast not eternal life in this world: our existence is as a ray of the sun. He hath given thee the grace of knowing us and of associating in our common life. Now the god Mictlantecutli and the goddess Mictecaciuatl [Lord and Lady of Hell] have made thee to share their abode. We shall all follow thee, for it is our destiny, and the abode is broad enough to receive the whole world. Thou wilt be heard of no longer among us. Behold, thou art gone to the domain of darkness, where there is neither light nor window. Never shalt thou come hither again, nor needst thou concern thyself for thy return, for thine absence is eternal. Thou dost leave thy children poor and orphaned, not knowing what will be their end nor how they will support the fatigues of this life. As for us, we shall not delay to go to join thee there where thou wilt be." Then upon the head of the body, like another baptism, the priest let fall a few drops of water and beside it placed a bowl of water: "Lo, the water of which in this life thou hast made use; this for thy journey." And like another Book of the Dead, in due order certain papers were laid upon the mummy-form corpse: "Lo, with this thou shalt pass the two clashing mountains. . . . With this thou shalt pass the road where the serpent awaiteth thee. . . . With this thou shalt pass the lair of the green lizard. . . . Lo, wherewith thou shalt cross the eight deserts. . . . And the eight hills. . . . And behold with what thou canst traverse the place of the winds that drive with obsidian knives." Thus the perils of the Underworld Way were to be passed, and the soul to arrive before Mictlantecutli, whence after four years he should fare onward until, by the aid of his dog, sacrificed at his grave, he should pass over the Ninefold Stream, and thence, hound with master, enter into the eternal house of the dead, Chicomemictlan, the Ninth Hell.

There are those who would see in this charting of the Perilous Way echoes of the teachings of Buddhist or even older Asiatic sages; but it is not necessary to go for its understanding beyond the simple analogies of human experience which prompt both the imagery of Greek mind and Oriental, Asian and American, everywhere yielding some strange continuation of death's journey after life's, such that death itself is but one fateful episode in a wider wayfaring. We need not turn to Asia for conceptions somewhat similar to those of the Nahua. In the mountains of southern Canada, among the Thompson River Indians, the country of the souls is held also to be in the Underworld, toward the sunset, whither the trail leads in dim twilight. Tracks of those who have gone over it, with their dogs, are there thought to be visible. The trail winds until it is cut by a shorter road used by shamans when seeking to intercept a departed soul and turn it backward into life. But beyond this the way is straight and smooth and it is painted red with ochre. Eventually it descends to a shallow stream of clear water, spanned by a slender log upon which are still to be seen the footprints of souls gone before. Beyond this lies the heap of their human possessions, here discarded, for the souls must proceed naked before their judges. There are three of these (like the three of the classical Underworld), and it is their duty to send back into life those who have not yet passed the trial of their appointed days; old men and venerable they are, and at times to the living they send back messages borne by returning souls—as Er, the son of Arminius brought back his Platonic message, or as Dante, in another age, returned with his vision of the three-fold depth and height of destined things. Finally, say the Thompson River people, at the end of the fire-bound trail is a great lodge, with doors at the eastern and western ends. When a spirit is expected, the souls of his friends gather to welcome him, so that when he reaches the entrance he hears within the sound of drums and the people laughing and singing. Some stand at the door to welcome him, and before him opens out a wide and beautiful country, sweet with the smell of flowers, abundant with grasses and berry-laden bushes. The air is still and pleasant and it is always warm and light in that land. His friends are delighted to greet the new-comer; they take him up on their shoulders and joyously dance about with him on their shoulders.[5] In this Elysian delight there is, to be sure, no echo of the sombre Aztecan termination of the journey, but it does not essentially differ from Pueblo beliefs—remotely of an identical stream of thought—that give rise to tales of the great Underworld Dancing Lodge of the Dead, whence the sound of the drumming and singing from time to time arises to the ears of those gifted with the power of hearing spirit voices.

In this Elysian form the dancings of the festal dead, whether in cavernous Underworlds or among the star-spirits on the floors of Heaven, share nothing with the *danse macabre* of European lore. But there are parallels to this latter conception also. They turn upon elementary duplicity of life and death as one in substance, such that each is, as it were, a mode of seeing one common reality, though myopic to the other's perception. From the Arctic North southward there recur, in legend, tales of beings which from before are men like other men, but seen from behind are flesh-denuded skeletons; and it is perhaps these Skeleton Men that most essentially image the Indian's dual and puzzled comprehension of a life which is neither wholly fleshed nor wholly spiritual. The two, physical being and spiritual, are united, but not inevitably. The securest of their ties, if we may trust their tales, is love, which, if primarily physical, is still some-how against nature and doomed to disaster. A young man falls in love with a star, which descends to him in the ravishing form of a maiden by whom he is lured into the star-lands above; but there he discovers the dead dancing as skeletons, and although in horror he escapes back to earth, the maiden calls after him, "You run away in vain; you shall soon return." [6] This is a grim South American version. In the northern continent there are stories, similar but more refined in motive, telling of a bereaved and despairing lover, youth or maid, who, while still in the flesh follows the dead beloved into the other world; there the living and the dead are joyously reunited, amid the rejoicings of an otherworld village; but on the ghastly morrow the lover awakens to find a skeleton arm clasping her mortal body.

With less of horror and far more of pathos are the tales which adorn most Indian mythologies of Orphean heroes who pass the ordeals and penetrate the land of the dead to bring back into a fugitive mortality the beloved spirit. The most beautiful of these is a Pawnee tale recorded in several versions.[7] A young man joined a war-party in order to win ponies as a bridal fee for the girl of his desire. During his absence the girl died and was buried. Learning of this upon his return with the successful party, he departed to the spot where the grave was—for the tribe had meantime followed the buffalo—and there he remained weeping. But he saw smoke arising from one of the lodges of the deserted village, and looking within, he beheld his beloved seated upon the blankets with which she had been buried. The spiritmaiden said: "You have been standing there a long time. Come into the lodge, but do not come near me. Sit down near the entrance." Night after night he returned, each time coming a little nearer to the girl, but never being allowed to touch her. Finally he saw himself surrounded by a dancing group of the girl's dead relatives—first their feet, then their limbs, then their bodies showing successively. Their leader said: "Young man, when you first started from the village where your people are you began to cry. We knew what you were crying about. You were poor in spirit because this girl had died. All of us agreed that we would send the girl back. You can see her now, but she is not real. You must be careful and not make her angry or you will lose her. You have been a brave man to stay with the girl when we came in, but this is the way we are. You cannot see us, but sometimes we can turn into people and you can see us, though we are not real. We are spirits. There is one thing you must do before the girl can stay with you. We have smoked." The feat demanded was that when her mortal kinsfolk returned and approached her grave with meat-offerings he must be able to seize and hold her in their presence. Thrice he was thrown, but the fourth time, with the aid of her uncles, he succeeded in holding her and she became his wife. Only the young man's mother remained suspicious; the old woman went to the grave and dug until she found the bones, but when she returned, the bride said to her: "Mother, I know what you have done. You do not believe that I am your daughter; but, mother, I am your daughter. My body lies up there, but I am here with you. I am not real, and if you people do not always treat me properly I will suddenly disappear." In due time she gave birth to a son, but the child was never allowed to touch the ground and the mother never made moccasins for her husband. Eventually, although warned by his spirit bride against it, the husband took a second wife. A quarrel arose. She said: "Do not strike me any more, for you know what I told you. For one thing I am glad, and that is I have a child. If I had remained in the spirit world I should never have been allowed to have a child. The child is mine. You do not love my child. . . . I love my child. When I am gone I shall take my child with me." The mother then disappeared in a whirlwind; the child lay dead; the man, too, died of grief and remorse. But the people buried him apart from the ghost-wife's grave. . . . The tale is stark and simple, but back of it lies the eternal theme of a love which cannot be defeated by death, of a life that cannot be sustained without love.

III

IT IS LITTLE wonder that with such vivid conceptions of the pathways of life and death certain of the Indians should have incorporated into their ceremonials Mysteries of the Way which, like those of the ancient classical world, taught to their initiates the meaning of the soul's journeyings, endowing them with power better to understand life's perplexities and more securely to meet its perils. Such mysteries, like the Orphic and Osirian of old, are in effect religions, and are regarded as such by their adherents. Two of these, the Big House ceremony of the Delaware tribe and the Midé wiwin of the Chippewa and related central Algonquian tribes, appear to be clearly of an origin preceding any contact with white man and to arise from a fund of thought anterior to any wide separation of the Algonquian peoples. Both of these have developed a ceremonial lodge and a ritual action which images the pathway of life and its otherworld continuation; both inculcate ideals of living essentially religious in inspiration; and both rest their appeal upon beliefs in a Creator-God who is actively the friend and helper of mankind. Life after death is, likewise for each, subject to moral measures and judgments.

The Big House ceremony, or doctrine of the Beautiful White Path, has been studied by M. R. Harrington, primarily from the ritual and social, and by Frank G. Speck, from the religious point of view.[8] At the core of its expression stands the symbolism of the Big House itself, the lodge or religious house in which the chief of its rites, the twelve-day ceremony, takes place. Writes Dr. Speck: [9]

The Big House stands for the Universe; its floor, the earth; its four walls, the four quarters; its vault, the sky dome, atop which resides the Creator in his indefinable supremacy. To use Delaware expressions, the Big House being the universe, the center post is the staff of the Great Spirit with its foot upon the earth, its pinnacle reaching to the hand of the Supreme Deity. The floor of the Big House is the flatness of the earth upon which sit the three grouped divisions of mankind, the human social groupings in their appropriate places; the eastern door is the point of sunrise where the day begins and at the same time the symbol of the beginnings of things; the western door the point of sunset and symbol of termination; the north and south walls assume the meaning of respective horizons; the roof of the temple is the visible sky vault. The ground beneath the Big House is the realm of the underworld while above the roof lie the extended planes or levels, twelve in number, stretched upward to the abode of the "Great Spirit, even the Creator," as Delaware form puts it. Here we might speak of the carved face images, . . . the representations on the center pole being the visible symbols of the Supreme Power, those on the upright posts, three on the north wall and three on the south wall, the manitu of these respective zones; those on the eastern and western door posts, those of the east and west. . . . But the most engrossing allegory of all stands forth in the concept of the

White Path, the symbol of the transit of life, which is met with in the oval, hard-trodden dancing path outlined on the floor of the Big House, from the east door passing to the right down the north side past the second fire to the west door and doubling back on the south side of the edifice around the eastern fire to its beginning. This is the path of life down which man wends his way to the western door where all ends. Its correspondent exists, I assume, in the Milky Way, where the passage of the soul after death continues in the spirit realm. As the dancers in the Big House ceremony wend their stately passage following the course of the White Path they "push something along," meaning existence, with their rhythmic tread. Not only the passage of life, but the journey of the soul after death is symbolically figured in the ceremony.

According to Delaware legend the rites of the Big House originated "long ago in the beginning" at a period of the quaking of the earth, when "the earth lay gaping open" and "dust and smoke were seen," allegedly the breath of the Evil Spirit. "Even the animals were so terrified, it is said, that those animals prayed." And among men certain ones arose saying, "This, behold, is my dream, and I can thus explain it and sing it in every way just as I saw it." And it was in the visions of these dreamers that the form of the lodge and of the rites to be observed were imparted. "And now this Big House when first built, they say of it, was the one great prayer-creed, that this carved post in the middle of the House, standing there reaches to the above through as many as ten and two strata. And the strata of sky light are as high as that post, it is said, this being the fastener. That is the Creator's staff. From that very staff branch off all prayer-creeds of the red-people given to them, whence come all other prayer-creeds of the world." [10]

The ceremony itself opened with the preparation of a sweathouse, into which the shamans entered. Oddly enough, the sweatbath was made a test of endurance rather than a simple healing, those able to endure its heat for any length of time being esteemed great men, and endowed with medicine power.[11] Thereafter followed twelve days of ceremonial, the features of which comprised the sending forth of hunters in quest of "pure" meat, the sharing of "pure" food after the manner of a communion, the daily singing and dancing of the course of the White Path, and also the narrations by the worshipers of the coming of their spiritual helpers, their tutelary manitos at times of fast or trial. Moral and spiritual instruction was also given by the elders conducting the ceremony, and at some time during its course was delivered an account of the journey of the soul after death. Vision of this came to Chief Elkhair in his earlier life, when he beheld a monstrous bird upon a mountain and was led toward this by a spirit that conducted him as far as the soul of the living could go. The path over which he passed was a crooked, hard road, always uphill, until he reached a crossroad, beyond which, he was told, none but the man who had led a righteous life could proceed; the unrighteous are here turned aside and wander away to unhappy fates. Of this crossroad the cross is symbol, and it is engraved upon the ceremonial drumsticks and used until the ninth night, when the ritual takes on an exclusive meaning and the sticks are decorated with maskforms representing the spiritual powers of salvation. Beyond the crossroad the spirit moves to the mountain where resides the great bird, and beyond this to the abode of the Thunders, and seen there is a second tier of mountains where the souls of the departed rest until the end of the world, when all shall pass the final gap and ascend to the highest place of all, where the Great Spirit sits, and where there is no illness or affliction. Chief Elkhair was permitted to ascend only to the heaven of the Thunders, for none but those disembodied by death could mount further; but from this height he could hear the joyous voices of the departed, awaiting their last ascent into the presence of the Supreme Spirit and the heaven which is called Delaware-where-he-goes.[12]

On the morning of the thirteenth day the worshipers assemble for a last dance around the sacred pole which symbolizes the staff wherewith the Creator guides his creation. For a last time the tortoise-shell rattles, emblems of the sustaining and life-producing earth, are shaken, and the final instructions and prayer are uttered by the leader: "My kindred, there remains one more matter, something I want to say for you to bear well in mind.

It is said traditionally, when anyone on Good meditates in his heart, there is formed the thought. And when he thinks of good it is easy to behave well, but when he misbehaves it is the Evil that a person seriously thinks about as concerns his life. It is exceedingly hard because it is necessary that we prepare the soul-spirit in order that we shall be able to take it back home again to where it belongs, to Our Father, when its use is finished here where we live. Here in this place it is the body that shall remain . . . because here is where it belongs in the ground. . . . At last we are ready to end this Our Father's service. And, my kindred, now from hence as we are going home, you must take good care, for you are carrying with you the spirit of Delaware worship. From now on for one year at least, we shall enjoy benefit from all the spirit-forces given us, those on top of the earth and those up above as they were created to have mercy upon us, and besides from him Our Father, the Great Spirit, even Our Creator." [13]

It is easy to find in this ritual of the White Path and its utterances Christian influences and teachings, especially since it is known that for more than two centuries the Delaware have listened to Christian missionaries. But it is also known that the ceremony was being celebrated in some form when the first Christian missionaries came to the tribes, and in addition that these people are peculiarly tenacious of their native tradition, which, in the *Walum Olam*,[14] reaches far back of the white man's coming. And it is certain that among Indian rituals this is only one of many in which what to us are Christian symbols and Christian thoughts are intimately, and to appearance agelessly, interwoven with native imagery and impulse. Far more than any local event, it is a universal human aspiration which the ceremony expresses and perpetuates.

IV

Strikingly analogous to the Big House Ceremony of the Delaware is the Great Medicine Lodge of the tribes dwelling about the western Great Lakes and in the northern Mississippi regions, tribes of Algonquian and Siouan stocks. With little question it is with the former, the Algonquian peoples, that the ritual takes its origin, and tradition points to the Chippewa if not as its remote instigators at least as its earliest transmitters. The rites are largely known by the Chippewa name *Midé wiwin,* meaning the Midé Society, which is a secret organization with ritual initiations, esoteric teachings, and a series of "lodges" or degrees. The latter vary in number among the different peoples who have accepted the Midé religion (for such it is), but the typical and apparently original division is into four degrees.[15]

What the Delaware religion and the Midé wiwin have in common is the belief that their central ceremonies are a direct revelation from the Great Spirit given to a blinded and afflicted humankind in order to lift men into a more suitable and spiritually understanding life. This is done in each case by the institution of a ritual which is emblematic of the pathway of life and of its after-death continuation. Again in each case, the ceremony is regarded as imparting to its participants powers and blessings not shared by others, while moral obligations meant to distinguish the mode of living of members or initiates are in both religions ritually enjoined. There are also similarities of ceremonial emblems and ritual acts which, while shared by many Indian groups in their ceremonial observances, nonetheless seem here to argue for a common conceptual source remote in Algonquian history.

Of the two, the Midé wiwin appears definitely the more archaic, as issuing from a more primitive level of thought, even if its ritual forms show the greater elaboration. It is associated with a body of myth of indubitable antiquity; the element of magic is noticeable; and the Midé rites are notably dramatic, in this respect contrasting strongly with the Quakerlike experientialism and individualism of the Big House meetings. Of the ritual elements which distinguish the Midé wiwin outstanding are the "shooting" and resurrection of the initiate, a veritable anastasis emblematic of birth into a new life. This rite is the core of the Midé initiation, and it is directly dependent upon the essential myth which recounts the descent from heaven of the divine Son, here born of a mortal woman, narrates his Passion and his conflict with the Lords of Hell, and tells of the institution of his Salvation for mankind. The outline is strangely Christian, but the substance is ancient and native.

The Midé wiwin ceremonial of initiation takes place whenever one or more candidates present themselves to a priestly leader as desirous of sharing the benefits of the society and as able to fulfill its obligations. The candidate's first task is to assemble the necessary fees and gifts. Thereafter he is placed under an assigned mentor and a period of instruction ensues, during which he learns little by little the meaning of the ritual, its songs, and the uses and efficacies of certain plants. This period also requires frequent resort to a small sweat-lodge near the site selected for the ceremonial lodge, and it is here that the candidate receives his instruction and undergoes purification; he is likewise expected to compose certain songs which are to find place in the ceremony itself. "When entering the society you will observe, as you are in the sweat-bath, that water is poured on the stones. This is a purification to take away your worldly life and make you a new creature. . . . The rock which is used in the sweat-bath is your Grandfather; it is one of the first things in the world to be created, and it possesses this song, which must be sung for it: 'But it is I who am so mysterious.' " [16] This is a portion of the instruction in the Wahpeton form of the rite, giving succinctly the conception of a new birth which underlies the ceremony.

The Midé wigan,[17] or ceremonial lodge, is a temporary rectangular shelter, having approximately the proportions of one to four, with an entrance door facing the east at one end, and an opposite door westward. For the fourth degree there are likewise openings to the north and the south, in the center of the sides. Fires may be built near the ends of the enclosed rectangle, while within it are placed, eastward, a sacred stone and, westward, a pole cut from a living tree and symbolically painted; the pole symbolizes the candidate himself and is known as his medicine pole, while the stone is emblematic of the Midé as a defense, and perhaps also of that Center of the World where the rite was first given to man. Between these two objects is a blanket, where the central act is to be performed, while above is a lengthened, suspended pole, from which are to be hung the gifts made by the candidate, and which typifies the added length of life which the ceremony is to bring him. The lodge is a simple modification of the "long house" of the Eastern Indians, but in every detail it is emblematic, and to the initiate it is peopled and surrounded by spirit beings. Thus, before the eastern entrance are demonic guardians, whose evil can be averted only by Midé power—according to the degree, serpent-beings, bear-beings, panther-beings, witches—and perched upon the summit of the candidate's pole there is the owl-being that guides, into the Land of the Setting Sun, the land of the dead. In the second and the third and fourth degrees the number of the poles is increased to two and three and four, but on one of these is always perched the owl, Ko-ko-ko-o, westward guiding. The last of the poles to be erected, in the fourth degree, has the form of a Roman cross; it rises above and westward of the symbolic stone and is painted on squared faces with the colors of Earth's quarters, while the upper trunk and the arms are white with red spots representing the medicine strength acquired by the candidate during his journey. It was such a cross that brought joy to the heart of Father Marquette when he arrived at what is now Green Bay, Wisconsin.

On the day of the initiation there is a preliminary rite at the sweat-house, with smoke-offerings, songs for a "blue day," and an interesting discourse setting forth the meaning of the ceremony about to be undertaken: "Now is the time he hears us all, he who made the Midé wiwin. Listen to what I am about to say: If you give heed to it your life shall continue always. Today I make known to you the Great Spirit, that which he says: that he loves you. White shall be the sacred object at the time when they shall let it be known, and this I say unto you as now saith the Great Spirit: Even if they say that they saw him dead, in this place he shall be raised again, in this place shall he put his trust. For the time of the duration of the world it shall never fail. That is what he says, the Great Spirit. My child, this shall give you life." [18] Thereafter occurs the processional, first around the outside and afterward making a circuit, four times, of the interior of the Lodge, there are also preliminary gift-givings and songs. But central is the shooting and resurrection of the candidate. The emblems employed are the otterskin medicine bag of the Midé members and the migis, a white shell which for each initiate typifies his own participation in the mystic power conferred. The bag is pointed gun-wise at the body of the initiate and "discharged" with a violent bodily action. After the fourth shooting the victim falls as dead or entranced. The medicine bags are then laid upon his body, which shortly is seemingly restored to life. These acts are accompanied by suitable songs, and theoretically by the reception into the candidate's body of the *migis* shot into it. When he arises he is already a Midé, fully initiated in the mystic sense, as one raised up from dead, reborn; but there are still songs to be sung, his own among others, and instructions to be given, and a communal feast supplied by the new initiate, who in his turn receives otterskin bag and *migis* from the priests. Except for details of symbolism and changes of songs and instruction, all four degrees have similar rituals: in each the path perilous is pursued, with evils of the unseen world overcome, and in each there is central the death and resurrection of the initiate.

The teaching itself is moral as well as mythical. The Wahpeton even make a decalogue of commandments to govern the conduct of their members, and while most of these relate to ritual observances, others lie at the foundation of moral law. Such are: "Respect your lodge; no quarreling may be done there. Whenever visitors come, you must respect them and welcome them." "Love your neighbors." "You must get up a feast for the relatives of deceased brothers and sisters of the lodge, and comfort them." "The members of the *Wakanwacipi* [Siouan name for the society] are as one and should regard each other equal." "All members are supposed to keep these rules and not tell them to non-members. They must not lie about their neighbors. They must not fornicate. They must be kind to all mankind." [19] In a similar vein is the Midé song: [20]

> Do not speak ill of the Midé,
> My Midé brethren,
> Wherever you may be;
> Do not speak ill of a woman,
> My Midé brethren.

But the inmost genius of the organization lies in another and a more truly mystic understanding:

> We may live by it always,
> My Midé brethren;
> It is spiritual,
> The inspiration we receive.

Simplest and most telling of all is a song which in the Chippewa tongue has but three words: "Beautiful as a star hanging in the sky is our Midé lodge!"

Like other Indian ceremonies the Midé ritual is the symbolical exegesis of a myth, which must be known in order that its fuller meaning may become apparent. This myth is an ancient one of the Algonquian peoples. It tells how the Uncreated Spirit, supreme over all, looked down from the uppermost of the four heavens and beheld upon earth the feeble and afflicted tribes of men. So he summoned a council of the Manitos of the four quarters of creation, and it was there decided that the Manito of the East should descend to men to help them. So he allowed himself to be born of a childless woman, and to become a man among men. This, by some of the Chippewa,[21] is said to have taken place on Madeline Island, in Lake Superior. The child grew, and as he grew, in many ways he showed magical powers and seemed of unusual fortune. It was at a certain time (still his boyhood according to several versions) that news came of the death of his beloved companion (cousin or brother), while he and his earthly father were upon the mainland. A storm seemed to prohibit approach to the island, but the son commanded that the canoe be placed upon the water, and this done, at once the waves subsided. When they arrived the companion had been four days dead, but the East Manito commanded the people not to weep for the youth, and he instructed them as to the build-

ing of the long lodge, such as is now used in the Midé ceremony.
Beside the pole (symbol of the initiate) he ordered placed the
coffin of the dead. Then he told his father to take the Midé drum
and sing. "I do not know how to sing," the old man said. But
the son replied, "Make the effort and you will be able to sing."
After that the East Manito departed for four days, and the days
of his absence were cloudless and there was no wind. The old
man drummed and sang, the songs coming to him one after the
other, for he was spiritually directed by his son even during the
latter's absence. A little before noon of the fourth day the four
Manitos of the Quarters, in the guise of Indians, descended
from the skies carrying otterskin medicine bags; and these, one
after the other, shot the body of the dead youth, until at the end
he arose, a living man.

Then these four manidó * began to talk to the Indians, and to tell
them that this was the method by which they were to treat the sick
and the dead, and that the East manidó would instruct them in all
they were to do. Then these manidó told the Indians they would
never see them again. The manidó would never come to earth again,
but the Indians must offer them gifts and sacrifices, which would be
spiritually received. They must always remember that the Midé was
given to them by the manidó. The East manidó taught them the
religion of the Midé and put souls in their bodies and arranged how
these souls should live in the next world. A great many times some of
these Midé people have a trance in which they follow the spirit path
and see their dead friends. They also receive messages in dreams. They
are especially liable to do this when sorrowing for their friends. It is
told to Midé mmbers that about half way to the Spirit Land there is
a punishment place where fire burns out all the evil that is in them.
Sometimes there is so little left of the person that he turns into a frog.
There are many little frogs in that place, but the good pass through
it unharmed. . . . Those initiated into the Midé are instructed how to
lead a good life.

If plausibly there are echoes of missionary teachings in
this native account of the Indian revelation, such influences
have certainly not inspired the myth itself. The East Manito is

* Miss Densmore's narrative uses spelling "manidó."

none other than the great Algonquian demiurge Manabozho, the White Hare, and also, it would appear, the White Light of Morning.[22] The cycles of his mythic labors have many variants, widespread through far-cast tribes, but always central is a typical tale. The Heaven Spirit above, looking down upon creation and finding it sorry, sends his son, the Light of the East, as his delegate to shape more happily the affairs of the world and of the men; Manabozho is born from a childless woman; he grows into a miraculous youth; he has for his beloved companion one who is sometimes represented as a kinsman ("brother" at least in spirit) and oftener and more aboriginally as a carnivorous animal, usually the wolf; this "brother," while hunting, is seized and drowned by the underworld monsters, the jealous and malignant gods below. Thereafter follows the mourning of Manabozho and the period of his grieving. So terrible is this that all nature, above and below, is disorganized and terrified, and the gods of the two regions send emissaries to the sorrowing demiurge seeking to appease his passion. The otter induces him to attend where the deities have erected a medicine lodge (the roof of which is the blue sky) and there Manabozho is initiated into the heavenly Midé, the songs and rites of which he brings to earth for the salvation of men. It is a ritual of healing and of life, but it withholds one gift, that of immortality upon earth, for even the gods cannot wholly conquer death. However, in another form, that of a soul or shade, the brother of Manabozho is allowed to revisit him, and from Manabozho he receives instructions as to the marking out of the path into the Lands Beyond and the erection there of the Dancing Lodge of the Dead.

There is no more affecting Indian narrative than the story of Manabozho's encounter with the shade of his brother, as recorded by Alanson Skinner from a Menomini version,[23] and recounted in connection with the memorial ceremony held for a dead member of the lodge. The instruction opens with a smoke-offering directed to the "Younger Brother of Manabus [Manabozho] gone to the west," and to the spirits of the dead who have gone to join him. The story of the encounter follows:

Manabus said, when he at last realized that his brother was dead, "I shall now wait four days to see if my brother will return." On the night of the fourth he said to himself as he lay down to rest, "Now is the time that he ought to come to me." When Manabus was almost dozing off, he began to feel and know that his brother Naxpatao [Little Wolf] was approaching. . . . So he looked and waited, but he saw only the shade of Naxpatao, like a shadow cast by the moonlight. Manabus sat up to look more closely, and when he saw his little brother's nature was changed, he arose and cried out to the shade, which was outside a little way, "Stop where you are!" Then Manabus cried: "Alas, little brother, I had supposed you had gone only for a short time, and would return to me in a natural way; I had thought that those Powers might have wanted to keep you only a little while and then let you return. But now you are disgusting to my sight, and therefore have turned my mind so I shall not let you enter my lodge in your present condition. Now, my little brother, I have decided what I shall do. Little brother, you will have to continue on your journey. Follow the sun's course to the west, where it sets, and go on a little farther; a little bit to the north of that place where the sun goes down shall be your abode."

Then Naxpatao answered Manabus and said: "Oh, alas, this is too bad, that you are now doing, by ordering me to continue my journey to that place! It will hurt our uncles and aunts in the future. The better way would have been, when our parents were missing or lost, to allow them to return to life on the fourth day, just as I have done."

Then Manabus said to his little brother, "No, it is my earnest intention to do as I have ordered you. I have planned it that way and I cannot change it. It would not be good to do as you say, for the benefit of our parents to come, and, moreover, the gods, the four gods under us, those nearest the surface, they have planned it this way with their terrible power. They have done this to you and to me, and have made it so. It cannot be bettered because they have conquered us from the very beginning; and I tell you this, my little brother, because the day has already passed with me that you were lost and I missed you. I looked for you the next day and lamented and wept and inquired for you all over the whole world, and in so doing I showed my grief so that all the great Grandfathers, the Powers that are between heaven and earth, and all the Powers beneath, have heard me in my sorrow and in my anguish, and that is why I refuse to receive you. I must have revenge upon them, and let them know that I am powerful on earth. I cannot turn back now, so I order you to take your course right on. Naxpatao, my younger brother, I might accept you, but cannot and will not, because if I do take you in your present condition, within a short time more trouble will be made for us by the same evil powers who hurt me, and I therefore insist on making an end of it. Moreover, if you are accepted in your shade it will be dreadful for your parents to return that way in the future, so keep on your way, Naxpatao."

Naxpatao replied: "You have told me all that you want me to do and made me understand it, so I now choose to obey you in every particular; but you must instruct me further how to proceed to this place, since you have power and must know all the things that I have to do. I bow to your will. It is good."

Manabus answered: "Well done, my dear little brother. Now I shall provide for you. You shall have our fire from earth." Manabus took a brand from the fire and handed it out to Naxpatao. "Here, I give you this to take along with you. . . . Make no mistake, because if you do it will be of great harm to our parents in the future, as they will suffer and derive no benefit; but if you accomplish all that I say it shall be good for them. This is what it is: As you have determined to go where I have ordered, you shall clear their road for them, and make good the path that they shall have to follow in the future."

Then said Manabus to Naxpatao: "As you are now about ready to take your departure, my little brother, I order you to make a visible open path. Make four plain spaces that can be seen." And surely enough there were already marked on the clear white sands four tracks where Naxpatao started. Manabus added: "After you make those four spaces, arrange it so that the trail will be good and cannot be missed. At intervals cause beautiful flowers to spring up and mark the road. This I ask you, so that our future parents may easily trace you and see the open road, and also that the babies may be lured on and kept in the path by the sight of the pretty blossoms, until they reach the goal that they are headed for. If you do this at my order it shall be well done, and will redound to the benefit of our relatives."

The myth narrative proceeds, telling how Manabozho visits the world beyond, finding the trail well-marked and adorned with flowers, as he had commanded, and how he arrives at the great lodge erected by Naxpatao for the souls of the dead. There he delivers his final instructions:

"Also take note of all this and be very careful. Our parents will keep coming, and especially the little innocent ones; when they die on the earth, you will note it, and see it from here; and our relatives inside the lodge, who have long ago been alive, must be told that there is one yonder on its way here, and because it is of their blood, kind, and people, and comes from where they too lived once, they must go out and meet it on the way, and shake hands with it and kiss it, to show their joy at the meeting. Another thing that you must do," Manabus added, "that I order you to do when those parents of ours come here, you too must meet them at the door. You must give them a fresh drink of your medicine, to revive, purify, and purge them. This will take away their earthly knowledge and give them new and heavenly understanding which is not quite as full and strong as theirs, yet of a different nature from what they had before. Moreover, be very careful to note that all those who come here are received and used well and cared for, for here you are the chief, who is supposed to have charge over them, and I, yonder where I am, I will care for the living ones. They shall direct prayers to you, knowing that you are here, and you shall have the power to know and hear them. Always have mercy on them and carry out what is desired of you. This I tell you to observe without fail. For my part, I shall be opposite in the east, and I shall care for the living ones of the earth. They shall petition me and ask me favors, and when they mention me, I shall never refuse them. I will do my part well, and you do yours, for those who desire it. Now, my little brother, observe these things that I came to tell you. Care for those who have once lived on earth, who afterward left their bodies and came to you in their shades, and this shall continue as long as the world and its people shall exist."

V

SUCH IS THE MYSTERY of Manabozho and its myth, whence is derived the religion of the Midé wiwin and its related societies. Early investigators were so struck with the likenesses of its lodge and degree organization and its moral code to those of the Society of Free Masons that they deemed that it might be a red man's imitation of the Masonic order. But its real analogies are to other and far more ancient societies, for in those Mysteries of the Path which in antique days taught their initiates the songs and chants which should safeguard their journey through life and into the Beyond, the Indian rites and faiths find their truest counterpart. In all of them the essential pattern includes, first, the advent and incarnation of a Son of Heaven, who comes as the guide and helper of mankind; second, the story of his conflict with the Powers of the Underworld; third, the wresting therefrom of a Salvation which is typified in the mystery of a death and resurrection; and lastly, the establishment of a teaching, moral and spiritual, which is the Doctrine of the Way. The Mystery of Isis and Osiris was of this character—early a rival of Christianity—and the mysteries of the Oriental corn cults; but of them all, most in harmony with the Indian were the Mysteries of Orpheus, lost to us in detail but in their general character discernible from the fragmentary allusions to them handed on from ancient times.[24]

Orpheus was a prophet and a singer, a magical musician who by the sweetness of his harmony tamed whatever was wild and monstrous in nature or in man's breast. He was also a teacher and the founder, mythical or real, of a religion which seems to have grown from mystic ceremonials which he inaugurated, in Thrace it is supposed, some time in the sixth century B.C. Of the teaching it is known that at its core was a cosmogony, telling how the world sprang forth from the union of heaven and earth in a kind of nuptial chaos, whence born first of all was Love, to give order to creation. Like Manabozho he is a heaven-coursing boy or youth, for on the vases he is shown as the winged Eros; and like Manabozho, one would guess, he is mortally incarnated, as the magical musician whose song should soothe and civilize the anarchy of the natal ages. But enemies arise, the untaught Titans and the leaderless passions of men, and these destroy the singer—except only his song, which floats deathless—until from the very anguish of creation he is restored to life, now as a spirit-guide, and as one who has formerly persuaded Hades himself in behalf of Love. Certainly in the Orphic Mysteries, as in the

Mysteries of Isis and Osiris, the central act of the drama was the symbolic death of the hero, attacked and torn by underworld monsters, and thereafter his resurrection to a newer life in which he is teacher and guide not only for the ways of mortal life but yet more for the paths that lead into the beyond. Already in Plato's day the Orphics were proclaiming the destinies of the dead, how festal joys awaited the souls of the pure initiate, while for base men frightful dooms were prepared; and two centuries after Plato, in the Greek colonial towns of Italy, the Orphic dead were being interred with golden tablets upon which were inscribed the songs and avowals which their souls should chant as they encountered the perils of the Path and came before the lords and judges of the Dead. There is pride and devotion expressed in these gold-inscribed hymns, and a triumph and joy of spirit, as of those who had drawn from death its sting.

Manabozho, like Orpheus, is a magical teacher and a song-giver, and the coming of Manabozho, too, is as a descent of divinity out of creative skies, to lift men from savagery and to reveal to them the ways of clean walking through life and the rites of purity. In the Mystery of Manabozho, no less than in the Orphic, the central episode is the symbolic death and new birth of the initiate, and the teaching is the teaching of the Songs of the Way, the path of life that leads beyond the terminations of mortality. In the myth, Manabozho like Orpheus carries on a struggle with the daemonic and Titanic powers of an untaught nature; both heroes suffer and know grief, and out of the anguish of each issues a fresh revelation which shall be for men's helping, for "our uncles and our aunts in the future," as the Indian myth phrases it. It is true that neither Orpheus nor Manabozho overcomes death utterly. The Gods of the Underworld "have conquered us from the beginning"; but if the mortality of the flesh is foredoomed, yet both the Greek and the Indian teachers lift up the hope of a more beautiful spiritual life which the faithful shall share—and which somehow shall be like a singing and a music. The plot and teaching of the two mysteries is essentially the same, and the emotional understanding for the

Midé and for the Orphic do not materially differ: each could chant—

Beautiful as a star hanging in the sky is our Midé lodge!

Indeed, it is obvious that for the religious spirit of mankind, when it has attained to a certain stature of insight, the pattern of the mystery is universal. Face to face with the elemental facts of love and death, the human spirit is touched not only with a pathetic sense of the tears of things, but is seized with a resentful consciousness of its own blindness and imperiously utters its demand for light and liberation. Animals join their flesh or encounter death with unpremeditated passion or with blank surprise; their affections, grievings and terrors are often intense, but they give no sign of thought penetrating their emotion nor of any aftermath of reflection; loves fade with their instinctive hour and bleached bones are meaningless. But with men it is different, for human love is revolted of death and decay, and pity and tears not less than dread preside over the valleys of dry bones. "My head is only a death's head, with no longer any flesh. So it is also with the head of even the greatest of princes; for it is the flesh alone that adorneth the visage: whence cometh the horror that besetteth men at the moment of death." Such is the grim and universal testament as given by the bones of Hunhun Ahpu, fruit of Death's Tree, in the tale of the Harrying of Hell in the *Popul Vuh*; [25] and it is the shudder of this horror which seizes Manabozho when in the moonlight he perceives the grisly shade of his little brother and realizes that Death is conqueror.

But against death's brutalities the outraged mind rises in rebellion. The tales of the descents *ad infernos,* not for mere oracle, as Odysseus and Aeneas, but for reaving the loved victim from the Lords of Hell, as Ishtar and Isis, as Hercules and Theseus and Orpheus in the hero cycles, as the Christ of the Book of Enoch, and as the wizard twins in the *Popul Vuh* (a version as vivid and stinging as Dante's own)—tales such as these are testimony to the fierce protest of the human spirit against death's apparent victory and love's seeming defeat. The mysteries embody a sense of this, and in a more tragic mode the far-cast cycle of the fateful tale of Orpheus and Eurydice in many forms, American and Old World, embody it. Perhaps, indeed, all tragedy is the issue of love and death, and all religion at bottom a demand that they be found conciliable.

It is thence that there arises a metaphysic, which is also an insight, and which assails the spirit of man wherever it is first awakened to a sense of its own humanity. Cardinal herein is the teaching that the world is a created and intended thing, and that its full meaning is not disclosed in the surfaces of events. Physically it is but a passing flesh, a formed and fleeting breath, a phantasm of reality. And this reality, which must be surmised more than read, is that for which the heart impulsively pleads. Deep in the creative intentions—from before the beginnings—it stirs and moves, and its action is the unfolding of time. If there be assault and terror and the dread drama of heroic strife and suffering and of loves torn by death's separations, there is also a saving descent from above of the Guide and Helper, and the trail of the White Path that leads through vision on to the flower-adorned lodge where the singing is eternal. In images this understanding takes form, for images are the renewed flesh of the world, and the one reality that can give forth its meaning without flaw.

VI

THERE IS ONE LAST FAITH of the religious imagination which, as upon other peoples, has made its impression upon the American Indian. This is the Messianic faith and the Messianic hope. Undoubtedly it reaches far back into the history of the development of the native spirit. The myth of Quetzalcoatl, the shining white god of the Nahua and their predecessors, who came to earth to bring men law and peace and prosperity, and when driven forth promised to return again once more to rule his people with righteousness, bringing joy unto their abode—this myth recurs in a score of forms and under many names, in both North and South America; and it is the type for the tales of other redeemers whose return in glory the Indian nations wistfully awaited. Quetzal-coatl's was an ancient myth, and long pre-Columbian. But prob-ably it was with accentuation, due to the fateful pressure exerted by the white man, a power beyond the Indian's valor to resist, that both the felt need for the Messiah, and the eager hope for his coming grew more and more vivid among the native peoples. It may well have been that the Aztec followers of the early Spanish invaders of New Mexico first brought thither the name of the tragic Montezuma—the last glorified monarch of the Indian peoples, whose image the passing time ever more magically en-dowed; but as the Pueblo folk themselves came to feel the heavy hand of the conqueror, they made of Montezuma their own lost leader and eventual hope, for they still tell tales of his rivalries with Christ, and they still faintly hold to the fable of his second coming, when on the wings of his eagle he will return as he as-cended, to restore once again the red man's world.

A similar motive has recurred in every century of the racial conflict which has wiped away the hunting grounds and confined the tribes to narrow and desecrated reservations; and the glamor of the hope of a deliverance and a restoration, under the guidance of one divinely instructed and led, has lifted the Indian prophets to illusory power and impelled them onward to the inevitable tragedy: the Tewa leader Popé in the seventeenth century, who raised up the Pueblo Rebellion; Pontiac in the eighteenth cen-tury, inspired by a visionary who had climbed the mountain of the Great Spirit thence to bring the message of liberation; and a generation later Tenskwatawa, who was regarded by his fol-lowers as the incarnation of Manabozho himself. Of the same tribe as Tenskwatawa, the Shawano, came Tecumseh, greatest of the Indian prophets and heroes; and later in the nineteenth century, Kanakuk, of a gentler and more spiritual type, also visited the Great Spirit, who revealed to him the pathways of destiny and promised to appear again when the people had marched forward a sufficient distance on "the straight way"—for there was a moral teaching as well as a message of hope in the utterances of these prophets. Most eloquent of all was Smohalla, who formed a new religion for the tribes of the Columbia basin in the middle of the nineteenth century and voiced the fundamental cause of all the great periods of Indian unrest:

You ask me to plow the ground! Shall I take a knife and tear my mother's bosom? Then when I die she will not take me to her bosom to rest.

You ask me to dig for stone! Shall I dig under her skin for her bones? Then when I die I can not enter her body to be born again.

You ask me to cut grass and make hay and sell it, and be rich like white men! But how dare I cut off my mother's hair?

It is a bad law and my people can not obey it. I want my people to stay with me here. All the dead men will come to life again. Their spirits will come to their bodies again. We must wait here in the homes of our fathers and be ready to meet them in the bosom of our mother.[26]

To complete the picture I would cite one final ritual which perhaps best of all images the red man's poetic philosophy. It was probably on January 1, 1889, on the occasion of an eclipse of the sun visible in the western states, that a Paiute sheepherder in Nevada beheld the great vision which made of him the Messiah of the Indian race. "When the sun died," he said,[27] "I went up to heaven and saw God and all the people who had died a long time ago. God told me to come back and tell my people they must be good and love one another, and not fight, or steal, or lie. He gave me this dance to give to my people." These were the commands. The people were to dance five days at a time, and they must wait patiently on this earth, for in a near time the old life of the Indian, as it was before the coming of the white man, would be restored. This was God's promise, and the restoration was near. The souls from beyond were already at the door. For the dead were to be restored to life; the sick and the decrepit were to be healed; the old were to be given their strength once more; the herds of the buffalo would return; game would be plentiful. The white men would disappear, drowned in a great flood which God would send to overwhelm them.

The dance, which came to be called the Ghost Dance, spread

rapidly from tribe to tribe over nearly half of the native West. The rite was not simply a dance, although this was its notable feature. For the dancers themselves, as in the Sun Dance, were in quest of visions. They danced until the dancers fell in trances, wherein their souls beheld their dead relatives returning and saw the vast herds of the buffalo issuing from the spirit past to become once more the cattle of the red man. Songs[28] innumerable were composed to celebrate the event, and the singing dancers were filled with fervor and excitement—

> The snow lies here—*ro'rani!*
> The snow lies here—*ro'rani!*
> The Pathway of Souls lies there!

The idea is the contrast between the trails of men in the snow here on earth and the trails of spirit moccasins returning down the Galaxy to rejoin those below. In other songs the dancer impersonates the returning dead:

> I circle around,
> I circle around
> The boundaries of the earth,
> Wearing the long wing-feathers as I fly!

This is the Song of the Whirlwind, "Father Whirlwind," within which the spirit is conceived to be snatched up. Most beautiful and pathetic of all is the Arapaho song which has been described as the Indian's "Lord's Prayer," voicing as it does his spiritual hunger:

> Father, have pity upon me!
> Father, have pity upon me!
> I am crying for thirst;
> There is nothing here to satisfy me!

In 1890 the dance reached the Sioux. It was then only a few years since peace had been made with this warlike tribe. When they began to dance with fervor, the settlers became alarmed; the Indians became difficult to control. In the autumn troops were called out to hold the Indians to their reservation. It was at the end of the year, amid snows, that the conflict at Wounded Knee took place, needless, with misunderstanding, and cruel. It was the last act in the tragedy of the encounter of the races, and it bloodily marked the setting of the Indian's sun. Mainly it was Indians who were killed. Many of the dead wore "ghost shirts" which marked them as followers of Wovoka. The medicine men had assured them that these were impervious to bullets. "Take it off," said one wounded woman, "take it off. They told me it would ward away bullets. I do not want it any more." And with the removal of the ceremonial shirt went the Indian faith, and hope of return of the old life was laid aside forever.

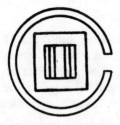

Epilogue

WHETHER with a conscious anxiety for some truth that can be made objective in statement, as with Europeans since Grecian times, or whether intuitively issuing into symbolic expression and mythic and ritual utterance, every group of mankind which has at all matured in its humanity has developed from its experience of the world some philosophy of life that determines its understanding and fashions the moral sense by which it lives. Its experiences are, in a sense, its instruction by nature, much as we regard the instinctive conduct of animals to be directed to some end of living and continuing for as long as nature may tolerate or for its own balance require the animal kind. The differences between a merely instinctive animal existence and the reflective life of human beings is from this angle not vast: among men the instruction is no less profoundly nature's own, but it takes the form of a conscious experience within which the reflective powers stir as inevitably as do the passions and appetites of animals, and they should be nature's revelation of herself, as genuinely as can any instinctive mode. In other words, human thinking is a truth-giving window into the world's reality. It is not an exclusive revelation, any more than animal hunger or procreation are exclusive in nature's operations, and there is no sound reason why we should regard its powers as adequate to any final appraisal of the world, or the forms of our reason as holding any inevitable hegemony over the illuminations of intuition. For human experience in all its forms cannot give us a last word upon creation. Nevertheless, it can and does give us some word; and by our own life's measures, it gives us philosophies which fulfill in their degree our deeply vital need of a mind's guidance, expressing such elements of nature's verity, of the world's reality, as our own human bodies and minds and societies are framed to understand. Truth *is* revealed in human thinking, and if this is often in clouded shapes, yet it is not apart from essential reality.

It is with such prepossession that American Indian thinking has here been examined in certain of its aspects. The interest lies not in the fact that America had bred a race distinct (for this race is not in any radical sense unique), but rather in the fact that this land, has held apart, in relative seclusion, bodies of human beings who, on the whole, had developed without contacts with other races. For some thousands of years nature had conducted, so to speak, separate schools of humanity, with comparable although differing curricula, inducing each to come to its own philosophical and religious interpretation of life; and, now that the ages of seclusion are passed, it is of no small concern to note wherein they have come to agreement in their thinking. Differences in the costume of thought we must allow for; these are no more than the uniforms of the schools, prescribed by the traditions which nature herself sets in differentiating the flora and fauna and the geographies of the continents. But if shearing these away uncovers elemental agreements, we are nearer to what is most genuine in that portion of world-being which a humanity can represent; and even in their distinctions they will add to our wealth of understanding of humanity—just as the decorative art of the red man adds to our total understanding of what art can do for man. Like art, philosophy, has grown out of each setting of human life with its own color and understanding.

And now, with the documents which have been reviewed, what are the salient features of this native American philosophy? Certain features are clear. The Indian, like any other man, conceives the physical world as a kind of projection from his own bodily life, which forms its topographical focus and dramatic center. This is what is called an anthropocentric view of the world, but it is one from which even in imagination we ourselves have not been able wholly to escape. For not from the remotest paths of light which we speculate has the ghost of an observer, a human eye, been eliminated; and human history still holds its place as somehow the center of time: the wheel of man's horizon and the wheel of man's time circumscribe his universe, and form the World's Rim, and this is the same for red man and white. But certainly the physical cannot mean for the Indian what lately it has come to mean for the Occidental of the Old World. It is not a material labyrinth in which the soul of man has been incidentally trapped, but it is rather a sense-born phantasm, as Plato held it to be. Nothing is more obvious in Indian thinking than his belief that the Powers are the Realities, and that shapes and functions of things are primarily the exercise of these powers. It is Pythagoras that the metaphysics of the Sioux suggests, and for the American as for the sages of the Ancient East the stars are fates. Nor should the glamour of myth conceal from us the fact that a world which is "held up" by the Spirits of the Quarters and the Elders of the Kinds is essentially a world of ideas, of agents, not of things. In the language of our own metaphysics, the Indian is an idealist, not a materialist. Were this false to his instinct, all his ritual symbolism would jibber into nonsense, but since it is true to it, this symbolism mounts into a poetry of cosmic understanding.

This, however, yields only the background of an understanding. Again as for us, the physical picture, be it matter or phantasm, can give only the frame of a life. To get at the *gignomenon* which lies behind the *phenomenon*, the growth that produces the appearance, it is necessary to go beyond sense to motive, beyond action to moral. In end and sum nothing else can satisfy man's reason. Indian myth universally tells of an Age of Stone Giants—huge, strong, stupid; like the earth-formed men of the Kiché myth their sight was veiled, they had no intelligence, they could not utter the name of their Creator; and this first race was destroyed, or transformed into its kindred rock. Life in a genuine and endowed form issues from another source, and it is instructive that in more than one account the living corn is the substance of man's first flesh, while his intelligence is from the breath of Heaven. Underlying the cosmogonies is almost universally the theory of an experimental creation of life, or, as we should say, an evolution. Only the Indian demands that this evolution be motivated by a moral end. There is a good which is its purpose, and that good leads beyond any mere pastime of the creators; it is serious and it is cosmically sought. Man is its immediate concern, as man sees it; but even as he sees it, there is no indifference as to the human quality; it is not merely the men who happen to be that are significant, but the men who find and display a certain character, a moral quality which to eyes more than human may justify their coming into being and their better passing. In the Indian view death is as important as life, and it is the manner of each that counts. This is the philosophy of life as ordeal; man is placed upon this earth to show his mettle; for life or death the triumph lies in its manner and quality, under the test of Creation. This is the dramatic conception of human living, turning away from its incidents to its honors—as if nature were to be glorified by the heraldries of deeds, and men's parts were the parts of the contenders. Something of the sort underlay Mithraism, in the old days, and the nobler spirit of the Crusaders. The fact that base metal is intermingled with the noble, for Old World as for New World man, does not detract from the conditions of the course, nor from the ends for which it is run.

That the sense-born world is phantasmic and that the action of the world, cosmic and human, is throughout an experiment and an ordeal, in which gods and men participate and the judgment falls to the heroic, are two of the features of the philosophy guiding the Indian's life. A third feature is his unwillingness to close his eyes with no more than this world as the visage of creation. His soul, like that of Old World men, sought its salvation. All his magic of "medicine" and his faiths in Messiahs turn to this end. That it was often blind and misguided and commingled with cruelties and bestialities is as true of him as of men of other human groups, but that it was maintained and kept glowing by a core of aspiration toward a good that is somehow nobler than its human best, is also as true of him as of other men. Centrally it was a belief in God as the only sufficiency of the human mind.

Dramatically this belief takes form in the mysteries in the

very fact that these are prayers for blessings. Spiritually it issues in the effort to define human virtues and the pattern of clean living, such that a man may examine his own life and judge it. But most profoundly it shows itself in that sense which calls for a supplementation and in some fashion a fulfillment of this world's life: for sight beyond the limitations of mortal vision and for powers beyond the weaknesses that beset us. Illumination and salvation are the words by which we most commonly express our demands for a being better than that which Nature has vouchsafed, and we look to God for their satisfaction—not, however, without a sense of responsibility or of participation on our own part. "We need your worship as you need ours," said the spirit who came to the young Indian fasting; and throughout Indian thought there is an omnipresence of this sense of partnership between mortal men and spirits, of life as being mortally given for immortal ends, which is after all perhaps the most fundamental as it is surely the most astonishing of nature's teachings, revealed only to the human spirit, never to the physical eye. Among all the races of mankind it has taken form, and we are prone to think that in the Christian faith it is seen most purely. Yet in the examination of American Indian rituals there repeatedly comes to mind, as it more than once recurs in the letters of the early missionaries, that phrase of Tertullian's which best summarizes the universality of nature's inner teaching: *Exclamant vocem naturaliter Christianam.*

Notes

THE NOTES for this volume have been checked by the author's son, Dr. H. G. Alexander. Brackets indicate insertions not in the original notes.

CHAPTER I. THE PIPE OF PEACE.

1. Lewis H. Morgan, *League of the Ho-Dé-No-Sau-Nee or Iroquois* (New York: Dodd, Mead and Company, 1901), Vol. II, Appendix B, Sect. 62, p. 232.

2. Hiram M. Chittenden and Alfred T. Richardson, *Life, Letters and Travels of Father Pierre-Jean De Smet, S. J.* (New York: Francis P. Harper, 1905), Vol. III, p. 1008.

3. *Ibid.*, Vol. II, pp. 681-2.

4. Journal of the first journey of Marquette, section vi: "Du naturel des Ilinois, de leurs moeurs et de leurs coustumes. De l'estime qu'ils ont pour le calumet ou pipe à prendre du tabac, et de la dance qu'ils font en son honneur."

5. See J. R. Walker, "The Sun Dance and other Ceremonies of the Oglala Division of the Teton Dakota," *American Museum of Natural History, Anthropological Papers*, Vol. XVI, Part II (New York, 1917), p. 157.

6. *Ibid.*, p. 80 and pp. 157-8.

7. Chief Standing Bear, *Land of the Spotted Eagle* (Boston and New York: Houghton Mifflin Company, 1933), pp. 201-2.

8. "Lakota" is a variant of "Dakota," the native name of the Sioux peoples.

9. See H. B. Alexander, *Mythology of All Races* (Boston: Marshall Jones Company, 1916), Vol. X, pp. 286-7, note 31, and the passages there cited. See also "Handbook of the American Indians," *Bur. of Am. Ethnol., Bul. 30*, Part I (Washington, 1907), art. "Color Symbolism."

10. James Stevenson, "Ceremonial of Hasjelti Dailjis," *Bur. of Am. Ethnol., Eighth Annual Report* (1891), pp. 275-6. [Stevenson's version should be contrasted with those recorded by Washington Matthews in *Navaho Legends* (Boston and New York, 1897) which differ in several respects.]

NOTES

11. Alice C. Fletcher, "The Hako: a Pawnee Ceremony," *Bur. of Am. Ethnol., Twenty-second Annual Report*, Part 2 (1904), p. 125. [Tahirussawichi is Miss Fletcher's Pawnee informant.]

12. *Tlachtli* or *tlaxtli* is the Nahuatlan name for a game played with a rubber ball which was struck with the thigh, head or shoulder of the contestants, the object being to hurl the ball through rings affixed well up on the sides of a court, such as the famous Ball Court of Chichen Itza. The game was a sport much favored, but that it was also a ceremony with cosmic significance is abundantly testified by tradition, by its place in myth (as in the *Popul Vuh*), and by its symbolism in the codices. See T. A. Joyce, *Mexican Archaeology* (London, 1914), pp. 301 f., and E. Seler, "Einiges über die natürlichen Grundlagen mexikanischer Mythen," *Zeitschrift f. Ethnologie,* Vol. XXXIX (1907), pp. 1-41.

13. [See Alexander, *God's Drum* (New York: E. P. Dutton and Company, 1927), "Tezcatlipoca," p. 211, and "The Sun's Last Ray," p. 23, for poetic renderings of these themes.]

14. The tale of the quest of eternal life has many versions. It is referred to in the *Jesuit Relations*, and fuller versions are to be found in S. T. Rand, *Legends of the Micmacs* (New York, 1894), nos. x, xxxv, xlii, and in W. J. Hoffman, "The Menomini Indians," *Bur. of Am. Ethnol., Fourteenth Annual Report*, Part I (1896), pp. 118, 206. For an interpretation of this legend, see H. B. Alexander, *Manito Masks* (New York: E. P. Dutton and Company, 1926).

15. See James Hastings, ed., *Encyclopedia of Religion and Ethics,* art. "Philosophy: Primitive," and authorities there cited. For details as to camp circles, consult especially James Dorsey, "Siouan Sociology," *Bur. of Am. Ethnol., Fifteenth Annual Report* (1897), pp. 205 ff., and Francis La Flesche, "The Osage Tribe," *Thirty-sixth Annual Report* (1921).

16. La Flesche, "The Symbolic Man of the Osage Tribe," *Art and Archaeology*, Vol. IX, No. 2 (1920), pp. 68-72.

17. Garrick Mallery, "Picture Writing of the American Indians," *Bur. of Am. Ethnol., Tenth Annual Report* (1893), p. 290. Further details regarding this important Dakota myth are to be found in Chapter V below.

18. Fletcher and La Flesche, "The Omaha Tribe," *Bur. of Am. Ethnol., Twenty-seventh Annual Report* (1911), p. 599.

CHAPTER II. The Tree of Life.

1. *Kinnikinnick* is an Algonquian word designating the mixture of native tobacco and other leaves or barks which form the smoking mixture of the North American tribes. In North Dakota, where the Arikara dwell, the inner bark of the red osier (*cornus stolonifera*), the leaves of the bearberry (*arctostaphylos uva-ursi*), and the dried tops of *nicotiana quadrivalvis,* the local tobacco, form the ingredients of the smoking mixtures, according to Dr. Melvin R. Gilmore.

NOTES

2. "Mother Corn" is an important being, essentially a goddess, in both the myth and ritual of the Caddoan peoples. Plausibly the "mother corn" is the seed-corn from which the yearly crop is raised, but as personified she is clearly a spiritual being and tribal tutelary. The origin of the Arikara "Mother Corn" is recounted in myth as follows: "Nesaru [the Creator] in the heavens planted corn in the heavens, to remind him that his people were put under ground. As soon as the corn in the heavens had matured, Nesaru took from the field an ear of corn. This corn he turned into a woman and Nesaru said, 'You must go down to the earth and bring my people from the earth.'" Then follows the story of the leading forth of the First People from the underworld. See G. A. Dorsey, "Tradition of the Arikara," *Carnegie Institution of Washington, Publication 17* (Washington, 1904), p. 13. See also Chapters IV and V below.

3. Four Rings, an Arikara priest, so expressed the rôle of Mother Corn in his ritualistic account of the myth of the emergence to Dr. Gilmore. See H. B. Alexander, *L'Art et la Philosophie des Indiens de l'Amérique du Nord* (Paris, 1926), pp. 60-1. For a more philosophical interpretation, see the words of a Pawnee priest, *Bur. of Am. Ethnol., Twenty-second Annual Report,* Part 2 (1904), pp. 44, 61.

4. An interesting feature is this comic negro. In the fiestas of the Pueblo Indians, with whom the Caddoan peoples were formerly in contact, a negro comedy rôle is not infrequently introduced as a comic interlude, there said to represent the negro, Estevan, who in company with Friar Marcos made the first discovery of the Pueblos, and who was killed at Hawikuh.

5. The source of the agriculture of the Plains peoples is as yet undetermined. It must have travelled up the Missouri and its tributaries at a period antedating even the coming of the tribes occupying this region in the eighteenth century, when a developed riparian agriculture was encountered. The Caddoan tribes, who are plausibly the eldest-seated of the still living Plains tribes, have myths only of the supernatural gift of the maize, while neighboring tribes according to tradition derived the cereal from Caddoan peoples. Coronado encountered Wichita or Pawnee (both Caddoan) Indians at the Pueblo of Pecos, and it is known that the Pawnee obtained the pony and the burro from New Mexico. It is of interest to note also that the Pawnee preserve ritual "Songs of the Mesas" together with the tradition of former association with these flat-topped hills. See page 109 below.

6. My sources for the description here given of the Arikara ceremony are my own notes and the notes of Dr. Melvin R. Gilmore on the performance of July, 1924, of the rite of the Sacred Cedar at the Fort Berthold Reservation, North Dakota. Dr. Gilmore, who has in charge the full notes, has published in *Prairie Smoke* (New York: Columbia University

Press, 1929), materials of value in the interpretation of Arikara thought. See also my "Lucky-in-the-House," *Theatre Arts Monthly* (August, 1933) from which portions of the present account are quoted.

7. An example is painted on the interior of the mission church, Santo Domingo Pueblo, New Mexico.

8. See H. B. Alexander, *Mythology of All Races*, Vol. X, Chs. VIII, ii, and IX, vi-vii.

9. Fletcher and La Flesche, "The Omaha Tribe," *Bur. of Am. Ethnol., Twenty-seventh Annual Report* (1911), sect. vi, p. 219.

10. *Ibid.*, pp. 251-60. Dr. Leslie Spier, "The Sun Dance of the Plains Indians," *Am. Mus. of Nat. Hist., Anthropol. Papers*, Vol. XVI, Part VII (1921), regards the Hedewachi of the Omaha as simply "resembling in some respects" (p. 460) the Sun Dance. But that there is some intimate, even if remote, common background of ritual idea can hardly be questioned. See Chapter VI below.

CHAPTER III. THE ABIDING ROCK.

1. The words of Sword, an Oglala priest, quoted by J. R. Walker, "The Sun Dance and other Ceremonies of the Oglala Division of the Teton Dakota," *Am. Mus. of Nat. Hist., Anthropol. Papers*, Vol. XVI, Part II (1917), p. 155. For color symbols, see p. 159.

2. Fletcher and La Flesche, "The Omaha Tribe," *Bur. of Am. Ethnol., Twenty-seventh Annual Report* (1911), pp. 570-1.

3. *Ibid.*, p. 570.

4. See Chapter I above, page 14. Also Alexander, *Mythology of All Races*, Vol. XI, pp. 179-80.

5. Fletcher and La Flesche, *op. cit.*, pp. 586-7.

6. *Timaeus*, 33-34.

7. William James, *A Pluralistic Universe* (New York: Longmans, Green, and Co., 1909), Lecture IV.

8. *Genesis*, 28: 18-19.

9. Fletcher and La Flesche, *op. cit.*, p. 133.

10. L. R. Farnell, *Cults of the Greek States* (Oxford: The Clarendon Press, 1896), Vol. I, p. 45.

11. Chr. Blinkenberg, *The Thunderweapon in Religion and Folklore, A Study in Comparative Archaeology* (Cambridge University Press, 1911), p. 31.

12. Garcilasso de la Vega, *Royal Commentaries of the Incas*, Bk. II, Ch. 1.

13. Fletcher and La Flesche, *op. cit.*, p. 218.

14. W. Robertson Smith, *Lectures on the Religion of the Semites* (London: Adam and Charles Black, 1901), pp. 185-6.

15. *Deuteronomy*, 16:21-22.

NOTES

16. W. W. Skeat, *Malay Magic* (London: Macmillan and Co., Ltd., 1900), p. 205.
17. *Ibid.*, p. 211.
18. Sir John Maundeville, *Travels*, Part II, Ch. XIX.
19. See Chapter I, above, page 14, and note 10.
20. J. N. B. Hewitt, "Iroquoian Cosmology," *Bur. of Am. Ethnol., Twenty-first Annual Report* (1903), p. 332.
21. *Ibid.*, pp. 218-220.
22. Jeremiah Curtin, *Creation Myths of Primitive America* (Boston: Little, Brown, and Company, 1911), p. 19. See entire account of "Olelbis."
23. *Ibid.*, pp. 15, 23, 25, 48. See also Alexander, *God's Drum*, pp. 75-85, for a poetic version.
24. See Chapter I, note 14 above.

CHAPTER IV. THE CORN MAIDENS.

1. Francis La Flesche, "The Osage Tribe," *Bur. of Am. Ethnol., Thirty-ninth Annual Report* (1925), pp. 197-8.
2. Ruth L. Bunzell, "Zuni Ritual Poetry," *Bur. of Am. Ethnol., Forty-seventh Annual Report* (1932), p. 701. See also p. 775: "When in the spring, your earth mother is wet," etc.
3. *Koshare* is a Keresan name for a society the members of which perform important rôles in the tribal ceremonies. Their function is clearly magical and associated with ideas of fertility; it appears also to be definitely connected with ideas of death, the underworld, and ancestral spirits (cf., e.g., the Isleta name for their analogous society, *qha'byonin*, "cold-dead-being," interpreted as "afraid-of-the-cold"). Such societies are found among all the Pueblo peoples. They combine magical and clowning functions, analogous to the *heyoka,* or half magical buffoon, of the Dakota.
4. Bunzell, *op. cit.,* p. 641.
5. Quoted by Daniel G. Brinton, *The Annals of the Cakchiquels* (Philadelphia, 1885), p. 14.
6. H. R. Schoolcraft, *The Myth of Hiawatha* (1856), pp. 99 ff. This is the source from which Longfellow drew his materials for the version contained in *Hiawatha.* See below, Chapter VII, note 8.
7. *Basket maker* is the term employed by archaeologists for the Indian culture of maize cultivators which preceded the Pueblo cultures on the Southwestern plateaus of North America. [The preferred opinion in recent archaeology is that maize developed first in the northern portions of South America, thence spreading, among other directions, northward into Mexico. The migration of maize cultivation into North

America is much more complicated than was formerly thought. The route along the Gulf shore and Atlantic Coast is less credible in view of the lack of evidence of early maize cultivation in southern Texas. Instead, it seems more probable that the cultivation of maize spread first into New Mexico and Arizona and then across the middle or northern plains. See P. C. Mangelsdorf and C. Earle Smith, Jr., "New Archaeological Evidence on Evolution in Maize," *Harvard University, Botanical Museum, Leaflets*, Vol. 13, No. 8 (Cambridge, Mar. 4, 1949), pp. 213-247; and H. W. Dick, "Evidence of Early Man in Bat Cave and on the Plains of San Augustin, New Mexico," *International Congress of Americanists, Papers, 29th,* Vol. III (1952), pp. 158-63.]

8. *Sub-Pedregal* is a term applied to the archaic agricultural civilization in the Valley of Mexico, remains of which have been found beneath the *Pedregal,* or volcanic flow in that area.

9. This interesting hypothesis has been advanced by N. Cordy, "The Origin of the Tonalamatl," *The Masterkey,* Vol. VII, No. 3 (May, 1933), p. 80. The relation of calendric units to maize cultivation is clear in a number of American Indian time schemes. See "Handbook of the American Indians," *Bur. of Am. Ethnol., Bul. 30,* Part I (1907), art. "Calendar."

10. For a general account of the character of Pueblo and pre-Columbian Mexican rituals in their agricultural relationships, see Alexander, *Mythology of All Races,* Vol. X, Ch. IX, iv-v, and Vol. XI, Chs. II, iv-v, and IV, iii-iv, and the authorities there cited.

11. Frank H. Cushing, "Outlines of Zuñi Creation Myths," *Bur. of Am. Ethnol., Thirteenth Annual Report* (1896), p. 386.

12. *Ibid.,* p. 391.

13. *Ibid.,* pp. 393-5.

14. For an account of the *Popul Vuh,* see Alexander, *op. cit.,* Vol. XI, Ch. V, ii, and especially p. 165. [See also Recinos, Goetz, and Morley, *Popol Vuh* (University of Oklahoma Press, 1950).] For the Sia and Siouan myths, see Alexander, *op. cit.,* Vol. X, Chs. IX, vi, and VI, vii.

15. From the ritual account given by Four Rings to Dr. Melvin R. Gilmore, to whom I am indebted for this. See Alexander, *L'Art et la Philosophie des Indiens de l'Amérique du Nord,* pp. 59-61.

16. See Alexander, *Mythology of All Races,* Vol. X, Ch. III, i-ii.

17. See H. W. Henshaw, "Animal Carvings from Mounds of the Mississippi Valley," *Bur. of Am. Ethnol., Second Annual Report* (1883), pp. 267 ff. See also Alexander, *op. cit.,* Vol. X, Ch. IX and Vol. XI, Chs. II, IV, VII.

18. My sources for Chinese color symbolism are primarily from Chinese students in America.

19. See Alexander, *op. cit.,* Vol. XI, p. 77.

20. *Ibid.,* pp. 160-2.

CHAPTER V. MANY CHILDREN.

1. Alice C. Fletcher, "The Hako: A Pawnee Ceremony," *Bur. of Am. Ethnol., Twenty-second Annual Report,* Part 2 (1904).

2. See Fletcher and La Flesche, "The Omaha Tribe," *Bur. of Am. Ethnol., Twenty-seventh Annual Report* (1911), for an account of the Omaha *Wawan* ceremony. See also Fletcher, "The Wawan, or Pipe Dance of the Omahas," *Peabody Museum of American Archaeology and Ethnology, Reports,* Vol. III, Nos. 3 and 4 (Cambridge, 1884), pp. 308-333. For the Dakota *Hunka* ceremony, see Edward S. Curtis, *The North American Indian* (Cambridge, U.S.A.: The University Press, 1908), Vol. III, pp. 71-87; also Frances Densmore, "Teton Sioux Music," *Bur. of Am. Ethnol., Bul. 61* (1918), pp. 68-77.

3. Curtis, *op. cit.,* p. 71.

4. Densmore, *op. cit.,* p. 70.

5. Fletcher, "The Hako," pp. 201, 23-4.

6. In the narrative which follows, the quoted passages are from Fletcher, *op. cit.,* pp. 17-278, being the comments of Tahirussawichi, Miss Fletcher's Pawnee informant, who acted as Kurahus in explaining the ritual. Occasionally the translations are those of Miss Fletcher's rhythmic renderings given in her "Analytical Recapitulation," pp. 279 ff.

7. L. R. Farnell, *Cults of the Greek States* (Oxford, 1907), Vol. III, p. 164.

8. Plato, *Cratylus* 397.

9. *Isaiah* 40: 12-22.

10. *Genesis* 1: 1-5.

11. *Psalms* 65: 8-11; 19: 1-5.

12. Fletcher, *op. cit.,* pp. 277-8.

CHAPTER VI. THE SUN DANCE.

1. See Alexander, Mythology of All Races, Vol. X, p. 300, note 50, and the authorities there cited. See especially J. W. Fewkes, "Tusayan Snake Ceremonies," *Bur. of Am. Ethnol., Sixteenth Annual Report* (1897), and "Tusayan Flute and Snake Ceremonies," *Nineteenth Annual Report,* Part 2. (1900).

2. The most important assemblage of materials upon the Sun Dance is comprised in Volume XVI of the *Anthropological Papers of the American Museum of Natural History.* See also Clark Wissler, *The Relation of Nature to Man in Aboriginal America* (Oxford University Press, 1926), pp. 82-93.

3. See *Voyages en Virginie et en Floride* (Paris, 1927), reproducing *Images des Indiens habitant la Province de Floride* which contains the plates and comments of Jacob le Moyne, first published in 1501. Note especially Plate XXXV and comment. See also Plate LXXIV from Picart, *Cere-*

monies and Religious Customs of the Various Nations of the Known World (London, 1733-39).

4. See Leslie Spier, "The Sun Dance of the Plains Indians: its Development and Diffusion," *Am. Mus. of Nat. Hist., Anthropol. Papers.* Vol. XVI, Part VII (1921), and Wissler, *loc. cit.*

5. See especially Spier, *op. cit.,* pp. 485-6, for accounts of the modes of the institution of the ritual.

6. For example, the tongue of the sacrificial animal has a similar significance in the Arikara festival already described in Chapter II.

7. Frances Densmore, "Teton Sioux Music," *Bur. of Am. Ethnol., Bul. 61* (1918), p. 120.

8. G. A. Dorsey, "The Cheyenne: Ceremonial Organization," *Field Columbian Museum* (now *Chicago Natural History Mueum*), *Anthropological Series,* Vol. IX, No. 1 (Chicago, 1905), pp. 46-9.

9. Dorsey, "The Arapaho Sun Dance," *Field Columbian Museum, Anthropol. Series,* Vol. IV (1903), p. 74.

10. Densmore, *op. cit.,* pp. 65-6.

11. *Ibid.,* p. 66.

12. George Catlin, *The Manners, Customs, and Condition of the North American Indians* (London, 1841), Letter No. 21, Vol. I, pp. 156-7.

13. Densmore, *op. cit.,* pp. 95-6.

14. *Ibid.,* p. 95.

15. J. R. Walker, "The Sun Dance and other Ceremonies of the Oglala Division of the Teton Dakota," *Am. Mus. of Nat. Hist., Anthropol. Papers,* Vol. XVI, Part II (1917), esp. pp. 78-92 and 152-8.

16. *Ibid.,* pp. 152-3.

17. Densmore, *op. cit.,* p. 216.

CHAPTER VII. LIFE AS ORDEAL.

1. Visitors and volunteers are permitted to enter certain of the ceremonial dances of the Pueblo peoples, although they are expected to dance in the division which corresponds with that of which they are members in their own village, the polity and ceremonial organization of the several villages being closely similar.

2. Section III below describes the widespread rite of vigil and fasting. But there are also societies of Eldermen organized for the express purpose of reflective study. Such are the Pawnee *Raristesharu,* the men who "try to be like the stars," or the Osage *Non-hon-zhin-ga,* the Little Old Men who debate the tribal metaphysics. See Fletcher, "The Hako," *Bur. of Am. Ethnol., Twenty-second Annual Report,* Part 2 (1904), p. 235, and La Flesche, "The Osage Tribe," *Thirty-sixth Annual Report* (1921), pp. 48, 55.

3. See Frances Densmore, "Chippewa Music," *Bur. of Am. Ethnol., Bul. 45* (1910), p. 24.

NOTES

4. Fletcher and La Flesche, "The Omaha Tribe," *Bur. of Am. Ethnol.. Twenty-seventh Annual Report* (1911), pp. 115-6.
5. Herbert J. Spinden, *Songs of the Tewa* (New York, 1933), No. XLVI.
6. Bernardino de Sahagún, *Historia de las cosas de la Nueva España,* Bk. VI, Ch. XXXII.
7. The word *totem* is an Algonquian term, properly applied to the personal guardian or tutelary which belongs to the individual man, and often represented by picture or emblem in his Medicine, or fetish parcel, or painted upon his clothing or accoutrements. It is in no sense hereditary or genealogical, nor has it anything to do with the social organization of tribe or clan. In this respect it differs entirely from the family heraldry of the Indians of the Northwest Coast, typified by their well-known "totem poles," and it has no relation to the social phenomena of "totemism," as commonly discussed. It is indeed unfortunate that the word should have come to be misapplied to forms and customs to which its proper meaning is diametrically opposed.
8. *The Song of Hiawatha,* Canto V. Longfellow's source for his materials was H. R. Schoolcraft, *Algic Researches* (New York, 1839), in which there is a confusion of Algonquian and Iroquoian materials. "Hiawatha" was historically an Iroquois (Onondaga) chieftain of the sixteenth century, while the myths recounted are of the Algonquian cosmogonical cycle. There is perhaps an especial interest in the confusion in this particular episode, in that it is wholly probable that it was from Iroquoian tribes that the Algonquians first derived their maize-culture. [*Algic Researches* is the earlier version later republished as *The Myth of Hiawatha* with some modifications. See Osborn and Osborn, *Schoolcraft— Longfellow—Hiawatha* (Lancaster, Pa.: The Jaques Cattell Press, 1942).]
9. Densmore, "Chippewa Music II," *Bur. of Am. Ethnol., Bul. 53* (1913), pp. 83-4.
10. Fletcher and La Flesche, *op. cit.,* Sect. VI. See also page 38 above.
11. Densmore, "Teton Sioux Music," *Bur. of Am. Ethnol., Bul. 61* (1918), pp. 159-63.
12. Densmore, "Chippewa Music II," p. 248.
13. See page 62 above and Chapter I, note 14.
14. Densmore, "Teton Sioux Music," p. 160.
15. This story was narrated to the author by Francis La Flesche who regarded it as an episode in the history of his own tribe, the Omaha. Equally romantic is the story of "The Weeper," as dramatized in Alexander, *Manito Masks,* a story also told by Dr. La Flesche who remembered "the Weeper" as an old man.
16. Densmore, *op. cit.,* Nos. 125, 126, 129, 136, 140, 143, 142, 144, 151, 153, 154, and 152.
17. Thos. L. McKenney and Jas. Hall, *History of the Indian Tribes* (Phila-

delphia, 1870), Vol. II, p. 312, gives the account of Red Bird's surrender. [This will be found in Vol. II, p. 431, of the three-volume edition edited by F. W. Hodge and published under the title *The Indian Tribes of North America* (Edinburgh: John Grant, 1933).]

18. James Mooney, "Calendar History of the Kiowa," *Bur. of Am. Ethnol., Seventeenth Annual Report*, Part I (1898), pp. 329, 332.

19. O. O. Howard, *My Life and Experiences among Our Hostile Indians* (Hartford: A. D. Worthington and Company, 1907), p. 114.

20. R. H. Lowie, "The Religion of the Crow Indians," *Am. Mus. of Nat. Hist., Anthropol. Papers*, Vol. XXV, Part II (1922), pp. 416-7.

21. Fletcher, "A Study of Omaha Indian Music," *Peabody Mus. of Am. Arch. and Ethnol., Papers*, Vol. I, No. 5 (1893), pp. 13-14, 46.

22. Melvin R. Gilmore, *Prairie Smoke*, p. 207.

23. Narrated to Dr. Clyde Kluckhohn by a cacique of Jemez Pueblo in 1934.

24. Wissler and Duvall, "Mythology of the Blackfoot Indians," *Am. Mus. of Nat. Hist., Anthropol. Papers*, Vol. II, Part I (1908), p. 21.

CHAPTER VIII. THE LAST TRAIL.

1. See page 98 above.

2. See Alexander, *Mythology of All Races*, Vol. X, pp. 9, 260, 263, 279-80, note 16, and passages there cited. [Also see *God's Drum*, p. 88.]

3. Jeremiah Curtin, *Creation Myths of Primitive America* (Boston, 1911), p. 169.

4. Sahagún, *Historia*, Bk. III, Appendix I.

5. Alexander, *op. cit.*, Vol. X, pp. 147-9.

6. *Ibid.*, Vol. XI, pp. 307-8.

7. Recorded especially by G. A. Dorsey, "Pawnee Mythology," *Carnegie Institution of Washington, Publication 59*, Part I (1906), No. 34. An interpretation of the myth in dramatic form will be found in Alexander, *Taiwa* (Los Angeles: Primavera Press, 1934).

8. M. R. Harrington, "Religion and Ceremonies of the Lenape," *Museum of the American Indian, Heye Foundation, Indian Notes and Monographs, Misc. 19* (New York, 1921); and Frank G. Speck, "A Study of the Delaware Indian Big House Ceremony," *Publications of the Pennsylvania Historical Commission*, Vol. 2 (Harrisburg, 1931).

9. Speck, *op. cit.*, pp. 22-3.

10. *Ibid.*, pp. 81-7.

11. The sweat-bath is a widely extended rite or treatment among North American tribes, generally regarded as therapeutic, but never clearly separated from religious or ritual ideas. There is a possibility that the Delaware adopted the sweat-bath from the Plains tribes after their removal to Kansas (see Speck, *op. cit.*, pp. 73-4). However, we find this rite in connection with the Midé wiwin (see page 211 below).

NOTES

12. *Ibid.*, pp. 174-7.
13. *Ibid.*, pp. 161-3.
14. D. G. Brinton, *The Lénapé and their Legends* (Philadelphia, 1885).
15. The primary sources for the Chippewa (Ojibwa) form of the ceremonial are W. J. Hoffman, "The Midē'wiwin or 'Grand Medicine Society' of the Ojibwa," *Bur. of Am. Ethnol., Seventh Annual Report* (1891), and Frances Densmore, "Chippewa Music," *Bur. of Am. Ethnol., Bul. 45* (1910). For the Menomini version the essential sources are Hoffman, "The Menomini Indians," *Bur. of Am. Ethnol., Fourteenth Annual Report*, Part I (1896), and Alanson Skinner, "Medicine Ceremony of the Menomini, Iowa, and Wahpeton Dakota," *Mus. of the Am. Ind., Heye Foundation, Indian Notes and Monographs*, Vol. IV. (1920).
16. Skinner, *op. cit.*, pp. 283-4.
17. The description here given is abridged from the diagrams and descriptions given by Hoffman and Densmore in their respective reports upon Chippewa (Ojibwa) performances, as cited above. The details of the construction vary with time, tribe, and ceremonial degree, but the essential form is constant.
18. Hoffman, "The Midē'wiwin," *op cit.*, pp. 211-2. [Quotation here slightly rephrased.]
19. Skinner, *op. cit.*, pp. 282-3.
20. Densmore, *op. cit.*, Nos. 49, 50, and 44.
21. *Ibid.*, pp. 21-3. The narrative is given by an initiate Chippewa, Nawajibigokwe, Woman-dwelling-among-the-Rocks.
22. For a discussion of Manabozho, see Alexander, *Mythology of All Races*, Vol. X, Ch. III, ii, and pp. 297-8, note 47.
23. Skinner, *op. cit.*, pp. 103ff.
24. See especially the discussion of Orphism in Jane E. Harrison, *Prolegomena to the Study of Greek Religion* (Cambridge University Press, 1903).
25. See Alexander, *op. cit.*, Vol. XI, Ch. V, ii-iii, esp. p. 171.
26. James Mooney, "The Ghost-Dance Religion," *Bur. of Am. Ethnol., Fourteenth Annual Report*, Part 2 (1896), p. 721.
27. *Ibid.*, pp. 764ff. [Quotation, pp. 771-2, here slightly rephrased.]
28. Of the three songs here cited, the first is a Paiute song, *ibid.*, p. 1052, the others are Arapaho, pp. 970, 977. [Songs slightly rephrased.]

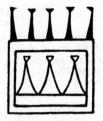

Index

Art, xv; of shell, stone and copper disc, 91; snake and serpent in Indian, 92-3; deerskin painting, 182; philosophy like art, 229; of Phidias and Michelangelo, 57.
Aryan, xvi.
Ashera, 55.
Ashtoreth (pl. Ashtaroth), 41, 88.
Ashur, eagle of, 92.
Asia Minor, Cybele and Attis in, 126.
Assyrian eagle and thunderbird compared, 90.
Astronomical doctrines further from ordinary view than those of Hako, 130.
Athens, initiates at, 28; *sacra* brought to, 127.
Atlantis, xvii.
Attis and Cybele, 126.
Australian Blackwoman, carries corpse of baby, 80.
Axe, as thunderstone, 52-3.
Aztec, Sun God, 17; symbolic trees, 36, 38; myth of Tezcatlipoca, 64; and Southeastern tribes, 76; maize deities, 77; tying of years, 79; poem, 95; birds as emblem of animal life, 151; prayer for new-born, 177; treatment of Tlascalans, 188; inevitability of death for, 194; descent into Hell (Aztec "Book of the Dead"), 201.

Baals, 87-8.
Babylon, mythic conceptions in, 16; Ishtar and Tammuz in, 126.
Baetyli, perhaps same as *bethel,* 51-2.
Banner, in Corn Dance, 68.
Baptismal ceremonies, bowl used in, 107; petition for life and welfare, 172; Christian, 173; Indian analogues, 175-7.
Basket Maker, 237; maize in times of, 75.
Bayreuth Parsifal, 159.
Bear, honored in Sun Dance, 144; God in Siouan cosmology, 166.
Bedaw, and Fellah, 88.
Bible, *Genesis,* 236, 239; *Deuteronomy,* 236; *Isaiah,* 239; *Psalms,* 239.
Big House ceremony, 205-9.
Birds, calumet embellished with, 6;

angelic messengers, 93, 132; songs about, 117-8; symbolic flocking of, 119-20; symbolic nesting of, 123-4; as emblem of animal life, 151; and butterflies in Pueblo ceremonies, 177; pictured on deerskin attached to trophy pole, 182.
Bison, magical corn bringer, 75; emblem of animal life, 151. (See Buffalo).
Blackfoot, 197; of Algonquian stock, 152.
Blinkenberg, Chr., *The Thunderweapon in Religion and Folklore,* 236.
Bowl, clay mixed in wooden, 106; used in baptismal ceremony, 107, 177; symbolic of sky, 107.
Breath, symbolism of in Zuñi ritual poetry, 68; of flute, 84; most perfect image of nature, 100; in Hako, 101, 121; of Tirawa beseeched, 125.
Brinton, Daniel G., *The Annals of the Cakchiquels,* 237; *The Lênapé and their Legends,* 243.
Brulé, legend of gift of maize, 23.
Bucranium, 151.
Buckeye bush, 59.
Buddhist, thinking, xvii; teachings echoed, 202.
Buffalo, legend of White Buffalo Cow, 23, 87, 155-7; effigy on Sun Pole, 138, meaning of in Sun Dance, 140-1; ornamenting of buffalo skull, 142; propitiated, 144; cranium placed on earth altar, 147; dance, 147-8; "cattle" of the Plains Indians, 151; God, 151, 166.
Buffalo-Stands-Upward, a Yankton pipe-keeper, 158.
Bullock, sacrificial, 151, 169.
Bunzell, Ruth L., "Zuni Ritual Poetry," 237.
Busk, an endurance dance, 160.
Butterfly, symbol of water, 79; associated with agricultural rituals, 137, 177.

Caddoan tribes, habitat, 33-4; early development of maize culture, 75, 88; The Hako among the, 101.
Caedmon, 131.

Genius in Siouan cosmology, 166; medicine, 180.
Fetishism behind anthropomorphism, 57.
Fewkes, J. W., "Tusayan Snake Ceremonies," and "Tusayan Flute and Snake Ceremonies," 239.
Fiat lux, fundamental metaphor of man's philosophy, 13.
Fire, oldest living thing, 27; flint, the prison of fire jinni, 45, 61; an element, 46; and shelter, gifts from Mother Earth, 116. (See Conflagration).
Fletcher, Alice, 103, 124, 125, 127, 130, 134; "The Hako: a Pawnee Ceremony," 234, 239, 240; "The Wawan or Pipe Dance of the Omahas," 239; "A Study of Omaha Indian Music," 242; and Francis La Flesche, "The Omaha Tribe," 234, 236, 239, 241.
Flint, prison of fire, 45, 61; and Sapling in Iroquois cosmogony, 57-8; magical, 59.
Flood in Wintun cosmogony, 60.
Florida Indians, sun worship, 40, 138; serpent on food bowls of, 92; deer emblem of animal life for, 150-1.
Flute, refreshing breath of (Zuñi myth), 84; associated with agricultural rituals, 137.
Four Hills of Life, Infancy, 174-7; Youth, 178-83; Maturity, 183-94; Old Age, 194-7.
Four Quarters, of earth's plane, 8-10, 14; in Arikara lodge, 26; scouts sent to, 29; in Omaha chant, 47; in maize rituals, 78; in Chinese and Mexican lore, 93; saluting the, 195; Manitos of the, 214-5; symbolized by Midé pole, 212; spirits of the, 230.
Four Rings, an Arikara priest, 235, 238.

Garcilasso de la Vega (el Inca), 54; *Royal Commentaries of the Incas,* 236.
Gawitayac, a Chippewa, 189.
Ge = Earth Mother, 80.

Genesis, Navaho, 13; Kiché and Semitic, 97; Hebrew, 132-3; Book of, 236, 239.
Geometry, the most human science, 11.
Georgia, 91.
Ghost, in Siouan cosmology, 166; laying of, 173; Dance Religion, 225-7.
Gifts, sought from Manabozho (Algonquian legend), 18, 62, 183; of dancers in Corn Dance, 71; of corn to Omaha by Arikara, 74; festal, 184.
Gignomenon and phenomenon, 230.
Gilmore, Melvin R., 235, 238; *Prairie Smoke,* 235, 242.
God, quest for, 101; visions of, 132; theory of, 158, 163-9; belief in as only sufficiency to human mind, 231-2. (See Father, Great Spirit, Tirawa atius, Wakantanka).
Good, meditation on, 209; as goal of evolution, 231.
Gopher and Mole in Wintun cosmogony, 60.
Great Spirit, smoking with, 5, 7-9; of Sioux, 23, 43; ministers of, 182; abode of, 206-9; revelation from, 210, 212; visited by prophets, 224.
Greek, mysteries, xvi, xx, 126-30; number systems, 11; myth of Phaethon, 13; *triaina,* 53; tragic chorus, 69; vase paintings of earth goddess, 89; gods, early, 131; Pindaric maxim, 183.
Green Bay, Wisconsin, 212.
Gucumatz, Kiché Creator, 95-8.

Hako Ceremony, xix, 89, 101-135.
Hall, James, and Thomas L. McKenney, *History of the Indian Tribes,* 241.
Hare, Great White, in Algonquian myth, 18, 152, 216.
Harrington, M. R., 206; *Religion and Ceremonies of the Lenape,* 242.
Harrison, Jane E., *Prolegomena to the Study of Greek Religion,* 243.
Hawikuh, 235.
Heaven, Father and Mother Corn, 31; Lord of, 91; Awahokshu (Pawnee), 104; mentioned in *Cratylus,* 131; like the walls of a lodge, 131.

INDEX

Hebrew, ark, 22; Lord of Heaven, 132; Genesis, 133.
He'dewachi ceremony, 39-40.
Hell (See Underworld).
Heraclitus, doctrine of fiery flux, 44; outer aspect vs. inner potencies, 195.
Hercules, 222.
Hereafter, journey of soul to, 195; symbolized in Big House ceremony, 207-8; visited by Manabozho, 218-9. (See Underworld).
Herms and Terms, 55.
Hero, in Mysteries, 220. (See Twin Gods).
Hesiod, *Theogony*, xvi.
Hestia, symbol of hearth center, 34.
Hewitt, J. N. B., 57; "Iroquoian Cosmology," 237.
Hiawatha, 179, 237, 241.
Hindu, thinking, xvii-xviii; *trisula*, 53.
Hittite Lion Queen, 41.
Hobowakan, 3. (See Calumet).
Hodge, F. W., 242.
Hoe, of shoulder bone used in Arikara ceremony, 31; -grown musculature of an earth cult, 137.
Hoffman, W. J., "The Menomini Indians," 234, 243; "The Midē'wiwin or 'Grand Medicine Society' of the Ojibwa," 243.
Holy, Big, 9; symbols hidden, 123.
Honga, Earth-people (Osage), 20-2.
Hopi, sky serpent (Polulukoñ), 94; snake dance, 79, 92, 136-7.
Howard, Gen. O. O., 192; *My Life and Experiences among Our Hostile Indians,* 242.
Huichol, evening prayer song, 17.
Human sacrifice, 75, 78.
Hunters and warriors of the prairies, 137.
Hunting, drama of in Arikara ceremony, 32; prowess requested as a gift, 18, 62, 183; and rearing of children, two most anxious concerns, 152-3.
Hymns (See Chants).

Iacchos, god of vegetation, 127.
Idols, 56-7.
Illinois, 5, 6, 91, 92.

Illumination (See Visions).
Inca, belief about lightning, 54-5; maize spread to, 77.
Individualism, of hunting culture, 141; even among Pueblos, 170; evidenced in prowess and romance, 171-2.
Indo-European languages, directions in, 10.
Inyan Kara, Wyoming, 43.
Isis, 41; and Osiris, 126; mystery of, 220-2.
Iroquois, use of pipe, 5; cosmogony, 57-9; corn-maiden cult among, 86.
Isaiah, 132; Book of, 239.
Ishtar, 41, 88, 126, 222.
Isleta, 237.
Israel, Urim and Thummim of high Priest, 45.
Italy, age of stone in, 45.
Iximche, capital city of the Cakchiquel, 44.

Jacal, decorated booth, 35, 71.
Jack-and-the-Beanstalk counterpart, 37.
Jacob, pillar set up by at Bethel, 52.
James, William, 49-50; *A Pluralistic Universe,* 236.
Japanese Samurai, 187.
Jemez Pueblo, 242.
Jesuit, missionaries, 5, 18; *Relations,* 62, 234.
Jinni, of fire, 45; magical, 166.
John Bull, 20.
Journey to the Son (Hako), 107-9.
Joy, expressed in Hako, 130; and peace, gift from Heaven, 134.
Joyce, T. A., *Mexican Archaeology,* 234.
Juppiter Lapis and Fulgur, 54.

Kanakuk, Kickapoo Indian prophet, 224.
Kansas, home of Wichita, 33.
Keening, of Arikara woman, 31; an Indian expression of emotion, 145.
Keokuk, Sauk Indian chief, 182.
Keraunos of Zeus (thunderbolt), 53.
Kiché Scripture (*Popul Vuh*), 87, 97, 230.
Kinnikinnic, 26, 234.

Kiowa, symbolism of pipe according to, 22; Holy Woman represents a captive, 40.
Kiva, place of assembly in Corn Dance, 71.
Korai (maidens), 86, 88.
Koshare, in Corn Dance, 68, 70-3, 237.
Kluckhohn, Clyde, 242.
Knossos, fetish idols found at, 51; image of double axe at, 52-3.
Kurahus, a Pawnee priest's title, 103-33.

La Flesche, Francis, 20; "The Osage Tribe," 234, 237, 240; "The Symbolic Man of the Osage Tribe," 234; and Alice Fletcher, "The Omaha Tribe," 234, 236, 239, 241.
Lakota, 8. (See Dakota).
Lang, Andrew, 128.
Law, and life, two facets of the world, 100; symbol as law or principle, 165. (See Destiny).
Lenape (See Delaware).
Life, Master of, 5; symbolism of, 16; three great treasures of, 17; tree of, 25ff.; of an object = its use, 51; restored on earth (Wintun cosmogony), 60; unending, requested as gift, 62; hours of, counted by drumbeats, 64; sense of continuity of, 73, 106, 153-4; of agricultural man, 81; and law, two facets of the world, 100; symbolized by child, 101; progress of, symbolized in Hako ceremony, 121-2; prayer for, 125, 175; Givers of, 154; meaning of, 170; personal and inward to Indian, 171; ceremonial petition for, 172-4; four ages of, 174; hunters dependent on seasonal, 183; conceived as ordeal, 170ff., 189, 231; and death confluent, 196; for duration of world, 212; issues from corn, 230.
Lightning, Zuñi belief about, 54; Inca belief about, 54-5; on Pueblo pottery, 79; sent forth by thunderbirds, 90; sign of Hurakan, 98; averted by woodpecker, 105.
Lodge, ceremonial open to east, 13; of Arikara, 26, 30; of Olelbis, 59; of Dawn, 62; in Hako ceremony,

108, 114-5; erection of Sun Pole, 143; trail to, 146-7; destroyed, 150; of the Manitos, 151; erected, 155; trophy pole beside, 181-2; of the Dead, 202-3, 216; of Great Lakes Indians, 209; sweat, 211; circuit of, in Big House and Midé ceremonies, 206-7, 213; beautiful as a star, 214, 222.
Lone Man, a Teton Sioux, 155-7, 180-1.
Longfellow, 179, 237, 241.
Looking Elk, a Teton Sioux, 103.
Louisiana, 91.
Love, valor and wisdom, life's treasures, 17; requested as a gift, 18, 62, 183; making during Sun Dance, 144; intensity in wooings, 187; underlies myth of origin of death, 197; and death, 203-5, 222-3; for man by Great Spirit, 212; winged Eros, 220.
Lowie, R. H., "The Religion of the Crow Indians," 242.
Lucky-in-the-House, an Arikara woman, 28.
Lupercals, 71.

Macaw, and parrot plumes, 68-9; plumes like corn leaves, 83.
Madeline Island, Lake Superior, 214.
Magic, sympathetic, in Corn Dance, 64-7; bison, bringer of corn, 75; jinni in Siouan cosmology, 166; teachers, 221.
Maize, Indian corn, 3; God and Lord of Death, 37; miracle of, 73-4; conquest of, 74; spread of, 75-7, 235, 237-8; goddesses of, 86; dicotyledon of, 91; = own flesh and blood, 96-7; literature of cultivators of, 99; symbolic ear of, 106. (See Corn.)
Malay, belief about speaking trees, 55; about tree souls, 56.
Male, in Pueblo Corn Dance, 63-5; element in nature typified by Sun (Hako), 113.
Mallery, Garrick, "Picture Writing of the American Indians," 234.
Man, advice of White Buffalo Woman to, 157; theory of God and, 158; Wakantanka more powerful than, 161; can understand animals, 162; interdependence with fellowman

INDEX

Smith, Earle C., Jr., and P. C. Mangelsdorf, "New Archaeological Evidence on Evolution in Maize," 238.

Smith, W. Robertson, *Lectures on the Religion of the Semites*, 236.

Smohalla, Wanapun Indian prophet, 182.

Smoking, 3-4, 116-7, 124, 143, 144, 195, 212, 216.

Snake, in Indian art, 92; Dance, 79, 92, 136-7.

Socrates, 131.

Sol Invictus, 17, 168.

Sophocles, 127.

Southwest Plateau, 75-6, 79.

Space, conception of, 8-10, 11-12, 14, 16, 18, 20, 27, 29, 34, 38; in Omaha chant, 47; in maize rituals, 78; divisions of, 165. (See Four Quarters).

Speck, Frank G., 206; "A Study of the Delaware Indian Big House Ceremony," 242.

Spier, Leslie, 140; "The Sun Dance of the Plains Indians," 236, 240.

Spinden, Herbert J., "Songs of the Tewa," 241.

Spotted Tail, a Dakota chief, 176.

Standing Bear, a Dakota chief, 8; *Land of the Spotted Eagle*, 233.

Standing Rock, South Dakota, 43.

Stars, 11, 80, 88, 91, 122, 200.

Steel, Age of in Northern Europe, 45.

Stevenson, James, "Ceremonial of Hasjelti Dailjis," 233.

Stocks and stones, as divinities, 51.

Stones, used in sweat-bath, 46; symbols of immovable being, 46; brought from Pergamum and Pessinus, 51, 53; of Mecca, 53; metamorphosis into, 61-2; giants, heads, masks, etc., 61, 230; symbolizes defense and center of world, 211.

Sub-Pedregal, 77, 238.

Sun, greeting the, 12; of time, 16; fourth oldest, 42; shows malediction by thunderbolt, 55; corn, offspring of, 78; = life-age, 86; sky-serpent dissolved by, 94; typifies male element, 113; ray of traced, 114; worship widespread, 137; Dance, 139-50; hero releases animal life, 151-2; greatest power, 161; in Siouan cosmology, 166; in Mithraism, 168-9; Land of Setting, 212; when died, 225.

Sweat-bath, significance of, 46; chant (Omaha), 47-8; Lodge of Olelbis, 59; powers of, 61; test of endurance in Big House ceremony, 207; used in Midé ceremony, 211-2.

Sword, a Dakota Indian, 7, 167, 236.

Symbolism of number, 120, 164-9. (See Color Symbolism).

Tablita, 65-6.

Tahirussawichi, a Pawnee priest, 15, 103, 130, 134-5, 239.

Tammuz, 75, 126, 222.

Tecumseh, Shawnee (or Shawano) Indian chief, 182, 224.

Temple, orientation of, 13.

Tenskwatawa, Shawnee Indian prophet, brother of Tecumseh, 224.

Tetralogies, 7. (See Quaternity).

Tewa Indian, sky serpent (Avanyu), 94; naming song, 176.

Thales, xvi.

Theogony, xvi, 126. (See Cosmogony).

Theophany, desire for, 48.

Theseus, 222.

Thompson River Indians, concept of underworld of, 202.

Thor, 90; the Hammer from heaven, 52-3.

Thunder, name of pillar in Arikara lodge, 26; masked, 73; Zeus lord of, 88; emblem of warriors, 90-1; bolt, sign of Hurakan, 98; god in Siouan cosmology, 166.

Thunderbird, on sacred tree, 38-9; emblem of warriors, 89-93, 96; of hawk family, 90-1; vision of implies inverted behavior, 180.

Thunderstone, considered a missile from heaven, 52-4.

Time, circle, symbol of, 8-9; wheel of, 9, 15, 18; rock as core of, 43; drumbeats as marks of, 64; in maize rituals, 78-9; dividers of, 165; four ages of life, 174; sense of consequences of, 187; end of our Sun of, 200; duration of world, life for, 212; schemes of American Indians, 238. (See Cosmogony).

DATE DUE